The Diaspora Writes Home

The Diaspora Writes Home

Subcontinental Narratives

Jasbir Jain

RAWAT PUBLICATIONS
Jaipur • New Delhi • Bangalore • Hyderabad • Guwahati • Kolkata

ISBN 978-81-316-0711-4

© Author, 2015

No part of this book may be reproduced or transmitted in any form or by any means, electronic or mechanical, including photocopying, recording or by any information storage and retrieval system, without permission in writing from the publishers.

Published by
Prem Rawat for **Rawat Publications**
Satyam Apts, Sector 3, Jawahar Nagar, Jaipur 302 004 (India)
Phone: 0141 265 1748 / 7006 Fax: 0141 265 1748
E-mail: info@rawatbooks.com
Website: www.rawatbooks.com

New Delhi Office
4858/24, Ansari Road, Daryaganj, New Delhi 110 002
Phone: 011 2326 3290

Also at *Bangalore, Hyderabad* and *Guwahati*

Typeset by Rawat Computers, Jaipur
Printed at Chaman Enterprises, New Delhi

For
Behn, Swaran Bedi
my eldest sister who gave so generously of
her love to all of us

Contents

Preface		ix
Introduction: Multiple Locations		1
1	Writing Home: Memory, History and Imagined Spaces	11
2	The Burden of Culture: Between Filiation and Affiliation	28
3	Geographical Dislocations and the Poetics of Exile: Ashis Gupta and Michael Ondaatje	40
4	Memory and Reflection in the Writing of the Diaspora	54
5	Writing in One's Own Language and the Grounds of *Being*	64
6	The New Parochialism: Homeland in the Writing of the Indian Diaspora	77
7	Out of the Colonial Cocoon? From *The Mimic Men* to *India: A Million Mutinies Now*	90
8	Routes of Passage: Identity, Home and Culture through Dislocations – Dabydeen, Bissoondath and the Naipaul Inheritance	105

9	A Bit of India: Under African Skies	116
10	In Search of Nationhood Across Borders	134
11	Mid-Air Tragedy: The *Emperor Kanishka* Crash	147
12	Call of the Homeland: The Civil War in Sri Lanka	162
13	Failed Hijrat? Cultural Mourning, Refugees and *Muhajirs*	178
14	The Diaspora Zeroes in on the Borders	194
15	The Children of Jahazi Bhai: Histories, Cultures and (Dis)Continuities	207
16	To India with Love: Rushdie, Ghosh and Mistry	221
17	Cultural Interpretations/ Representations in Film of the Indian Diaspora: Nostalgia, Memory or Spoofing?	234
18	Overwriting Memory: The Diaspora and Its Present	247
	Index	263

Preface

The subject of diaspora has been with me for several years. One could go back to the nineties, the decade which witnessed a subtle change from expatriate to diaspora, and accordingly moved from the politics of exile to hyphenated identities and 'translated' men. During this long period, my relationship with the diaspora has gone through several phases, inevitable when one realises that the initial response is to a work of literature, it is only later that one looks at the numerous locations, politics and theories that surround it.

Over the years, one has had to consider the poetics and the aesthetics of the diaspora, to debate its postcoloniality and to place its work alongside with those writing in India, not only in English but in its many languages. The question as to what goes to make a classic has also arisen. Further, how do we read it, evaluate it and judge it? Where does it belong: to 'us', whose countries it writes about whether with love, disapproval or derision, or to 'them' who read it as representative of the home culture and literature, and what about language when the dominant language subdues the dialogicity of the native tongue leading to a dilution of cultural references?

The double location – one physical, the other of the mind – and the transcendence of that distance raise many questions which cannot be answered by any generalisations on account of the multiple differences that crowd diasporic writing. The present work attempts to answer some of these. Except for a few essays, the rest have been written for this volume, focusing on the questions related to representation and memory. The world 'write' has many connotations and the first chapter, 'Writing Home', dwells on some of them. The act of 'representation', capturing the 'reality' of the moment and reflecting it in a literary artefact, brings in languages. I have no desire to credit either 'representation' or 'reality' with any fixed meaning. They are constantly evolving into new meanings and have a tendency to be provocative through their rapid shifts. 'Writing Home' consists of memories from a distance and perspectives from the outside. Yet, no cast-iron division can exist, the boundaries will collapse and merge. Literature opens out and creates new contexts.

Some of these essays have appeared earlier. 'The New Parochialism' was presented at a JNU seminar and first published in *In Diaspora* edited by Makarand Paranjpe (New Delhi: Indialog, 2000), 'Out of the Colonial Cocoon?' in *South Asian Review* (Fall 2003), 'Films of the Indian Diaspora' in the bilingual – French and English – *Indian Cinema* edited by Emmanuel Grimand and Kirstie Gormley, (Lyon, 2008), 'Geographical Dislocations' in *Writers of the Indian Diaspora* edited by Jasbir Jain (Jaipur: Rawat, 1998) and 'Mid-Air Tragedy' in *Bharati Mukherjee* edited by Somdatta Mandal (Delhi: Pencraft International, 2010).

Jasbir Jain

Introduction
Multiple Locations

To undertake any work on the diaspora raises the question as to how many diasporas? Even if we move away from the origins of the Jewish diaspora, the Indian one has acquired a multiplicity – the indentured labour, the early migrants in search of trade, adventure or prosperity, the political exiles, the professionals; the seventies witnessed the emigration of engineering and medical graduates, later came the IT professionals clustering Silicon Valley and now one can see the effects of globalisation. Each one works differently. And spread over the world as they are, many trace their beginnings abroad back through four generations or more, and some have even lost knowledge of their beginnings. History tells us that these different phases overlap. They do not terminate when a new phase begins, even the practice of slavery extended beyond the indentured labour. England has its own history of slaves and even in the present the hired and underpaid domestic help and nurses from India, if we pay attention to the exploitation that exists, fall perhaps into the same category. They fill up the gaps in labour which developed countries are unable to fill on their own. In addition, there are all those manual workers in the Middle East whose passports are kept in the employers' custody, stealing their freedom and sealing any voluntary exit. All of them are diaspora, many of them are slaves in one sense. In addition, there is also the specificity of political history between any host and home culture. No matter where one begins the diaspora is subject to a network of considerations.

Yet, a great deal is being written to unfold this multiplicity of the diasporic presence and interpret and reflect upon it. Our early writers and political exiles' relationship to India was marked by an emotional closeness and social concern. Among them are writers like Santha Rama Rau, Kamala Markandaya, G.V. Desani and Raja Rao. We have hardly ever asked the question of the location of their perspective, but have simply gone ahead and worked on the texts as literature. The political exiles and the freedom movements launched abroad have found limited representation. Nayantara Sahgal, herself not a diaspora writer, is one writer who has a fictional character Kalyan Sinha very much like Krishna Menon, working in the interest of the freedom movement abroad in *This Time of Morning* (1965)[1] and Kamala Markandaya's *The Nowhere Man* (1972) is the narrative of a political refugee. Markandaya's novels are dominantly about cultural differences, confrontations and adjustments. Santha Rama Rau in *Home to India* (1944) and *Remember the House* (1956) looks at India through a young girl's eyes who has grown up abroad, on account of her father's work, and who is just learning to be an Indian. Though in language literatures the ongoing migrations to Burma are taken note of, especially by a writer like Sarat Chandra Chatterjee, whose well-known novel *Pathar Dabi* has the character of Sabyasaachi engaged in the freedom struggle. All of the above are realities of the diaspora discourse and need to be placed within that perspective, if at any point of time, the definite history of the diaspora is to be written.

Others who were travellers, like Nehru and Tagore, remained grounded in India. It would be interesting to assess the contribution of those writers, artists and thinkers who were temporary residents abroad like Balraj Sahni, Mulk Raj Anand and Sajjad Zaheer. What they gave to the west and what they brought home from it, runs like a steady strand in their literary or artistic expressions. Anand's non-fictional work *An Apology for Heroism* (1946) and Sajjad Zaheer's Urdu work *London Ki Ek Raat* (1938) translated as *A Night in London* (2011) are works which write about these encounters. In the Foreword, Zaheer writes:

> It is one thing to sit down in Paris at the culmination of several years of study in Europe and, under the spell of private emotional conflict, to write a book of a hundred to a hundred

and fifty pages. But to have spent two-and-half years since then taking part in the revolutionary movement of workers and peasants in India, breathing in unison with millions of people and listening to the beating of their hearts, is entirely another matter. (v)²

The two-nation theory became a political reality in the 1930s at Oxford when Jinnah was there. Muhammad Iqbal's study abroad transformed him. And Fatima Meer wrote the book in South Africa on which Benegal's *The Making of Mahatma* is based. All these movements of travellers, refugees, exiles, students were forging new relationships, widening horizons and making their presence felt in innumerable ways. We do not think of them as separate from us or our past, even when history may label them 'diaspora'. Literally, Giriraj Kishore is correct when he titles his novel *Pahla Girmilya* (*The First Contractee*)³ for Gandhi did go to South Africa on a job contract and earned the right to be called so on account of his sensitivity to the colonial issues. The significant point is the nature of the cultural discourse and the journeys of ideologies; the ruffling that these impacts brought with them and also sent out. But these were wrapped up in the postcolonial phenomenon, often referred to as the theory of migrancy.⁴

This early identification of diasporic writing with postcolonialism was damaging to all concerned: the writing abroad, the writing at home and the manner of reading. It located writing in a particular historical happening colonialism and after – and all phenomenological realities fell by the wayside. The tag 'The Empire Writes Back' soon graduated into a dead metaphor. Even Chinua Achebe titled the middle chapter of *Home and Exile*⁵, as 'The Empire Fights Back.' To some extent this was true of the times. Writing from the erstwhile colonies had literally to fight for every inch of space. But then, in that case, we do not distinguish as to *where* cultural representation is located. This erasure of location is a denial of individual space. The writing does not have to worry about as to 'how the west reads it' or that it should be to their taste. Achebe's slim book *Home and Exile*, part autobiographical and part a reflection on writing and cultural difference, makes a very significant point. Postcolonial writing is not merely an account of resistance but it is an *un-writing* of the western representations of the colonies, through stereotypes, exoticism, magic, darkness, smallness and powerlessness. Though Achebe uses Joseph Conrad and Joyce Cary as two main examples, he also points out towards the 'postcolonial' Naipaul's disdain for his fellow human beings. He gives examples from *A Bend in the River* and the narrator Salim whose attitude was 'to look down on the Africans' and although Naipaul was writing about Africa, 'he was not writing for Africans' (*Home and Exile* 87–88). Postcolonial writing is a questioning of history, of perceptions of reality as seen by one side and seeks to present the other, not merely as a response but as an understanding of one's own position. It is a questioning as well as a re-making but the journey is always difficult and arduous as one has to wade through layers of records, histories and hybrid formations in order to find out the truth about oneself. It compels us to work through literary traditions of the home country, where somewhere or the other, lie the roots of our difference.

Homi Bhabha in *The Location of Culture* is evidently engaged in one such project. Where is culture located? A main thrust is that it needs to be dis-located from assumed positions, and in order to demonstrate this he gives examples about conversion in the chapter 'Sly Civility'.[6] As opposed to this is Naipaul's proclamation that the west is the producer of a universal civilisation. Apparently there is a missing link here and the debate between culture and civilisation between the east and the west carried out in the years 1880–1920 has been missed out. Achebe, quoting from Naipaul's *A Bend in the River*, writes in response and points out that the dusty road leading to the third world, 'is my link to other destinations. To ask everybody to shut down their history, pack their bag, and buy a one-way ticket to Europe or America is just crazy ... to be wilfully blind to our present reality ... .' (91).

Many of the writers we thoughtlessly label postcolonial are not postcolonial, they are sitting at the altar of the top layer, not able to discover either their histories or their subjectivities. A mere date in history does not define the postcolonial. It needs to be a position of questioning and it invariably demands a different way of reading. The more important aspect of postcolonial is not history, not geographical location, but as Ella Shohat observes its 'political agency' (100).[7] It is in the nineties that the term 'post-colonial' was reformed and its ossification broken. Arun Prabha Mukherjee, Gayatri Spivak, Ella Shohat, all from their different locations and disciplines questioned the way it was being generalised, over-used and working on the basis of a universal, flat applicability. Shohat questioned the absence of the term in the academic opposition to the Gulf War and asked: 'Is there something about the term "post-colonial" which does not lend itself to geo-political critique, or to a critique of the dominant media's Gulf-War macro-narratives?' (99). Overloaded with theoretical and political ambiguities, the term was in need of a constant questioning, redefinition and opening out, if it was to be meaningful and stand guard against erasure and extinction of differences.

Similarly, its closeness or identification with the writing of the diaspora, needs a constant interrogation and calls for discriminatory reading. How does it represent the homeland, how far is it a cultural analysis or a representation, or how alien and distant it is? Criticism of the home culture is valid enough but not disdain. The writer's emotional location, intellectual perceptions, a certain sense of at home-ness, all come into play. The non-culture reader may or may not be able to judge a falsity. The transfer of the word postcolonial from an adjective to a noun needs to be viewed critically. In many ways, postcolonial writing continues with the resistance narrative but now it seeks to go beyond the reference point of the empire's end; it needs to look within and around.

The present essays do not make any liberal use of the word postcolonial. Their postcoloniality maybe there at some level but it is not a dominant presence or even a conscious approach either in these essays or in the writings. They do work with ways of reading the diaspora, reading it through its many complex shades references and meaning. The essays work with subcontinental writing so as not to collapse all cultural differences. Somewhere Edward Said's 'Secular Criticism' is at the back of my mind. Said categorises critical approaches into four schools of criticism: theory based, text-based, literary appreciation variety and ideology based. To these he adds a fifth, secular criticism and works with 'existential actualities of human life', politics, societies and events. These, he continues, include 'the realities of power and authority as well as resistances offered by men and women and movements to institutions, authorities and orthodoxies – are the realities that made texts possible ... .'.[8]

Said's approach is comprehensive as it advises the same 'contrapuntality' while reading as he does in writing. One also has to realise, that in this he goes beyond the hermeneutic approach. 'Contrapuntal' has several resonances and carries both centripetal and centrifugal movements and runs like a constant strand in Said's reading and writing. Abdul JanMohammed refers to this view as 'extraordinarily persistent residual sense of his own marginality, he instinctively protected his vision with an aesthetic restraint of someone who stood forever at the very juncture of this (the Colonial) world with another, always unspecified but different one'.[9] It is this which leads JanMohammed to proceed to yet another categorisation – the specular intellectual, who is a border intellectual and who even while equally familiar with both cultures 'finds himself or herself unable or unwilling to be "at home" in these societies' (JanMohammed 97).

Suppose we grant this position of a border intellectual to the writer located abroad, then what happens? The term 'specular' is not without its own problems. First, his examples are from written texts and their thematic inclusiveness. In this regard most of us who have grown up in the erstwhile colonies have had a continued exposure to western literatures and histories, including the cultural, theological and mythological structures. Hence, we are theoretically syncretic, even if we practically may not be. But the same cannot be true of the west in equal measure, for they have read our cultures through western histories, translated texts and often diluted cultures. Achebe's comments about the perception of African culture (*Home and Exile*) are also applicable to many an Asian country. We ourselves do not know enough about our South Asian or East Asian neighbours. Thus, we are all border intellectuals living on the margins and in the in-between areas.

Diasporas too have a multiplicity of origins and locations. These essays have recognised this fact and have attempted to represent work across geographical areas, different kinds of migrations, and concerns through a mapping of the varying shades of memories. The title 'Writing Home', carries the meaning of representing as well as relating, hence memory and narrative are two factors that shape them. Memory is central to all kinds of writing but to the writing of the diaspora, it is much more central. How far back do these memories go, how filtered are they and what have been their mediums of remembering: stories, epics read or heard, gods, methods of worship, festivals, customs and rituals, colour, race, names or/and languages? Each one mentioned in the above list has contributed individually or collectively. Besides these, letters, home remedies, cooking recipes and anecdotes have created their own clusters.

One could problematise 'memory' in highly philosophical terms, as Derrida did the memory of an absent object or past. At some level, the idea of 'pure' or 'real' memory has to be dismissed. First, it is never self-contained or isolated, second, it has a personal perception: the same event may be seen differently by different people and also by the same person in different contexts and times. Third, memory is likely to be embedded in a continuum of other events, people or environments. And fourth and also most important of all of them is that memory inevitably gets intermixed with imagination. Though Aristotle's definition has two categories *mnēmē* or a simple evocation of the past and *anamnēsis*, an active reproduction of the past,[10] it is doubtful whether the distinction is possible or can be preserved at all times. All memory is an emotional going back in the first instance, whether personal or political. And the moment it is expressed through words, it acquires language, and is a little distanced from the mental idea and thus placed in an imaginative process. Verbal evocation or expression shakes it free of the purely personal and gives it a body. Memory seeks narration in multiple ways: vivid recollections, silent references cloaked in something else, metaphors, symbols, parallel events, or by working with consequences of a particular event, which sends the listener back to his own memories or perceptions of the same. Evocation of the past is not merely an individual act: memory may be evoked by many things as the treatment recommended for patients of amnesia – photographs, places, re-enactments of past events, people – the whole lot of it. As Myrian Sepúlveda Santos asks:

> How are these two ways of relating to the past intertwined? The problems concerning the definitions of memory involve

how different forms of time consciousness can be related. To what extent is the act of telling stories, which involves *anamnēsis* that is creative thinking and imagination, opposed to *mnēmē*? (169)

The past in its pastness is outside our reach. Its relationship to the present and its likely impact on the future are also embedded in it. Migration, in its third or fourth generation, may thrust the past under layers of dust, distance it but the past has a tendency to resurface as the stories of the progeny of the indentured workers, record. It remains with us, whether we choose to recognise it or not.

The writing of the diaspora differs from the writing at home, primarily in its location. Thus, when it looks back at the home country and writes about it, it depends on memory and re-construction. If it locates itself in its present, then moves back, as in Ramabai Espinet's *Swinging Bridge*, it locates the narrative physically in its own location and is true to its locational reality but the moment it locates itself in the homeland, its authenticity is tested. The reading of diasporic writing demands this approach else the reader is taken in by a framing which is not truly representative, and from our location at home, this is an important consideration – how do they 'write' us? To what extent is the representation somewhere reflective of the 'real'? I use the word 'real' very cautiously, as in itself there is no 'real'. It is always related to space, time and the individual's location. But its proximity to what is or was actual – a hermeneutic reading of the past is important and an indication of the authenticity of feeling, comprehension and expression. Uma Parameswaran uses the term 'authenticity' in her essay 'What Price Expatriation?' and writes, 'the novel, more than any other genre, demands authenticity in the portrayal of society and sensibility'.[11] She equates it with realism, but I want to de-link it from 'realism'. The authentic goes further than that to relate to sensibility and relationships, both to the self and the subject. It is an ontological identification. I fall back on Lionel Trilling's 1972 work *Sincerity and Authenticity*[12], where Trilling makes a distinction between the two terms of his title. While sincerity is mainly concerned with relationship to the self as in Shakespeare's 'To thy own self be true', authenticity goes on to embrace a while civilisational discourse. It is concerned with the human, the humanity of the human being which is under constant threat. The authentic, then, is often in opposition to environmental pressures – cultural, economic, technological and global. It defines the human ability to explore the underside of modern civilisation as well as the human 'unconscious'. It is, at one level, an inbuilt warning signal in the whole discourse of modernity.[13]

It is a huge demand we place on the writer, but it is the demand on every good writing and goes to justify its position in the times to come, it tells us why we read it and remember it. It also helps us identify the 'classic' as it takes shape right before our eyes.

In the essays in this collection, the homeland/homelands is are placed at the centre and around it are assembled the various acts and modes of remembering the past across time and distance, moving from the immediate past to the distanced past and work with the various issues that the writers raise. In the writing of these subcontinental diasporic writings, several different narrative styles and modes are evident. Narrative styles vary from the *katha*, the *Tuti-Maina* stories, the *Thousand and One Nights* to modern and postmodern modes. The dominant concerns of poetics, aesthetics, memory and representation, form an underlying strand of continuity. Besides this, there is also a continuity of ideas and texts.

But no single volume can hope to cover the immensity of the philosophical and ontological issues because writing changes, realities shift and perceptions differ. And may they continue to do so, else a static world would be dead and boring.

NOTES & REFERENCES

1. Refer Nayantara Sahgal, *This Time of Morning* (New York: W.W. Norton, 1962. Published in India by Orient Paperbacks. n.d.).
2. Sajjad Zaheer, *A Night in London* (New Delhi: Harper Perennial, 2012).
3. Refer Giriraj Kishore, *Pahla Girimitiya* (Hindi), (New Delhi: Bharatiya Jnanpith, 1999).
4. I refer the reader to the Introduction in Jasbir Jain's *Writers of the Indian Diaspora* (Jaipur: Rawat Publications, 1998), 11–20. The Introduction brings together my view on postcolonialism as I saw it at that time and refers to several contemporary critics Arif Dirlik, Arun Prabha Mukherjee and Abdul JanMohammed – all of who have done significant work in this area and raised important issues.

5. Chinua Achebe's *Home and Exile* (New York: Anchor Books, 2001), is a slim volume in itself but a very honest (and moving) account of colonialism and its aftermath. It offers an insight into several issues: educational apparatus, the writing of the fifties and sixties, the way towards decolinisation of the mind with the human being at the centre of it all.
6. Refer Homi Bhabha, *The Location of Culture* (London and New York: Routledge, 1994). The blurb describing the contents of the book goes on to state: 'In *The Location of Culture*, Homi Bhabha sets out the conceptual imperative and the political consistency of a postcolonial intellectual project ... he explains why the culture of western modernity must be *relocated* from the postcolonial perspective', (emphasis mine). The chapter 'Sly Civility' (93–101) is the one I refer to later in this very essay.
7. Ella Shohat, 'Notes on the "Post-Colonial"', internet ref. http://www.jstor.org accessed 12 November 2014. originally published in *Social Text* No. 31/32. *Third World and Postcolonial Issues* (1992) 99–113.
8. Edward Said, 'Secular Criticism'. *The World, The Text and The Critic* (Cambridge: Massachusetts. Harvard University Press, 1983. 1–30, 5. Also see *Edward Said's Translocations* Ed. Tobias Doring and Mark Stein (New York: Routledge, 2012), essays written by several critics on Said's concepts and their practice.
9. Abdul JanMohamad, 'Worldiness – without world, homelessness as home: Toward a Definition of the Specular Border Intellectual', in *Edward Said: A Critical Reader* (Oxford UK: Blackwell, 1992). 96–109.
10. Myrian Sepúlveda Santos, 'Memory and Narrative in Social Theory. The Contribution of Jacques Derrida and Walter Benjamin' in *Time and Society*. Vol 10 (2/3) 163–189 (London, Thousand Oaks, CA and New Delhi, 2001). Internet download, Accessed 14 October 2014, 163–189: Sage, 169.
11. Uma Parameswaran, 'What Price Expatriation?,' in *Writing the Diaspora* (Jaipur: Rawat, 2006) 20–36, 23.
12. Lionel Trilling, *Sincerity and Authenticity* (Cambridge, Massachusetts: Harvard University Press, 1972).
13. For more background reference see Freud, *Civilisation and Its Discontents*. Trilling works with it in fair detail. I would also like to draw attention to Tagore's 1941 essay 'Crisis in Civilisation' (*The Crisis of Civilisation and Other Essays*, New Delhi: Rupa & Co. 2003). It would be of interest to refer to U.R. Ananthamurthy's 'The Search for an Identity: A Kannada Writer's Viewpoint', (Jasbir Jain Ed. *Creating Theory: Writers on Writing*, Delhi: Pencraft International, 2000) 145–158.

1

Writing Home

Memory, History and Imagined Spaces

Locations, space and time – each one of these categories moves into a double or a multiple discourse, the moment the diaspora decides to 'write' home. I use the word 'write' in all its multiplicity: writing – the fact of creative expression; writing – as an inscription, a mark, a definition, and 'writing' as a connectivity as if being called back, answering a summon. Memory is both process and raw material; process as it covers many journeys back and forth as a new subjectivity is defined, as relationships are reviewed and very often cleansed of bitterness and regret and the raw material as it is the only reality which has been experienced either by them or their ancestors, that has created them, made them what they are. All the cultural nuances so imperceptibly imbibed and internalised and often fretted against, are now highlighted and framed through the act of remembrance – an act which is simultaneously a process of self-analysis, self-discovery and relocation. It is raw material for, no matter how distanced they feel from it, it is the *primary* baggage they have lugged along the route, the context that provides a meaning. And it is through this they have inhabited familial, social and national spaces. Both history and geography coalesce in this memory as 'a place on the map is also a place in history'.[1] Space becomes an important category through a double process – one of experience, the other of memory. The two may not reveal the same vision. Experiencing as a participant is different from witnessing as an observer. The recollected space is defined through a process of selection or through an experiential reality which too has undergone a transformation through a sifting and an evaluatory hindsight.

Memories work through spatial images as wide-ranging as houses, landscapes, battle-fields and innerscapes. And even as they work through time, they are non-synchronous in time with contrary images clashing with each other. The narratives I wish to discuss bring together memories of the homeland with all their complexity of history, politics and exile and are predominantly narratives of 'mourning'. Sara Suleri's two memoirs are elegies; one – *Boys Will Be Boys* – carries *A Daughter's Elegy* as a descriptive subtitle.[2] The other *Meatless Days*[3] is a mellow homage to her Welsh mother, who lived her life in an adopted space. Khaled Hosseini's *The Kite Runner*[4] is also a mourning for a lost homeland, a dead half-brother, a dead father, and an unborn child. It is also an elegy for the loss of innocence. Rohinton Mistry apparently writes about Nariman Vakil and his divided family which becomes a story of the past and the destruction of a city. *Family Matters*[5] is, in fact, about a nation which needs to rework its model of space. Sorayya Khan in her very first novel *Noor*[6] works with histories of difference, war, defeat, loss and of coming together. Memories, both conscious and unconscious, lived through or inherited through a pre-birth trauma crowd the space as surrealistic images flow out in the coloured drawings of Noor.

These are the diaspora writers, all first generation diaspora – and their memories are involved with their past in active association. But mourning as Vijay Mishra has stated, is a continuing process[7] which works itself through residual cultural inputs, a search for roots, in an attempt to explain the fact of this permanent migrancy. But then there are also the floating diaspora like Kamila Shamsie, Vikram Seth and in some measure Mohsin Hamid who too 'write' home where history and culture are concerned. The manner in which they use time, memory and space offers an insight into the difference in rooted memories, those of the temporary diaspora who flit in and out of their home-countries and are constantly in touch with its raw reality, and floating memories, which represent the permanent diaspora with a selection of montages like a photo album. Their different mourning strategies are reflected in these narratives through the use they make of exterior space in relation to the space of the mind.

One is always very hesitant in making general statements: the creative mind eludes them all. Yet, unless we begin with the difference, the sharpness of individual processes remains hidden. Kamila Shamsie's *Broken Verses*[8] like Suleri's memoirs, is a narrative of mourning – for a mother, who Aasmani believes is still alive, for the poet who was pushed into prison, exile and death, and also for a nation gone awry. The novel begins with a dream. But dreams have a tendency to go sour. Hamid, through an unputable-down monologue in *The Reluctant Fundamentalist*[9] writes home through the wide view of cultural clashes, racial subjectivities, ambition-driven youth and the collectivity of a nation through the narrow space of a wayside cafe in Lahore. This memory is laced with self-critiquing, contrastive studies in culture and is a frontal attack on hegemonic self-conceit whether of the east or the west.

These narratives, falling in different genres and spread over a writing period of nearly two decades (1989 to 2007) choose to work with memories of the past, that refuse to be buried, memories that have a living presence and a foot in the future. They go back in time from a standpoint in the present to histories way back to more than half-a-century, when 'freedom' was an obsessive value. The hedging in of this freedom, the felt need to take escape-routes, the closing-in of spaces – the prison cells, the fractured legs, the battered bodies, the closing-in of the human mind all work criss-cross in these engagements with subcontinental histories.

At a sub-narrational level there is the muted rationality for travelling abroad, for rejecting the nation, and an equally poignant realisation that despite it all, the homeland calls. Hosseini's semi-autobiographical narrative very succinctly states, 'For me, America was a place to bury my memories. For Baba, a place to mourn his' (Hosseini 112). In fact, graves too are a space. And they can be of different kinds – some where we can place flowers as a fragrant presence of a memory, others which are mass graves, badly dug, in which bodies are lying over one-another, dead – or perhaps even half-alive, and a lost child searches for a mother or a father. Sorayya Khan's four-generational family is built upon the memories of the mass grave where Ali, as a Pakistani soldier, fighting a war in East Pakistan, is organising a mass burial: 'Then he stood next to others, if there were others, to offer namaaz-e-janazah, funeral prayers, for it was his duty to respect the dead' (Khan 207). But these burials are also a battleground. As the Bengalis crowd in around the grave, the soldiers unable to cope with it, use their guns. Shot follows shot – and the living join the dead (212). Graves can also be appropriated as Ifat does her father's grave, dying in an accident – a hit-and-miss murder, and following close on the heels of her dead mother. And graves also get erased. When Sara goes back home to visit her mother's grave she cannot locate it and offers her flowers at some other grave.[10] Memory may pursue one, be resurrected out of the past as it happens in *Noor*, but it may be forcibly resisted and a conscious effort made to reduce it to silence as it happens in *Meatless Days*. The 1971 war was one such moment. On Javed's return from Bangladesh, Suleri comments, that the prisoners came back to 'a world that did not really want to hear kind of stories they had to tell' … 'My terror asked me, how will Ifat do it, make Javed's mind a human home again and take those stories from his head?' (*Meatless Days* 144). Ali in *Noor* gets no such helping hand. Instead, years later his mother digs out his memories, prodded by the uncanny remembrance of his granddaughter and the confessional scene reenacted for Sajida's benefit. Written more than a decade apart, the two writers, Khan and Suleri, work through the different facets of national memories in their work.

There are some memories which refuses to be buried, because they have intertwined themselves in countless little ways into the living present. Amir, Hosseini's narrator in *The Kite Runner*, is repeatedly caught unawares by images of the past – his own hurt lip as a memory of Hassan's hare-lip, the child Sohrab's uncanny skill at the slingshot, the kite that separates and brings together, Hassan's rapist, resurfacing as his son's and Amir's enemy, and the centrality of the orphanage which his father had built, replaced by the orphanage where Sohrab was kept. Memory is also constantly kept alive by a nagging sense of guilt. And more than all else by the compulsion to go over the same ground, the same landscape and feel the overlaying of the past by a grim reality. Baba's house has literally become a grave of history, dreams and individual and collective futures as the Hitlerian racism travels to far-off places across geography and time.

Mistry's *Family Matters* and Hosseini's *The Kite Runner*, narratives located in different geographical spaces – Kabul and far-off America in one, and Bombay/Mumbai in the other – share the story of Rustum and Sohrab, reaching beyond both temporal and spatial memories to histories lying buried in the Persian past. Firdausi's *Shahnama* is also a record of war, of victory interwoven with defeat, a son threatened by death at his father's hands, of separation and illegitimate children. Amir, taking advantage of the illiterate Hassan, never discloses to him the true ending; for Nariman Vakil the past unfolds itself as a relationship and as a crossing-over, when rejected by his step-daughter, he finds refuge in the cramped space of his own daughter's house.

These writers look toward the homeland, though in entirely different ways. Sara Suleri negotiates the past, and through her recollections, travels through the failures of the nation, the sorrows of her father and the silences of her mother, created by her vociferous husband, the strangeness of language and a resistant culture and 'the centuries' worth of mistrust of English women.' She learned to abnegate power (*Meatless Days* 163). The shadow of political uncertainty is always there, always looming large even as an island of evanescent bonhomie and laughter is created inside the four walls of their home. Hosseini's is a journey twice taken in search of guilt and forgiveness as Amir struggles against his personal sense of failure and observes the sliding down of his childhood ideals. Habits long cultivated by aristocratic conditioning and the practice of feudalism, give way to a more realistic pattern of behaviour as refugeedom claims them.

Mistry, moving away from a direct confrontation with politics, constructs a micro-family which works with its internal divisions. Nariman's love for Lucy, thwarted by his parents, is an unfulfilled relationship which haunts him his whole life. Marriage to a widow with two children gives him a ready-made family. Significantly enough, all these texts, whether autobiographical or imagined, project half-families grafted on to another part. Amir discovers his half-brother, only after his father's death. There are several families – Amir's, his father's and Ali's. None of them is made up of a single unit. Ali's first wife had left him, the second had been seduced by his master and had subsequently eloped. His son is not his own –

not engendered by him. Baba, Amir's father, a rich Afghan merchant, holds on to his friendship with Ali and his fatherhood of the hare-lipped Hassan. His is a family divided by caste. Ali and therefore Hassan are Hazaras. Later Amir's own family consists of his wife and the adopted Hazara nephew, Sohrab. None of the families is genealogically pure. Sara knows Nuz is their step-sister (*Meatless Days*), Coomy and Jal are Nariman's step-children (*Family Matters*) and in *Noor* the family is one solely of adoption, a creation of love, when a Pakistani soldier adopts a forlorn *waif* of a Bengali fisherman crossing barriers of race, region and language, and brings her to Pakistan a family is born. Similarly *Broken Verses* has a double set of mothers and a half-sister. These half-families move across caste hierarchy, strict religious boundaries (such as the Zoroastrian), cross racial differences, or fail to cross them thus throwing into prominence relationships. They raise questions about the nature of fatherhood, the construct of a nation, about love and hatred, guilt and forgiveness. Not that they all yield or work towards similar answers. Both the nature of experience and the truth of history are different in each case; the genres are also different.

In some measure, these narratives also question the whole concept of a nation when they present critiques (Suleri), internal divisions and external aggression (Hosseini), one fragment of a nation (Mistry) and convergences of languages, cultures and histories (Sorayya Khan), Through the extensions of self and questioning of stable cultures, they also seem to state that there is something deeply wrong with methodological nationalism when we relate to plural societies and placing of migrancy in the modern context. As Daniel Chernilo observes, the very idea that the nation-state is 'the natural or necessary container of modern social life' is a mistaken one.[11] The link between 'cultures, peoples, or identities and specific places' is no longer immutable or valid.[12] Cultures and identities spill over into other spaces.

The important question to ask is – why recall? Are the obvious reasons the real reasons; are Suleri's memoirs an elegy, a homage or a personal account of mourning and search for solace? Are they also recounting the collapse of personal and collective dreams? The political history of Pakistan punctuates the narrative – the birth of the nation, the hold of the leader on the imagination of its followers, Gen Ayub Khan's regime, the wars with India, Bhutto, his decline and execution, Yayha Khan and Zia-ul-Haq. But between these markers and the personal narrative, there is a constant criss-crossing with prison terms and hit and miss deaths. One begins to wonder how easily the charges of sedition can be levied putting into question the concepts of loyalty, patriotism and freedom. Through the chinks of political control, one can sense the need for freedom.

Memory, even of historical events, is personal; it is rooted in a personal perspective. In Sara's case it is generated by the family environment. The events are also, perhaps, differently seen than they were at that time. Memory, no matter how personal, acquires a double layer. The lens is now focused on an event which is seen through a time lapse, which at that particular time, also constituted the unknown future. As it captures, or attempts to capture, the emotion of the moment in the past, there is an inevitable conjunction between two lines of vision. As each sibling is lovingly chalked out, the search for a plot beings. The reference to the teacher, who first told Shahid that he was going to write a book about him, is crucial to the understanding of the work. All that he writes of Shahid is 'Shahid is a good boy', a text designed for didactic religious purposes. 'Shahid is a good boy' dwells on the idea of goodness as defined in a patriarchal, theological society. But goodness, if cramped by rules, loses its merit. Suleri comments on this, 'It never had a plot to it, anyway, the story of your goodness' (*Meatless Days* 108). The point has already been made in the first chapter. Women did not count – 'the concept of a woman was not really part of an available vocabulary ...' (*ibid*. 1), the negotiation was with roles – a sister or a child or a wife or a mother or a servant'. Suleri is aware of the communicative nature of this writing home, 'My audience is lost, and angry to be lost, and both of us must find some token of exchange for this failed conversation' (*Meatless Days* 2). The narrative, thus, needs to continue from a female location – a matriarch who is unable to achieve that strange self-contained authority which would define a rootedness. The politics of dislocation have overtaken Dadi – she 'resented independence for the distances it made' (*ibid*. 2).

The luminosity of an Islamic culture which she is at pains to capture the code which is stressed in 'Shahid is a good boy', surfaces to the topmost layer with religion being taken to the streets. These were the years of the rise of Islamisation involved the suppression of individual freedom (the 70s, the period of the Tableeg, the Hudood Ordinance which was proclaimed and legislated in 1979–80), 'I think that we dimly know we were about to witness Islam's departure from the land of Pakistan'. The romance was over. God 'could now leave the home and soon would join the government' (*Meatless Days* 15).

Suleri's language works simultaneously at several levels – straightforward, poetic, personal, cryptic. There is no hesitation in stating the truth but the truth is dressed in an emotional response. The laughter which we find in the relationship of the siblings, is lost in the silence of the house as they decide to scatter – Tillat moves to Kuwait after marriage, Sara to the States. And then their mother dies – apparently in a meaningless accident – but in actuality a murder. Ifat joins her through another accident.

The other side of memory is forgetting. We remember lest we forget. But we forget because we do not want to remember. We remember to keep alive the past; we forget in order to create new communities.[13] Suleri writes 'One morning I awoke to find that, during the course of the night, my mind had completely ejected the names of all the streets in Pakistan, as though to assure that I could not return, or that if I did, it would be returning to a loss' (*Meatless Days* 18). A loss represented by young deaths and younger graves.

Memory and history are supposed to contrast with each other – memory is personal, akin to commonsense, history is systematic and a critical collective memory.[14] But who represents the collectivity? Whose voice is it? And how does the distancing or the framing take place? Is it through objectivity or emotion objectified? Does a witness-participant have greater legitimacy over an observer? In Suleri's case memory and history are interwoven, her experience of history is through the emotional range of her family as each individual reacts to the situation either through death, escape or flight or alternately by being put into prison. These recalls cannot be labeled as revisionists, they unveil the human side of history.

The memoirs work through memories and responses – to womanhood, to politics, to the lives of the siblings, the shared space and through language and the deaths she was part of at times from a distance, only through emotions. The recall is also through dreams (*Meatless Days* 44). From births of nation and self, to deaths and then to education, to America, back to the past, all through there is a movement to and fro from Bhutto to 1947, to Zia-ul-Haq to Jinnah, back to the present. We had, she writes, 'lost the art of location' (81). Thus when she wants to pay her respects to the dead – to her mother and sister Ifat – she is unable to locate the graves (87–88).

Meatless Days recounts in innumerable ways the reasons for her migration – the womenless world, the overpowering of history, the cramping of freedom (123). *Boys Will Be Boys* follows a somewhat different course. It is both a proxy writing – stepping in to fulfil her father's unfulfilled intentions, and a peri-autobiography, fully demonstrating the limits of stepping into someone else's place – across gender, age and politics and a constant dialogue with her dead father. What is most touching and valuable about it is the return to Urdu poetry, inscribed in the Arabic script, going back to poets like Ghalib and Hali; poets of a shared past. These epigraphs evoke emotional memories and the aura of a culture still surviving under the political web. They also single out the issue of language as the immigrant goes back to dwell on the sound, and the syllables of the past. Subtitled 'a daughter's elegy', the memoir begins with a rare collectivity of sibling fragrances as the opening chapter signifies. The sisters decided they would wear the same perfume, each identified with her smell. The perfumes change, Ifat and Nuz die, others are scattered – and the verses of Urdu poetry linger untranslatable into a less resonant language (4–5). The references to Pip – their father – interrupt or interlace the narrative.

The past resurfaces, through cities and landscapes, through monuments, and wars. It is almost a parallel account of the events described in *Meatless Days* but the central character is Pip. Pip is also the listener. The memories are all evoked for him, he is addressed, drawn into her own memory. The father-children relationships with their surprises, restraints and teasing are knitted in and alternately she takes in his presence and his absence, his anger and petulance, his hopes and the shattering of these hopes. *Boys Will Be Boys* is also an account of how individual lives are lost in the making of dreams and nations. At the fag end of the memoir, there is a reference to Faiz. Kamila Shamsie in *Broken Verses* gives us an account of the poet's loves, confinement and efforts at eluding confinement. But Shamsie does not mention the poet's name. Turning it into a personal narrative, a fiction of interrupted emotions, Shamsie creates a mystical reality. Is it the difficulty of living in a society which one is trying to recall in its pain? Suleri's account of history on the other hand does not have to go in search of fiction; it stands by itself as a comment on the nature of censure and censorship as well as on the capacity of art to circumvent them.

Broken Verses covers almost the same period as Suleri's memoirs, with two differences – it has the freedom of fiction, and it is located in Pakistan. The politics of the period also asserts itself more strongly for it is a politics which intervenes with all kinds of relationships – mother-daughter, wife-husband, a woman and her lover. Freedom is gauged in terms of certainty, knowing what is happening in terms of sexuality – the freedom to choose who you love and how you love. It is also defined as the freedom to write. Hence the poet's figure is chosen as a representative of freedom, history, love and exile. Woven together through dreams, coded language and memory, *Broken Verses* faces politics frontally. Politics, as it is enacted through an ordinance (the Hudood Ordinance), gender discrimination and repressive authority (Bhutto's execution, confinement, exile and murder)[15], steps right into one's home. it has a degree of materiality in its use of space – the *Save the Date* studio, the bedroom with the open window, the public meetings Aasmani's mother addresses, and the chopped ingredients for biryani. There are other spaces of the mind – memories of separate bedrooms, of exile, of cities abroad. It also happens to be a novel of transgressions of all kinds – of conventions and character blueprints (142–143), and of the stereotyped cultural feminist norms, for solidarity amongst women can produce superwomen who can 'take on governments, buy the groceries, wrest religion out of the hands of patriarchs ...' (184). Memory, for Shamsie, is an inhabited space.

Khaled Hosseini's *The Kite Runner* runs a different course, close to history even as it narrates a story of personal evolvement. It is a narrative of how countries are ravaged, cultures shorn alike of their negative fixities and of their strengths, and replanted in other locales. Amir and his father leave home as refugees and migrate to States in search of peace and a better future. Here they are almost land-locked into their migrant community, where blood ties and kinship patterns, segregated womanhood, concepts of honour and the rituals of honour still prevail carried over from the native home. The real agency of change still remains the individual who, when placed in alien circumstances, needs to select, preserve and rebel. More significantly, the narrative works through a trope of guilt and forgiveness. How does one ask for forgiveness and is it possible to get it? Do the dead forgive? If not then who forgives? Does it have to be earned through a personal act of expiation? It is in this intermixing of history with individual life that the Ricoeurian description of 'the epistemology of history borders on the ontology of being-in-the-world'.[16]

Fiction does not depend on historical veracity, it depends on historical truth. To that extent, veracity, reality and truth, each is different from the other – veracity cannot be measured, cannot be known unless it is subjected to a multi-focus. Reality is limited to a single experience: again everyone's perception and sensibility of reality is different. Truth, despite its multi-dimensionality and indefinability, is capable of being defined in terms of human loss, pain and anguish. Those who live in the moment touch shoulders with truth, and fiction enables a reliving in a partially sanitised atmosphere. The aesthetics of narration, even as it ignites and re-awakens the pain, allows it to be bearable. *The Kite Runner*, through its circuitous geographical and emotional moves, travels across a period of more than a quarter century – 1975 to 2002, moves back even further in time, to a period not recalled personally but through others, moves across space from Afghanistan to States, back again to Afghanistan via Pakistan – Peshawar, Khyber Pass, Islamabad, through traditions of honour, military glory and peace to the weekly flea market and petrol pump jobs, from freedom of the streets to coats and uniforms hanging loosely on ageing shoulders. Throughout the narrative certain themes hold it in place and one such connectivity is the phrase 'For you a thousand times over' (*The Kite Runner* 59, 61, 323). Kite-flying itself is a symbol of the spirit of independence of the Afghan people: 'Afghans cherish custom but abhor rules. And so it is with kite-fighting .... Fly your kite. Cut the opponents. Good Luck' (*ibid*. 45).

Assef's rape of Hassan is a symbol of power gone wrong, of the rape of a country, aided by its own people. And Sohrab's attack on Assef with his sling is, on the face of it, a rescue operation for Amir but also the hand of fate with the son settling his father's debts. Hassan's rape is parallelled by the narration of the lamb being sacrificed for Eid (*ibid*. 67); it happens in Amir's moment of celebration. Beneath these recurring metaphors the central concern of morality and ethics; is woven throughout. Amir in his personal relations violates the code of ethics in his relation to his conscience and of morality.[17] The journey back to Afghanistan is necessary for his redemption. Rahim Khan acts as his conscience as well as his father's conscience. He protects the child Amir from his father's wrath, realising full well the guilt of young Amir's lie, shields him. In this he fails as his conscience. Thus, Rahim Khan's summoning him back for a purpose only half-stated, giving him the name of a non-existent orphanage is justified on account of the Polaroid photograph he has with him of Hassan and his son Sohrab. It is essential for Rahim Khan to summon him back. In 1988 he had gone to Bamiyan in search of Ali and Hassan, in order to bring them back: again an act of restoration. Now Amir is handed over the responsibility of bringing Sohrab out of the Taliban-infested Afghanistan, back to some semblance of life.

It is in the journey back that the personal narrative expands to take into itself the larger narrative of war, aggression, poverty and hunger as the war between power and the powerless is fought on many fronts. There is a silent questioning of the justification of choices – Assef's who stays to destroy rather than leave with his parents, of the Russians, then the Americans and all the proxy powers who fight their wars on alien territory. There is a questioning of the meaning of development and of prosperity. The larger ends of life are constantly lost to smaller gains.

At the heart of *The Kite Runner* is the critiquing of a feudalistic culture, a careful sifting of its values that can survive on an alien soil, and its expansion into a larger discourse of guilt, expiation and forgiveness. Amir, in addition to his own guilt was also the 'unwitting embodiment of Baba's guilt'. He was the legitimate half, inheritor of the guilt and Hassan the 'unentitled, unprivileged half' who had inherited what had been 'pure and noble in Baba' (313). Forgiveness and trust go together. As Amir asks Sohrab's forgiveness, he wonders 'how long before Sohrab smiled again. How long before he trusted me. If ever.'

Hosseini's recounting of history is a statement of facts, his recounting of human lives what historical events do to them, how they toss people around, dislocate them and eject them from their cultures. His *'writing'* home is a writing *of* home, meant for both sides of the cultural divide, a writing for the outsider summoning him to probe his conscience as well as the insider for his divisionary approach. *Noor* coming out the same year (2003) as *The Kite Runner*, is also a novel about self-reflection, guilt, the difficulty of living with the past and a need for forgiveness, if family communities wish to relate. Ali's sector becomes a representative home with an inner compulsion to face the ghosts before they can be exorcised. It is not only collective memory, but memory transmitted through the body, obsessed with the past and its dead. Words, names and actions echo back; dress codes, tailoring techniques rise up from the river waters which are coloured red as is the blood of the menstrual flow (*Noor* 130), and the blood which continues to ooze even after one is dead (128-130). Haunted by memories, one gives up praying, one gives up talking about the past and also gives up certain kinds of food.

Family Matters, again like *The Kite Runner*, is addressed to both the host country and the country of origin. Through this family narrative, the idea is to reshape the nation along filial lines. Mistry writes about a Parsi household, comprising of three generations but Nariman Vakil's parents, who were responsible for the damage done to Nariman are the fourth generation looming large in the background even as they are absent from the period under review. Historical events fill in the background – the demolition of Babri Masjid, the Bombay riots, the Shiv Sena, but what is central is the relationship at home. Two kinds of space – the big, roomy flat that Nariman owns and has willed to his stepchildren and the small flat he has bought his daughter – are contrasted. Unwanted in the first he is bundled off to the second with a broken ankle. His son-in-law washes his hands off all responsibility. Then follows a narrative of forced closeness, age old smells, economic pressures and inner debates about right and wrong. Pressed for money Yezad thinks of gambling, the two grandsons Murad and Jehangir make their own contribution. Murad saves on bus fares, Jehangir is tempted by his co-students' bribes. A lesson in morality is lived out and Yezad can finally bring himself to offer nursing care to his father-in-law. In the other flat, Coomy has the plaster knocked off in order to delay

Nariman's return but in the process she meets her end and Jal, who had always resented her rejection of Nariman, offers help to his half-sister. The two families come together and the economic situation is eased. But two issues remain worrisome – Yezad's increased religiosity and the distancing in relationships when there is adequate space. Why this turn to religion – a return to purity, a holding on to the past? At the end of the novel we learn that Yezad during the past few years has read nothing but religious books, as though making up for lost time. The house is full of books about 'Parsi history and Zoroastrianism, various translations of the Zend-Avesta, interpretations of the Gathas ...' (451). There is a withdrawal from the world of politics, the materialism of Mrs Kapur, the black money transactions and tax evasions of Mr Kapur. Yezad is no longer employed. But religion has made him serious, obsessed, perpetually scurrying for a bath at the slightest touch from another. Once again the question of marrying someone from outside the community crops up; it has come full circle from Nariman to Murad. Can a community lock itself in the past or is there a way of relating to others without hatred, manipulation and corruption? Yezad now cordons off space, and is in no mood to continue old ties – almost an anti-social attitude that rejects without examining. His journey is a journey into the past, triggered off by the photographs of Bombay as it once was, neat and clean and not crowded, shorn of all ugliness. These photographs represent the transference of someone else's memory into Yezad's imagination – a coming together of time and space.

Religious orthodoxy, in itself, closes-in the world, creates barriers, sends out messages of closure. Yezad, like Assef in *The Kite Runner* and like Changez, in *The Reluctant Fundamentalist*, turns to a closure of identity. But they are not similarly motivated except that all three feel shaken in their historical bearings. All else is different. Assef is driven by a streak of cruelty, a sense of power and a desire of conquest: human life has no value for him. Yezad is driven to it by frustration, rejection, fading hopes and a family divided by personal interests. One needs to think how far are Mrs Kapur and the Shiv Sena responsible for his orthodoxy – how when territories are being fenced in, religion becomes the refuge. The reluctant fundamentalist is not overtly obsessed. He closes in for reasons of self-preservation. The Lacanian mirror reveals to him, his racial self cloaked in a religious identity. What price white colour, the

Princetonian education, the competitive edge, if they are all going to rule out relationships. Erica is a half-alive, half dead monument to relationships; and Juan-Bautista in far-off Chile, as he presides over a failing publishing house, touches a respondent chord in him (Hamid 141–143, 145) when he draws his attention to the fact of self-destruction indulged in through self-interest. Juan Buatista's reference to the janissaries who fought for the Ottoman Empire with fierce loyalty to 'erase their own civilizations' (151) is an eye-opener and a conscience-pricker. Which side is one on? This is the litmus test for the diaspora. Changez resolves to look around with an ex-janissary's gaze and consider reality from a holistic perspective. Changez's fundamentalism is not religious, it is not even cultural; it is more a question of nationhood, location and perspective, a search for freedom from serfdom and indentured labour. The blanket of suspicion subsequent to his resignation, disturbs him as his whole identity, nationality and religious affiliation are under question.

Fundamentalism resurfaces as a measure of self-defence, as resistance to being entirely take over by alienness, or being incorporated in a larger whole or slotted in a marginal role. In Changez's case it is the impact of exteriority on the making of his self. The encroachment of outer space into his inner being leads him to realise that boundaries cannot be restored, once they have been blurred – 'Something of us is now outside, and something of the outside is now within us' (174). Changez locates the struggle for national identity in a power-struggle, as a result of the dangerous game of power politics.[18]

Suleri and Mistry as they 'write' home, expose its many myths and deconstruct its many stereotypes. They both juxtapose closed worlds with open worlds where boundaries can be crossed. If Suleri's memoirs are dominated by aura, Mistry's novel is dominated by images – the image of old age – upright by the seashore, prostrate, crumpled upon a bed, and the beautiful image of Daisy, fully dressed for a stage performance, giving a deathbed performance. These novels deal with the past both in their historical and fictive presence. But Sorayya Khan in *Noor* projects an imagined space, made up of pieces of history.

Briefly *Noor* is a plea for peace. The oddly constructed family with affiliations going across race, colour, language and history becomes both a utopia and a human space with the little children of a fourth generation being born there, with the son-in-law – the outsider – moving in. The youngest child who is limited in her mental capacities throws her father out of the room, he sleeps in the dining space and rolls his bed back before anyone else is up. Her possessiveness is an assertion of her claim to space. And she expresses herself through her colours and drawings, which uncannily portray the scenes of the cyclone in Bangladesh, the rolling of trucks, the rescue, the tall palm trees swaying. How on earth did the child imagine those scenes of loss and aggression? Is it inherited, anguish and fear of the mother as a child passed on to a future embryo? How much continuity is there in terror? When imagined constructs of peace are transferred, they address the question both of self-imposed exile and deep cultural and emotional affiliations. At a deeper level, the novel engages with the issues of guilt, expiation, forgiveness and the need for a relationship that heals.

The diaspora 'writes' home to fulfil its many psychological, emotional and historical needs; it also feels free to comment on the political or religious happenings that push the nation into orthodoxies, fundamentalism and closed spaces. There are other reasons: it writes home to be 'visible' in the host culture, not as a waif but a person with a meaningful, valuable past. It also writes to establish a two-way connectivity and constantly chisel at a past which it claims. And then, that part of the diaspora which 'writes' home, does it also for the future. It combines a necessary exorcism with a convergence of polarities, which it seeks to dismantle through its repetitive journeys. It is a self-questioning and becomes for the writer a simultaneous habitation of plural spaces even as it critiques ingrowing and inbreeding of cultures. *Noor* carries the epigraph from Agha Shahid Ali's verse 'Your history gets in the way of my memory.' Memory, in the end is subversive of history and is an account of all that has slipped through the gaps – the interstices.

NOTES & REFERENCES

1. Adrienne Rich, 'Notes Towards a Politics of Location' *Feminist Postcolonial Theory: A Reader.* Eds. Reina Lewis and Sara Mills (Edinburgh: Edinburgh University Press), 2003. 30. Rich's comments are related to the location of identity in terms of nation, race, ideology, sex and sexual preference.

2. Sara Suleri, *Boys Will Be Boys: A Daughter's Elegy* (2003, New Delhi: Penguin, 2004).
3. Sara Suleri, *Meatless Days* (1989, London: Flamingo, 1991).
4. Khaled Hosseini, *The Kite Runner* (2003, London: Bloomsbury, 2004).
5. Rohinton Mistry, *Family Matters* (London: Faber and Faber, 2008).
6. Sorayya Khan, *Noor* (New Delhi: Penguin, 2003).
7. Vijay Mishra, 'The Impossible Mourning', *In Diaspora*, Ed. Makarand Paranjape, (New Delhi: Indialog), 24–51.
8. Kamila Shamsie, *Broken Verses* (London: Bloomsbury, 2005).
9. Mohsin Hamid, *The Reluctant Fundamentalist* (New Delhi: Viking), 2007.
10. Also see *The Kite Runner*, 152–153.
11. See Daniel Chernilo, *A Social Theory of the Nation-State* (London: Routledge), 2001. 1.
12. See Introduction, *Displacement, Diaspora and Geographies of Identity*. Eds. Smader Lavie and Ted Swedenburg (Durham: Duke University, 1996).
13. Also see Avishai Margalit, *The Ethics of Memory* (Cambridge, Mass: Harvard University Press, 2002, 2004) 'Preface' viii–ix
14. Margalit, 63.
15. See Kamila Shamsie, *Broken Verses* (New Delhi: Penguin). 92–96.
16. See Paul Ricoeur, *Memory, History and Forgetting*. Trans. By Kathleen Blamey and David Pallauer (Chicago: University of Chicago Press, 2004) 208.
17. See *The Ethics of Memory*, 7. Margalit makes a distinction between the morality of ethics and the morality of memory. The first is concerned with loyalty and betrayal, the second with respect and humiliation. Amir is guilty of violating both. By accusing Hassan of being a thief he is doubly betraying him, and Hassan is aware of this. His silence is a constant reproach. As Rahim realises the truth, Amir thus also suffers a loss of respect (as well as self-respect) and humiliation. His many attempts to push it aside do not put the gnawing of the spirit to an end. The guilt has to be replayed, this time alongside expiation, for even a temporary rehabilitation of the self.
18. For more details of power politics, refer Tariq Ali's *The Clash of Fundamentalisms* (London: Verso), 2002.

2

The Burden of Culture
Between Filiation and Affiliation

Culture is what defines us, a burden we carry wherever we go. The word 'burden' is meant to convey its positive as well as the negative meaning – a cross to be borne as well as the mainstay, the recurring refrain of our existence. A huge abstraction in itself, the word culture moves easily from being a noun to an adjective and a verb, implying impositions, design and education. Over the centuries cultures have changed; the major agencies of change being: time in its historical flow, migration as dislocation and belief manifested in religion or through religious conversion. The carriers of culture are multiple, languages and rhythms being only some of them. Nations have for long dealt with cultural pluralities wisely or unwisely but when cultures move outside a nation state, the issues of visibility and power, of rights and acceptability bring the cultural differences to the fore, and 'difference' again is a problematic term. I deliberately use the word plurality here rather than diversity. Allow me to explain why diversity emphasises difference and assumes a norm; it implies strangeness and unfamiliarity. The OED explains that even in 1691 the word diverse was used to indicate differing from what is right, good, or profitable, while the world plurality signifies a co-existence that is more than one existing side by side. When people of different cultures live together within a nation, the sense of both belonging and equality can best be indicated through plurality. One needs then to ask, why is it that diasporic people in a land not of their origin, at times not even of their birth, with their umbilical cord buried in some far off place, need to work out different strategies of self-definition and cultural co-existence?

I propose to examine two main issues: what happens when cultures travel and how is this change reflected in intellectual life at the level of theory and in creative writing. Cultures travel, perhaps in the same way as ideas travel. Earlier missionaries, whether Buddhist or Christians, carried their beliefs into other regions; refugees and exiles too have done the same. In his essay 'Traveling Theory,' Edward Said has placed circulation of ideas across time and space at the centre of his argument. He asks the question whether ideas when shifted from one historical period and culture to another become altogether different or not, thus drawing our attention to the changes of locations and contexts. Anything foreign or unfamiliar is met by an initial resistance. Outlining four stages in this journey – point of origin, distance traversed, set of conditions of receptivity or resistance and the measure of transformation required by the new location – he warns against ideas hardening into cultural dogmas.[1]

Taking up the argument further, Vivek Dharweshwar relates it to the postcolonial identity focusing not on the travelling of ideas but the travelling of men who are both more porous and more resistant to change in his essay, 'Fortunate Traveling: Location, Theory and Post-colonial Identity'.[2] He carries forth the dialectic process between filiation and affiliation into theory and cultural formation. Like Said's reference to power implicated in the formation of a dogma, Dharweshwar brings in the Fanonian argument of filiative processes often resulting in 'a concentration on a hard core of culture which [becomes] more and more shrivelled up, inert and empty' as it resists the impact of external influences.[3] This is the beginning of a fundamentalist attitude. We can, perhaps, state the problem in different terms – how much of the home culture is the diaspora prepared to give up for purposes of adaptation of the host culture's values? Is change going to constitute a marginal place and is difference the target of discrimination? Again, using Said's emphasis on the changed context – is change inevitable or is it likely to lead to a schizophrenic split? Distance, in itself, is of material significance. Cultures when they travel only physically and through memory, tend to freeze. One of the reasons for this is the split that takes place in the individual's mind and the dialectic process between filiation and affiliation that does not take place.

But writers who are engaged in the interrogation of this reality, also have no easy solution to offer. Neil Bissoondath in *Selling Illusions: The Cult of Multiculturalism in Canada* is unhappy with the hyphen (118), and uneasy with ethnicity. The problem is of receptivity and acceptance in the new nation – of affiliation. He considers the implications of past loyalties as they function within the new citizenship in fairly strong terms and states: 'Any country that does not claim full loyalty of its citizens old or new, any country that embraces citizens old or new who treat it as a public washroom ... accepts for itself an internal weakening.'[4] Staying away and outside the outer world is also a condition of 'internal exile', a ghetto mentality.[5] Himani Bannerjee proceeds to look at the professed policy of Multiculturalism through another lens, as the diffusion of an internal debate between the French and the English and a distraction from it by shifting the focus to other immigrant minorities. Bannerjee underlines the discriminatory effects even of the laws of abortion and the control the state exercises over the bodies of women.[6] Canadian history (and that of the States), are full of laws that have gone to racialise society. Canada as a nation is not a given but a construct, a set of representations; as a population the 'non-whites are living in a specific territory', described as visible minorities or people of colour and the like. Immigrants are 'left with the paradox of both belonging and non-belonging, simultaneously' (64–65). *The Dark Side of the Nation* is a close examination of the histories of the various people who have come together to live in a land, but the different timings of their arrival have constructed a pattern of power and subordination (The Caribbeans are another example of plural societies going awry in terms of the hierarchies of power).

Plurality is the result of travelling on one hand and expansion on the other. Often it is in response to the laws of demand and supply in economic terms and the pursuit of ideas in intellectual terms. The legendary *'pardesi'* in India is placed within notions of the romantic 'other' while the family man's travels have been placed within trade and necessity. The journeys of exile in both the *Ramayana* and the *Mahabharata* have been journeys of experience as well as of adventure, through which the self has been transformed, but in none of the two have these internecine conflicts destabilised the hierarchy. The notion of social equality is foreign to them. But in present day migration, it needs to be problematised if the process of racial and economic colonisation has to be halted.

It is when plural societies fail to accommodate the democratic aspirations of its members that resentment is high. Arun Mukherjee's *Oppositional Aesthetics* is an assertion of the right to carry over the culture of origin to the new land and focuses on the problematics of finding ways of relocating a cultural sensibility. The unequal functioning of hybridity in imperial and colonial cultures has ironically enough provided an edge to the colonial people – we know more of the west, than the west knows of us. Compared to our exposure and our knowledge of their past, their cultures are insular and closed. The degree of 'foreignness' they perceive in our cultural artifacts is much higher than what we see in theirs. Mukherjee's struggle is partly a pedagogical one and partly one of highlighting the 'difference', which is of great importance for purposes of individual assertion and cultural identity. The fear of erasure pursues one if this difference becomes the cause either of homogenisation or of discrimination. The 'margins' at home acquire an added significance for the diaspora. Arun Prabha Mukherjee, like Gayatri Spivak, turns to the writing of other languages available back home – be it about the tribal or the dalit, be it in Hindi, Bengali or Marathi. The 'newness' of the self is important to the immigrant just as other models of margins are. Spivak turns to Mahasweta Devi's 'Draupadi' in *Other Worlds: Essays in Cultural Politics*[7] and Mukherjee to Phaneshwarnath 'Renu' in *Oppositional Aesthetics*[8] and later to Omprakash Valmiki's *Jhootan*.[9] It remains questionable whether these are issues of ideology, social commitment or the need for margins to get away from one's own self marginalisation. Or, is it that power structures can best be deconstructed, through an encounter of extremes? It is a complex problem and has both its merits and demerits in socio-psychological terms and needs a deeper analysis than what it has received till now.

In contrast to the oppositional position of Arun Prabha Mukherjee, Uma Parameswaran works with different strategies both in her work and in life. In her plays she reworks interpretations of the *Ramayana* in *Sita's Promise* and the Meera-Krishna relationship in *Meera*.[10] She works the Hindu religious symbolisation of the Ganga in her many essays thus carrying over the river into a new landscape.[11] In her essay, 'Dispelling the Spells of Memory: Another Approach to Reading Our Yesterdays,' she problematises the contradictions inherent in a diasporic situation. An identification with Canada and the capitalistic west, makes her part of the 'oppressor group', but again as a Canadian, she also feels a victim vis-à-vis the Big Brother America. Emotionally she relates more closely to the people of South India than to her country people, yet condemns self-ghettoisation. She, thus, wants to make space for herself, on her own terms and that would be through joining the mainstream in politics, culture and history so that Komagatu Maru becomes a part of Canadian history. She writes, 'we have to write about these events, talk about them, cross-reference them at every turn until they become literary and cultural archetypes of the history in Canada.'[12]

Good, practical sense. An acceptance requires that the immigrant has to adjust as well as assert. But somewhere there is snag. One, I find in her location of acceptance within a gender dimension, comparing the dislocation to a woman's dislocation from a parental home to her marriage home, totally unacceptable. It introduces a stereotype, a heavily loaded one with inequality and docility as its major characteristics, it may be also a degree of wishful survival strategy in order to validate migration.[13] Again, the easy acceptance of a 'divided' self – expressed here as well as in 'Diaspora Consciousness: Going Beyond the Hyphen Without Erasing It,' sidelines the conflict and projects the maxim, 'when in Rome do as the Romans do'. I wonder whether this division does not reflect a deeper division and undermines the identity of 'self', which needs to be more stable than what Parameswaran concedes. The acceptance of location, being a determinant of where one belongs, is a pragmatic solution to an issue of grave importance. The moral dimensions of the act of belonging are not debated expressly by any of the above critics.

One fall-out of this awareness of plurality that developed in the twentieth century is that the two-dimensional encounter between 'self' and the 'other', or between east and west that characterised the imperial incursions has been replaced by an exchange between the 'self' and its multiple 'others' that refuse to be contained within categories like, race, gender and religion and bring in a criss-cross of loyalties simultaneously anchored in several different categories, affiliations that run across one to another in terms of language, geographical regions and economic interests, loyalties that are also often at odds with each other. While the imperial discourse had used condescension as a major plank, the Gandhian discourse had problematised the issue of 'hatred' and Gandhi spent a lifetime working out strategies which could bring about freedom and equality without violence and the resultant hatred, the inevitable fall out of conflict. In this pursuit, Gandhi turned away from oppositional political categories to individuals and relationships framed in a cultural dialogue. Both Gandhi and Tagore debated the question of culture versus civilisation and the artificial schism created by the west in separating the two terms.[14]

The creative mind (as opposed to the analytical mind) has also framed this conflict within the orbit of human relationship, beginning with individual memory. Diasporic writers have used memory and history to understand not only the nature of the 'self' but also the nature of the 'other'. They have worked with a cultural past and woven it with the history of their ancestors, have explored the construction of the 'self' in a political world and experimented with the aesthetics of writing, negotiating not only their migratory experience but also their own cultural pluralities. This is applicable even more to the work of the twice-dislocated people like Ramabai Espinet and M.G. Vassanji. Vassanji's gunny sack becomes for Espinet the boxes in the storeroom back home and the remembered echoes of the songs her great grandmother has left come alive to her in the songs of Babooni, the beggar woman.

Ramabai Espinet's autobiographical novel *The Swinging Bridge* is about the slow discarding of several pasts and the gradual retrieval of those very pasts in order to discover the real self. The title *The Swinging Bridge* brings together the constant movement between the different pasts moving forward as well as sideways. At one point in the novel she describes it in the following terms:

> I made for the bridge and ran smoothly along until suddenly the spider web began to rock violently from side to side. The

ropes at the side picked up speed and swung high in the air – exactly like a swing. A swinging bridge … . I was terrified. I heard myself screaming loudly, but I continued to run the length of the bridge … . At any movement, I feared, the fine silk threads would break and I would be flung into the roaring river below.[15]

It is one of the finest descriptions of the fear, the compulsion and the desire to prove oneself that live side by side in the diasporic self as it tries to adjust the world of its inheritance with its contextual world. The novel is a 'retrieval' novel, where bits and parts of the past, fragments scattered in various places – childhood memories, overheard conversations, hearsay, prayer songs, a beggar woman, tales from the distant homeland – all come together. It is also a woman's novel despite the fact that agencies of both the migrations, the conversion to Christianity and other alliances may have been patriarchal. The language that carries memories belongs to domesticity – 'domestic words from long ago, a far-off time and place,' patois words of the courtyard. Ramabai writes, 'Words are ghosts, ancestors on this side' (5). When they are sung, they become songs of various moods, romantic, religious or nostalgic. Written they become records and refuse to be ignored. They rise out of diaries and relate to the future. Da-da, the protagonist Mona's grandfather, had made it a habit to write letters to newspapers, letters full of outrage and a growing sense of despair, letters against the racist attitude and refusal to allow community isolation. Da-da had asked the question, 'How can we contribute to the enterprise of nationhood, trapped as we are by this perception of ourselves which is lodged in the hearts and minds of our fellow countrymen of other races?' a question that lays bare the real problem of a plural society – the need of relationships between self and the other, between peoples of different communities and races, a mutual self-respect. When these are missing, and racial hierarchies continue to persist, conflict-situations will continue.

The illness of Mona's brother Kello becomes symbolic of several other ills. As the family rushes to be with him, the migration to Canada is bemoaned, because every dislocation brings its own share of stress and struggle against hostility. Migration remains an enigma. Why do people 'leave the place they were born for an illusion of a better life?' (25). The answers are many – racism, feared erasure of identity, a continual draining of self-image, political marginalisation – all these push people to the margins. People also leave in order to protect their children (202–203), to save them from social criticism and sexual exploitation. More than ideas, origins and cultures, it is the colour of the skin and the sex of the body that come to be negotiating factors in any plural society.

The Swinging Bridge follows two connecting patterns – one is the reference to the migration of a young thirteen year-old widow in 1879, '*my own great-grandmother Gainder, crossing the unknown of the kala pani, the black waters that lie between India and the Caribbean,*' and the story of Baboonie which connects up with Gainder's. Baboonie's voice rises above the sound of the rain as she sings of the *Ramayana*, 'breaking up the classical words of the *Ramayana* with her own tale of exile and banishment ... . Of racial and tribal grief, of banishment, of the test of purity' (108). These two women trace similar histories across time. As Mona reflects upon their lives, her early insistence on the inclusion of Cecile Fatiman in the film they were making on Haitian history, surfaces once again. Fatiman a black woman, was a priestess who had played a part in the Bois Ritual that had launched the Haitian revolution, but history had pushed her to a secondary position. Mona regrets the fact that another woman is 'edited out of history' (10–11). Mona's fear of erasure is real, as Fatiman does not find a place even in the film. If recorded histories leave women out, then women's histories choose to dwell in the oral tradition, in the songs that Baboonie sings and Gainder had sung. The family had insisted that the songs be included in the family history despite the objections of Grandpa James. Through her Mona traces her matrilineage, 'my great-grandmother who bore grandma Lil, who in turned produced five children ... who bore Muddie, who bore me ... . I made up my mind that when I went to Trinidad I would search for her songs until I found them' (257). The anchorage of the immigrant returns to history, which becomes a substitute for land, and is an attempt to preserve 'difference' and avoid erasure.[16] Imaginary constructs and strategies may differ from person to person.

Briefly, I want to look at two other writers who choose to travel in a different direction – Michael Ondaatje and Amitav

Ghosh. Rather than remain confined to the homeland or east-west encounter, they explore their difference amongst other pluralities. Naipaul, in his travelogues, has also partly done that, but the observer's eye prevents self-reflection. Ondaatje on the other hand first travels away, then zeroes in. There are three works which mark the route: *Running in the Family, The English Patient* and *Anil's Ghost*.[17] In between are other myths and histories he has opened out in *The Collected Works of Billy the Kid, Coming Through Slaughter, The Cinnamon Peeler* and *In the Skin of the Lion*. Of the three works dealing with homeward spaces, the first *Running in the Family*, as Anisur Rahman has described it, is a search for mythic space, a condition of the mind[18] while in *The English Patient*, one can see it as 'nowhere'. The novel is located in a villa in Italy, turned into a temporary hospital, with a patient with a burnt out face, and a Canadian nurse who is incidentally also nursing her broken relationships. Out of these broken lives, Ondaatje constructs a mixed group who trace their own histories. Kirpal Singh, the Indian, is also part of this group. They explore national histories, histories of civilisation, personal histories, literary texts and pour over maps. They expand to include the world in themselves, ruling out marginalisation. Almásy traces his kinship with Kip (Kirpal Singh) and remarks that both he and Kip are international bastards, 'born in one place and choosing to live elsewhere' one can perhaps link them to a later work, Pico Iyer's *Global Soul*. Almásy expresses his dislike for nations, and his admiration for the desert tribes. To belong nowhere and to belong everywhere are both states of freedom but nation states deform us (112). Perhaps this nowhere position is equally disturbing as Kip returns to India and Hara to Canada. Past histories claim their right.

In *Anil's Ghost* (2000) Ondaatje returns to Sri Lanka, and to broken bones and broken lives. Anil Tissera is a forensic expert and has come to Sri Lanka, her homeland, on a Human Rights mission. Significantly her work involves digging up histories and examining the dimensions of violence. Sarath an archaeologist is deputed to work with her. Together they dig up dead bodies and match soils. It is like digging up history. The burial of the recently dead in ancient sites is a cause for suspicion and the novel is the working out of this disjunction. It becomes Anil's obsession, as they try to reconstruct the face of the victim for purposes of identification. It takes them to meet Palipana – the seventy-six-year-old-scholar – a historian and an archaeologist. Palipana is also a semi-hermit, a permanent dissident, accused of forging a history of the sixth century. It is this controversial scholar that they turn to – and the novel asks several questions, all at the same time: are all histories not forgeries, where is the neutral, indisputable evidence and where the record of dissidence? The main narrative goes on to explore these three questions. Anil's pursuit of factual truth places her life in danger, in the end she is rescued to safety through Sarath's efforts even as her father's friend has given orders for her to be imprisoned with the implication of death.

Anil's Ghost is an amazing novel and a very complex one at that, with destruction and reconstruction working from opposite ends, with knowledge systems relying equally on science and on intuition, with excavacations being equated with putting together the past, and reconstruction of a dead man's face gradually turning into the Netra-Mangala ceremony, tracing the oneness under difference. For Ananda, the artist, every face becomes the face of Buddha. Each of the participants has suffered – Palipana, Sarath, Gamini and Ananda and Anil who is the youngest is preparing her own suffering. Palipana first talks of Netra Mangala: 'It is the ritual of the eyes … . It is what gives the image life' and it alone makes a statue holy … . Without the eyes there is not just blindness, there is nothing' (97–99). And it is this ceremony that again comes at the end of the novel, beautifully described and linking up with Anil's discovery of herself, her land and human limitations. Nature, landscape, birds – are the sign of recognition and of change. Ondaatje's excursions into other cultures and other myths merge with the past and the present of his homeland.

Amitav Ghosh is another writer whose work ranges from rural India, to Egypt, England, Africa and the United States.[19] His characters travel as do his stories not only to western lands but to other ancient civilisations. They move to Bangladesh and Myanmar as past connections, oppositions, histories are opened out and as science and intuition become co-partners in search of knowledge. Land and sea fascinate him in equal measure as he looks at their conflictual bonding in *The Hungry Tide*, a novel located in the

Sunderbans. This cluster of islands, between them, have a plural society and a plural history – a Scotsman's estate, a researcher's paradise, a refuge for the unwanted, an escape for the politically persecuted, the home of the tribals. This is the margin and this is the centre when Pia, a woman of Indian origin but now a foreigner and Fokir, a peasant come together in an unexpressed relationship that crosses all differences. The novel addresses the significance of relationships in a plural society and leaves one with the hope that the world can be more human and compassionate if fixities of identity can be transcended.

Plurality of cultures, it is suggested by these writers, has first to be internalised prior to any meaningful negotiation with one's own historical past – this alone can prevent a ghettoisation or an inclination towards fundamentalism. Plurality does not rule out history; instead national histories acquire an additional importance for the diaspora for the sustenance of their self. Acceptability and belonging are related to the culture of adoption, but the self that moves forth to belonging has first to come to terms with its own multiplicity of pasts and inheritances.

NOTES & REFERENCES

1. Edward Said, 'Traveling Theory', *The World, the Text and the Critic* (Cambridge, Massachusetts: Harvard Univ. Press, 1983), 226–247.
2. Vivek Dhareshwar, 'Fortunate Traveling: Location, Theory and Post-colonial Identity', *Journal of Contemporary Thought* (Baroda, 1992).
3. *Ibid.*, 39. Dharweshwar quotes from Fanon's essay 'On National Culture' from *The Wretched of the Earth*.
4. Bissoondath, (Toronto: Penguin, 1994).
5. *Ibid.*, 134. '... The largest and the most dangerous pitfall would be the adoption of a ghetto mentality. To forget that there is a world beyond the community to which we belong, to confine ourselves within narrowly defined cultural frontiers, would be, I believe, to go voluntarily into that form of internal exile which in South Africa is called the "homeland"'.
6. Himani Bannerjee, *The Dark Side of the Nation: Essays on Multiculturalism, Nationalism and Gender* (Toronto: Scholars' Press Inc., 2000), 68–70.

7. Spivak, (New York: Routledge, 1988)
8. Mukherjee, (Toronto: Tsar Publications, 1994).
9. Translated by Mukherjee (Calcutta: Samya, 2003).
10. For further elaboration see Jancy James's essay on Parameswaran in *Writers of the Indian Diaspora*. Ed. Jasbir Jain (Jaipur: Rawat) 1998. 199–208.
11. Refer 'Ganga in the Assiniboine: Prospects for Indo-Canadian Literature' and 'Ganga in the Assiniboine: A Reading of Poems from *Trishanku*,' both included in her recent collection of essays. *Writing the Diaspora* (Jaipur: Rawat, 2006). 70–91.
12. Ibid., 325
13. See 'Home is Where Your Feet Are, and May Your Heart Be There Too,' *Writing the Diaspora*, 208–217. 210.
14. Gandhi in *Hind Swaraj* (1909) discusses this, while Tagore also debates this in several essays on culture and civilisation, specifically 'Crisis in Civilization' and 'Civilization and Progress', *Crisis in Civilization and Other Essays* (New Delhi: Rupa and Co., 2003).
15. Ramabai Espinet, *The Swinging Bridge* (New Delhi: Penguin, 2004), 83.
16. Interestingly enough, V.S. Naipaul in his acceptance speech of the Nobel Award, also talked at length about history – of the family, of his origins, of migration and culture. See internet sources.
17. Ondaatje, *Running in the Family* (London: Picador, 1984). *The English Patient* (Vintage Books, 1993) and *Anil's Ghost* (New York, Random House, 2000).
18. See Anisur Rahman, 'Versions of Subversion: *Running in the Family*' *Writers of the Indian Diaspora*, ed. Jasbir Jain (Jaipur: Rawat Publications, 1998), 145–155.149.
19. Amitav Ghosh's *The Circle of Reason* locates itself initially in a village before moving abroad, *In An Antique Land* to Egypt, *Calcutta Chromosome* to the States, *The Glass Palace* to Burma and Malaysia and the *Sea of Poppies*, and *The River of Smoke* to China. All these novels travel across space, cultures and histories. *The Hungry Tide* (New Delhi: Harper Collins, 2005) brings in the world of politics.

3

Geographical Dislocations and the Poetics of Exile

Ashis Gupta and Michael Ondaatje

Writers who have moved away from one culture to another are caught between two cultures and are very often engaged either in a process of self-recovery through resort to history and memory or in a process of self-preservation through an act of transformation.[1] Expatriate writers have also been engaged in a permanent act of uprootedness and dislocation through travel and travelogues like Naipaul.[2] Moving outside the nostalgia-protest syndrome, both Ashis Gupta and Michael Ondaatje create a 'third space', by moving away both from the culture of their adoption and the culture of their origin and setting their novels – Gupta in *The Toymaker from Wiesbaden* (1993) and Ondaatje in *The English Patient* (1992) – against the backdrop of the Second World War and its aftermath and locating them in Germany and Italy respectively. They project a world which rests on geographical and culture dislocation. Both move away from the implicatory position of involved participation to a postured position of apparent neutrality. Both the novels project multicultural situations in an attempt to minimise polarisation and individual pulls of identity.

The geographical dislocation raises several questions with respect to the poetics of exile, the nature of expatriate writing, the writer's relationship to his culture and his work, the specifics which govern identity-construction and the concept of decentring.

Is it, at one level, a move out of the expatriate's dilemma of avoiding a schizophrenic split, of being pulled in two contradictory directions, and if so, does it promise release or does it inscribe a new kind of meaning?[3] The creation of this third space does also, at another level, destroy the concept of 'purity' of cultures and brings into being a self-reflexive self and a self-reflexive text. As Homi Bhabha has pointed out in *The Location of Culture*, the creation of a Third Space disrupts 'the logics of synchronicity and evolution which traditionally authorize the subject of cultural knowledge'.[4] It makes 'the structure of meaning and reference an ambivalent process' and 'destroys this mirror of representation in which cultural knowledge is customarily revealed as an integrated, open, expanding code' (Bhabha 37).

A sense of place is one of the imperatives of a writer's being, an imperative increasingly being dislocated through extra-territoriality. Nineteenth century writing had privileged the sense of rootedness. Referring to Mark Twain, Henry B. Wonham has pointed out that literary creativity depends on the 'unconscious accumulation of local knowledge', and the writer has only one reservoir of unconscious material from which to draw.[5] Similarly, Barry Lopez, commenting upon 'A Literature of Place', writes:

> I want to talk about geography as a shaping force, not a subject ... . A specific and particular setting for human experience and endeavour is, indeed central to the work of many nature writers, I would say a sense of place is also critical to the development of a sense of morality and of human identity.[6]

Natural surroundings, the flow of streams, the direction of winds affect creative imagination as well as the sense of identity. A sense of place, the architectures which the imagination encounters, the openness towards one's surroundings, these impart a sense of belonging and reduce the sense of being isolated. How does the expatriate writer move from one kind of affiliation (culture of his origin) to another kind (culture of his adoption)? When the writer creates a third space, is it because he wants to 'escape from conflictual situations and self-division, or is it an attempt to negotiate alternate realities? Can this creation of a third space be equated with the use which writers make of fantasy in their narratives and is it comparable in anyway with the Foucauldian definition of heterotopias?[7] Soja draws attention to what he calls the 'ambivalent spatiality' of Foucault which was interwoven into 'brilliant whirls of historical insight'. Space and time are interrelated. History unfolds itself through constructions of space. Heterotopia, Foucault explained, is to be contrasted with utopias. Heterotopia is a countersite like a resting place, a sanatorium, a prison or a theatre, a countersite where 'all the other real sites that can be found within a culture are simultaneously represented, contested and inverted' and where a juxtaposition of the otherwise incompatible can take place.[8] If this negotiation within a third space is determinative of identity construction, how does it relate to the writer's native culture? Identity is constructed through multiple specifics – language, myth, history, psychology, gender and race. It is directly connected with the subject's self-image and the unconsciously inherited positioning. The creation of this third space reflects these complexities.

Space in itself provides a dynamics for history. Writers from erstwhile colonised countries and marginalised or inferiorised societies are engaged in a process of reconstructing both national and personal histories with the objectives of analysing and understanding their own past and also as a historical intervention in the master narrative of the imperial races. Space is an important determinant of the kind of relationships which are produced. Power structures indicating exclusion and inclusion are spatial in nature. As Edward Soja has pointed out, 'The historical imagination is never completely spaceless and critical. Social historians have written, and continue to write, some of the best geographies of the past' (Soja 14).

Gupta's *The Toymaker from Wiesbaden* (1993)[9] is his second novel. The first, *Dying Traditions* is set in post-Partition India and takes cognisance both of Pakistan and Bangladesh with characters travelling to Bangladesh, United States and Europe. Europeans and Americans also travel to India. Thus, these dislocations work in both directions and both exile and attraction work simultaneously. While some characters are exiled, or ousted, or choose self-exile to ignominy, others seek affiliation with alien cultures and are reluctant to return. In *The Toymaker*, however, the spatial structure is constructed differently. The movement is not to and fro in both directions, instead it is Hans Schroeder who moves first to Siberia as a Russian prisoner, and later, after a stay in Germany, migrates to America. There are two journeys and both of these take Hans to limited enclosed worlds, prisons or prison-like, loveless and airless. *The Toymaker* opens with conjunctions of past and present. Memories float from one to the other. The present is represented by the window protected by barbed wire, the sky dark and featureless and the past by memories of a mice-free world of open spaces and hearsay memories of people scavenging for food (1–2). Hans's childhood memories are of Wiesbaden as a place seemingly full of magic and unreal happiness. The narrative framing which takes place right at the beginning is a contrast between a world of faith and one bereft of faith. God, if he is not dead, is a distant presence, no longer reachable. It is within this framing that the narrative plunges straight into a trial for a double murder. Hans Schroeder is charged with the murder of his wife Eva and his daughter Katarina. The dominant image is of a closed space and of unknown terror. The conscious or unconscious intertextuality goes back to Orwell's *Nineteen Eighty-Four*.[10] The voice of God and the presence of mice are juxtaposed:

> I've heard the voice of God from time to time. The last time I heard him the voice sounded somewhat faint, like a call from a far away place. I thought about it for a long time, until the mice took over. Now they run in and out of the corners of my mind. Yes, mice have been very much on my mind the last few days. I hate mice. They're sly, small, crafty, you never win against mice (Gupta 1)

The first person narration is an entry into the prisoner's consciousness, and alternates with the third person world describing the trial – the long legal advice to the jury, the passages of argument and defence, the prosecution's charges, the medical evidence of emotional instability, the judgement that while one murder is first degree murder, the second a second degree committed in a moment of madness. The inconsistent verdict recognises a split personality which within minutes has moved from sanity to insanity. The alternating narrative voices are worked out quite meticulously. Hans is the narrator of almost every alternate chapter – one, three, five, seven, nine, eleven, thirteen, fifteen and in some measure seventeen and eighteen. The intervening voices are of the narrator, the neutral voice of legal advice, the prosecution's lawyer Concannon's presentation of the case, the opinions of two psychoanalysts, Dr Woodward and Dr Mezer, the defence lawyer Piscitelli's argument, a flashback of Hans's courtship of Eva, and letters to Peggy Constanza.

Woven into this narrative are several other narratives – Hans's childhood memories, his life in the army, and his prison term in Siberia where he has witnessed extreme brutality. This prison term is variously described as a period of three years (29), six years (63) and seven years (42) positing an unreliable narrative consciousness which indicates the nature of shifting reality as Rushdie in his essay, ' "Errata": Unreliable Narration in *Midnight's Children*' has pointed out, unreliable narration can be caused by interested parties as also by the unreliability of memory. In *Midnight's Children*, Saleem is an interested narrator as also Rushdie (23–24).[11] Similarly, the accounts in *The Toymaker* are provided by the two counsels. Mr Concannon mentions the period of Hans's imprisonment as one of three years from 1944 to 1947 (29), while Robert Piscitelli mentions it as a period of six years (62) which would cover the entire period of the Second World War. Hans's own account refers to the period as seven years (42–43). This period in the prison influences the entire course of his future life.

Hans is unable to resume the earlier pattern of life after return to Germany. The past overshadows everything. The national agenda of purity of blood, the persecution of the Jews, the helplessness experienced in the concentration camp and the 'witnessing of Tulla's gangrape' affect the future course of his life. There is a conflict between his internal being and the external reality, and there is also the humiliation he experiences as member of a defeated nation, when German girls have American lovers (39, 56). The world of Hans's childhood is now totally distanced. Wiesbaden had been a magic place with memories of the past, the Romans who had been there, the baths which people visited in search of lost youth, the Rhine maidens, the opera house which introduced him to the world of passion. Wagner's music opens out a world of infinite possibilities, 'I quickly realised I could be anyone

I wished inside the walls of the opera house' (4). Faith and music are in some mysterious way connected for him. Later, on his return from Siberia, and during his courtship of Eva, he never visited the opera. It was a world which excluded him, not merely because they were poor but be cause he had lost god (76).

Hans is twice removed from Germany, once because of the war, and the second time through emigration. His return from Siberia does not really fully rehabilitate him. The seven years had been without any contact with his family and friends. Slowly and gradually he tries to put the pieces of his life together. There is an abnormal concentration on the concept of 'self', his surroundings temporarily fall into insignificance. The destruction around him is symbolic of his own emptiness. Hans as he narrates the experience of this homecoming recounts, 'I circled aimlessly through the centre of the city. The life on the streets was utterly new to me, and yet I paid no attention to it. I was looking for the past, my own and that of my fellow Germans' (38). Wiesbaden is an escape route from war-torn Munich, from self-pity and hatred, just as the toymaking is a continuation of his humanity. He had first made toys for Tulla's child, then in Wiesbaden for the shop where he worked, and still later for Peggy's son. Toymaking symbolises for him an identity and is expressive of creativity (37). It offers him a haven from the onslaughts of the outer world, 'The toys that I shaped out of wood, the figures I moulded out of clay, all these were pleasurable experiences by themselves. More importantly, they kept me close to children and made me feel like a child' (54). His second dislocation is set in motion by his wife's betrayal. It is the beginning of a second withdrawal and the collapse of his identity when he submits to the possibility of his daughter being 'just like any other American kid' (58). Hans Schroeder's efforts to resume a normal life are interrupted when his wife is depressed and attempts suicide (64). It is at this point that the claims made on him get him down, that he murders his wife Eva and daughter Katarina. Having spent time in the concentration camp, and having witnessed the helplessness of Tulla, he kills Katarina as he himself admits, because 'She was a prisoner of her mortal self and I wanted to set her free. I wanted to preserve her innocence for all times, like the Elizabethan from my very first encounter with the opera .... It was my way of returning to my God' (135).

One recurring reference is to Wagner (76) and his operas *Tannhauser* and *Siegfried* (4, 23, 136), to the stories of Brunnhilde who is laid to sleep by Wotan and surrounded by a ring of fire. It is Siegfried, the son of Siegmond and Sieglinde, who obtains the magic ring and passes through the flames to awaken Brunnhilde (123). When he first sees Peggy Constanza, Hans feels it was like Brunnhilde's awakening. There was 'music in the air' as he sensed the 'unusual beauty of the oval face and the smooth, browned complexion' (123). The references to the Valkyries include references to the mythic hall of Odin where the heroes who have died bravely are received (76, 135). The act of killing Katarina is a way of cleansing, it is the supreme sacrifice he can offer to his God and his fatherland. In Katarina he sees Tulla reflected. First he had found Tulla in Peggy. Peggy had brought music to his life, just like Tulla and brought him close to a child's world, 'It made me alive once again, made me feel complete. Like Tulla she lost her child. like Tulla she lost her mind' (135). He is aware of Tulla's presence in Katarina as well. He would have liked to name her Tulla, only Eva wouldn't hear of it. Hans's world of the unconscious is a world where dreams and nightmares merge into each other. It is the erosion of his self-image and the loss of his identity (133) which renders him a victim. He feels humiliated, as if he had sold himself by coming to America (95), it seems to him to be the betrayal of his fatherland (77). He would even crawl to Germany (75) to salve his conscience.

To begin with, Ashis Gupta is working out a strategy of distancing himself from any involvement in the historical process. Hans is a German, and the narrative is based on a true life account offered to the writer by a lawyer friend. The exploration of Hans's psychological and historical world is conducted through focusing on it through multiple points of view. But underneath this concern, the concern is with the manner in which nations are constructed (the idea of racial purity), the internalisation of the humiliation of defeat, the loss of identity, the conflict which accompanies dislocation, the constant intervention of the past into the present, the denial of freedom and the constraints on the self. Hans's need for Harry is a need for the 'other', is a need to seek verifiability in a world where almost everything is unverifiable. A story, Hans elaborates at one point, is like a toy, much 'like the wooden toy I used to make. You whittle away at the wood with a knife, and little by little a face, a figure begins to show. Meanwhile, on the floor below lies a scattered pile of wood shavings and pieces of wood. Are they not part of the toy?' (118). Similarly the gaps in the narrative, the irreconcilability of the different versions, the hallucinatory memories of Hans's himself are part of the narrative which is about enclosures – the box car, the nine by nine space, the barbed window, the prison, the closures of memories, the exclusion from the world of opera and happiness, and about power structures which hold human life to ransom.

Ondaatje's *The English Patient*[12] shared the Booker Prize with Barry Unsworth's *The Sacred Hunger* in 1992, and has recently been made into a much discussed film. In one of the early reviews, Nilufer Bharucha viewed it as a laboured attempt at postmodernist fiction and found it difficult to defend it against the attack of the critics who viewed it as 'now you see it, now you don't kind of contemporary fiction'[13] The novel is located in Italy in a villa, Villa San Girolamo, a former nunnery used as a hospital, and now declared unsafe because of the bombing and landmining which has taken place. In it lies an 'English' patient whose face has been burnt out of recognition in a plane accident in the Libyan desert during the war. He is being nursed by a twenty-year-old Canadian nurse who has had a broken relationship and an abortion and is herself the child of a broken marriage. She has gone through this war with the knowledge that her father is dead, again the victim of a fire accident. Hana has enclosed herself in her passivity and the placing of this man and woman in this ruined villa is an act of willed seclusion. Both are in a kind of hibernation. But their seclusion cannot continue for long. It is interrupted first by the arrival of Caraviggio, her father's Italian friend, a thief and a spy, and then by Kirpal Singh's arrival who is an Indian sapper deputed to clear the mines in the area. With the coming of these two outsiders, disruptive and regenerative forces enter the villa. The patient has long confessional sessions with Caraviggio and as he goes over the past, the account of the expeditions into the Libyan desert are also accounts of a geographical location subject to shifts and obliteration by the sandstorms. The patient's account of his love relationship with Katharine also uncovers his identity. He is the

Hungarian spy, Almásy. Similarly Kirpal Singh's full-bodied presence in this world of mutilated men awakens desire in Hana. Both the narratives work in opposite directions. While the English patient's case states that identities cannot be shed or camouflaged, and the past cannot be discarded, the Hana-Kirpal relationship pretends, for a while, that they can be. Enclosed in the villa, temporarily they concede that the racial or political pulls are irrelevant.

There are several subnarratives within these two main narratives. Caraviggio has a past of his own, there is an implicit involvement in politics and spying. The English patient has also been a double agent. There is Kirpal's training period in England which brings in the colonial-imperial relationship. They are all of a nomadic kind who have traversed different distances. It is only now that they are at a still point, either analysing and evaluating the past, or hiding it and hiding from it. The narrative moves outwards in various directions. There are in all ten sections of the novel. The first, 'The Villa', is the central setting, in the second both Caraviggio and the sapper arrive, the third develops the relationship between Hana and the sapper, the fourth is concerned with the expeditions into the desert, the fifth is about Katharine, the sixth, 'A Buried Plane', is the patient's journey into the past, the buried city, the search for the oasis Zerzura, the interconnection with Kipling's Kim. The seventh, 'In Situ', meaning back to the original position, is about Kirpal Singh's training period in England with Lord Suffolk and Miss Morden, where Kip's fears of racial discrimination are belied and he wins a place of equality through his own intelligence and merit. The eighth section is titled 'The Holy Forest' and is about the Kip-Hana relationship, and the interconnections between Lahore, London and Toronto. The ninth section, 'Cave of Swimmers', returns to the Katharine-Almásy relationship and the last section, 'August', is the end of the war and its aftermath, the return of hostilities and national pulls. Kip is unable to continue in this idyllic isolation. The atomic explosions of Hiroshima and Nagasaki, he believes, happened only because Japan was an Asian country (286). Racial differences and ideological hostilities cannot be overcome so simply.

Repeated fire incidents also trace a pattern. A universal symbol of destruction and violence and of cleansing of all violence underlines the narrative. The Clifton-Katharine suicide pact ends in a plane crash, Almásy is burnt in a plane explosion, Hana's father dies in a fire accident, Lord Suffolk dies while defusing a bomb, while Kip saves Caraviggio by defusing a bomb. He is engaged in clearing the area of the mines but realises the irrelevance of the task he has undertaken when the enormity of the destruction in Japan stares him in the face.

Of the four people in the villa, three are social or political outcasts, or marginalised people while Hana is a self-exile. This grouping functions simultaneously in two ways, centrifugally through pushing acceptance, merger, truth away and centripetally in bringing people together across ideological and racial differences. The English are dealt with only in oblique ways. None of the four people in the villa is English. The English are, however, there in the background and determine the grouping as well as the dispersal. James Clifton is English whose identity gets lost and merged in Almásy's and whose wife is loved by the Hungarian. Lord Suffolk is English and he attempts to rise above the imperial power – structure by transcending racial discrimination. Miss Morden is able to provide Kip with a sense of comfort and belonging. There are other English connections. The whole question of the civilising mission is taken up and Kipling's *Kim* is interwoven into the text through repeated references. Hana reads passages from *Kim* to the English patient who comments on the way Kipling should be read (93–94). When Hana observes Kip in the English patient's company, 'it seemed to her a reversal of Kim. The young student was now Indian, the wise old teacher was English' (111). *Kim* resurfaces again when the English patient rejects all books in favour of Herodotus' *The Histories*. On one occasion, Caraviggio and Almásy pour over the map in *Kim* 'a map with a dotted line for the path the boy and the Holy one' had taken.

The English patient's room becomes a central place for people to relate to and interact with each other. There is a spirit of bonhomie between Kip and Almásy as they share a can of condensed milk. Almásy expresses the view that both he and Kip are international bastards 'born in one place and choosing to live elsewhere' (176). On another occasion, while describing his accident in the desert, he again uses the term, when they hauled him up as 'just another possible second-rate spy. Just another international bastard' (251). The implications of this term are ambivalent. If on the one hand there is a crossing of barriers, there is on the other hand a feeling of being anchorless, disowned and rejected. There is also a comment on the construction of identity and nations and on their relevance or otherwise. There are occasions when people are removed from the claims of civilisation and placed in a state of crisis, or seclusion and during these periods one is at one's most natural. Describing the expeditions in the desert, Almásy comments: 'There were rivers of desert tribes, the most beautiful humans I've met in my life. We were German, English, Hungarian, African all of us insignificant to them. Gradually we become nationals. I came to hate nations. We are deformed by nation states' (138).

If this is to be taken seriously, it is a comment on the hegemonic imperial structures. Kip's background substantiates this comment. Nationalities can be ignored when there is a felt need for the Other, or for the skills the Other has, but in all else they are reflected. The Kip-Hana relationship cannot follow its natural course because of the impossibility of a long-term seclusion. While Kip is interested in the clues to Hana's nature, she wants him to know her only in the present. Each is wary of the other's past. She is unable to find any key to him, 'Everywhere she touches braille doorways' but 'he has mapped her sadness more than any other. Just as she knows the strange path of love he has for his dangerous brother' (270). Kip's whole being is determined by his background. He is tentative in his relationships with people as he comes from an invisible race. At every step he carries his race with him and has to wait for acceptance before he proceeds. His brother on the other hand is more of a rebel, refusing to accept the authority of the English. While his brother rebelled publicly, Kip had worked out silent strategies of becoming invisible. But when Hiroshima happens, Kip has to discard this invisibility:

> When he closes his eyes he sees fire, people leaping into rivers into reservoirs to avoid flame or heat that within seconds burns everything, whatever they hold, their own skin and hair, even the water they leap into. The brilliant bomb carried over the sea in a plane, passing the moon in the east, towards the Green archipelago. And released. (286–87)

Kip can no longer continue to be in Italy. He leaves the other three in search of some semblance of peace. Hana too feels that Europe is too much for her and wants to go back to Canada (296) and thus they go their separate ways to lead their own lives.

Space is used in a variety of ways in the novel. First there are the enclosures – the English patient's room, Kip's tent and Kip's brother's prison, and the cave in which Katharine seeks shelter. As contrasted with this are the vast stretches of sand in the Libyan desert. Landscape and cityscapes are also pronounced. Lahore, the land of five rivers, London, Toronto, these are described in detail. But there are dislocations of space, especially when the process of historicising takes over. This is done through Herodotus' history and his records of the journeys to Egypt (see the several references, 96, 133, 142, 237, 240) and through Almásy's account. This is also done through intertextuality. There are references to *The Last of the Mohicans*, to *Kim* and to *The Charterhouse of Parma*. This is also done through Biblical references which are interwoven throughout but are dominant specially in the final section as the four characters are now in the process of dispersal and disposal. *The English Patient* offers no easy solutions. Nations and cultures demand their own and the past refuses to be obliterated. There is in both *The Toymaker from Wiesbaden* and *The English Patient* the creation of a European world of memory through references to art, to music – Wagner, Mozart and Verdi – to European history, to its flora and fauna, to city landmarks. How does the creation of this world relate to the writer's relationship with his material and what does it say about literary imagination? And in both, the writer's identity and cultural roots do not surface directly; the adult entry of the literary imagination into the cultural world of Europe is remarkably authentic. Is it then expressive of a need to transcend the limits of culture and relocate human identity within existential dimensions of being? Or is it a search for neutral ground as a strategy of distancing oneself, and does this search rest on historicising narrative?

The Toymaker, through a Kafkasque trial and contradictory narrations of the same happening, opens out existential questions regarding freedom, identity, sensitivity and desire for truth. These questions while they universalise issues also reflect ontological concerns. Hans's problems project a colonial situation, and the way brutality affects mankind. Ondaatje, who at first sight appears even more neutral than Gupta, is even more concerned with questions of identity and cultural pulls. Through the character of Almásy, the identity or lack of it is projected, and through Kip the racial differences which refuse obliteration and reject invisibility and the national pulls which summon him back. The process of historicising which engages both the writers, Ondaatje more than Gupta, is dominantly western. The Asian references are through *Kim* and the Indian landscape, not through history.

In this construction of a third space, these writers are moving away from engagement with their own cultural and historical pasts – and are also partly rejecting fantasy and personal memory in favour of the process of historicising the European past. They are not even engaged with the reality of their present world. Instead they move into backgrounds of violence and a culture which is acquired, not born into. Is this a measure of success, a search for a new readership, an escape from the immigrant self, an absorption into a new construct? If it is an absorption into a new construct it would be very different from all evolutionary strategies for the move into history is a move into the past and does not take into account new combinations. As poetics of exile, the strategy is one of projection through proxy.

NOTES & REFERENCES

1. Writers of the erstwhile colonies whether expatriates or stay-at-home have expressed their anger and dissatisfaction with the suppression of the native self. They have turned to history in an attempt to identify their strengths. This is perceptible in the work of a host of Indian writers like Raja Rao, Bhabani Bhattacharya, Manohar Malgonkar. This trait also characterises the work of several African writers. More recently postcolonial writing has been engaged with history and a reconstruction of the historical self like Nayantara Sahgal's novels of the 80s, Rushdie's *Midnight's Children*, Romesh Gunesekera's *Reef* and Abdul Rajak Gurnah's *Paradise*. As contrasted with these Bharati Mukherjee's thrust has been on transformation and metamorphosis as in *Jasmine*.

2. V.S. Naipaul is a classic example of the permanent nomad whose identity now appears to be vested in a condition of homelessness.

Geographical Dislocations and the Poetics of Exile 53

3. Writing about a third culture can also be an attempt at opting out of a dilemma. Anita Desai in an essay entitled 'The Indian Writer's Problem' admits to having sidestepped the problems writing in English is likely to create, 'by not writing the kind of social document that demands the creation of realistic and typical dialogue by writing novels that have been catalogued by critics as psychological, and that purely subjective, I have been left free to employ, simply, the languages of the interior.' *Explorations in Modern Indo-English Fiction* ed. R.K. Dhawan (New Delhi: Bahri Publications, 1982).
4. Homi K. Bhabha, *The Location of Culture* (London: Routledge, 1994).
5. Henry B. Wonman, *Mark Twain and the Art of the Tall Tale* (NY: OUP, 1993).
6. Barry Lopez, 'A Literature of Place', *A Sense of Place: Regional American Literature*. Delhi: USIS. August 1996.
7. Edward Soja, *Postmodern Geographies: The Reassertion of Space in Critical Theory* (Jaipur: Rawat Publications, 1997).
8. Michel Foucault, 'Texts/Contexts: Of Other Spaces', *Diacritics*, Spring, 1986
9. Ashis Gupta, *The Toymaker from Wiesbaden* (Surrey: Spantech and Lancer, 1993).
10. Winston Smith in George Orwell's *Nineteen Eighty-Four* is obsessed by the fear of mice and it is this fear which leads to his betrayal of Julia. The presence of mice is indicative of filth and poverty, and lack of interest in human survival. Their scurrying away represents a structure on the verge of collapse.
11. Rushdie, '"Errata": Or, Unreliable Narration in *Midnight's Children*,' *Imaginary Homelands* (London: Granta Books), 1991. 22-24.
12. Michael Ondaatje, *The English Patient* (1992, Vintage Books, 1993.
13. Nilofer Bharucha, '*The English Patient*', *Literature Alive*, Vol. 5 No. 3 January 1993.

4

Memory and Reflection in the Writing of the Diaspora

The immigrants through passage of time acquire two homes: one, the native country with its linguistic and cultural ties and other, the country to which they have migrated. And even while living in the four walls of a house abroad, they confront this division. How different are the inside spaces from life outside it in the streets, in the workplace and in social circles, and how does the immigrant negotiate this difference everyday and how much of it he is able to resolve or not resolve – are two very important questions which acquire added importance when we read the work of the writers who write in their native languages. Unlike the writer in English, they do not translate their homeland experiences and memories but translate their daily experience into their own language. The nature, material and span of the experience being translated are very different when a whole inherited culture is being translated and the confrontation with the writer both with reality and memory is very different from what happens when English is adopted as the medium of communication. The image that strikes me is the nature of the 'cradling' of this experience in a language not native to it.

The world 'diaspora' forever seems to be expanding in its meaning and application. It is fast merging into transnationalism, an attempt to transcend geographical and cultural spaces of the nation-state. But the fact remains, that though geographical boundaries require a twelve, or seventeen or more hours of flight, cultural spaces take a much longer time. They take several decades and a couple of generations if the traces of nursery rhymes, kinship patterns, ideas of romance, lingering verses of folk songs, and social and political histories are completely to be wiped out. But when there are frequent trips home, which is now increasingly possible and if the interaction with home and same-language people is a recurring one, there possibly cannot be any breaking point. Where Punjabi diaspora is concerned, the same language groups have a tendency to herd together. And the community has a strong collectivity in Canada with their own language clusters. Does this island community create a satisfactory substitute for the homeland, and does the homeland, where their ancestors have lived, where they still own land, still hold any significance for them? Punjab, despite being exposed to multiple invasions and forced into a semi-nomadic life at times, remains an agricultural society, where landholding signifies belonging and pride. How does the Punjabi migrant relate to his homeland? And how does the writer relate to it and represent it? These are the two issues which I wish to focus on as the embedding and the journey of memory is different from the route it adopts in the writing in English. Punjabi or for that matter, any other diasporic writing in native languages resists the kind of diffusion which writing in English permits. The native language in order to carry the burden of culture needs to survive in a foreign land. One wonders how much of change does it allow oneself or to what extent the emotions and thoughts reflected undergo a change.

In the above connection, the relationship of both writing and culture with the socio-economic environment is crucial. I refer to Pierre Bourdieu's work, *The Field of Cultural Production*[1] where Bourdieu has raised the subject of aesthetics and pointed out that literature has a direct relationship with the place of stay and the surrounding cultural patterns. Globalisation cannot erase the cultural differences or level them up in any uniform way. It is, therefore, imperative for cultures to be fluid and keep pace with the world around. It is of importance for cultures to be dialogic in the Bakhtinain sense. Bakhtin, in his 'Discourse in the Novel' has differentiated between poetic and novelistic discourse primarily because the novel inhabits reality in a more solid way than a poem.[2] The speech in a novel or a prose narrative explores nooks and corners, works with everyday life and wide range of experiences. This dialogicity is also applicable to development. It calls for filteration of new ideas and an openness of mind. The right to select remains with the subject. If one brings to one's minds the travels of Guru Nanak Dev, one realises of how much of openness he carried with him during those sixteen years, absorbing views, learning languages, dialoguing with men of other faiths, thinking with them as well as in opposition to them, a counter-questioning. Had he not travelled, or debated or learnt from these experiences, nor reacted to the divisionary social structure at home, the Sikh religion would not have been born.[3]

The diasporic writing in Punjabi has a wide range. Several of the works are testimonies of cultural conflicts and reflect other cultures available in the environment. Different kinds of employment, available directly related to the skill, education and willingness of the worker also make a difference to the nature of experience and self-image in the new society. Very often the immigrant is at the periphery of society and is motivated by a desire to climb up the social ladder. The diasporic community occupies a double space: it is visible on grounds of race and economic status but it is invisible in terms of social recognition, reduced as they often are to manual workers. Very often this social condition leads to the narrowing down of social space. Conscious of the need to preserve their home culture, very often artificial barriers are constructed and prohibitions imposed.

The diaspora's relationship with the homeland is very varied and complex. Rushdie's essay on 'Imaginary Homelands'[4] is often mentioned but other writers too pose the same question. Chandra Talpade Mohanty takes up this question from the gender perspective. It is an issue which is problematic for almost all immigrants: how long can one remain a foreigner and not take root? When does citizenship really become meaningful? She asks, 'What is home? The place where I was born? Where I grew up? Where my parents live? Where I live and work as an adult? Where I locate my community, my people? Who are "my people"? Is home a geographical space, a historical space, an emotional, sensory space? ... . What interests me is the meaning of home for immigrants and migrants. I am convinced that this question – how one understands and defines home – is a profoundly political one.'[5]

Home, nation, country and abroad – each one of them reflects the change that is happening both in the emotional world and in the socio-political world. There is no way one can escape it. An easy term which is applied is hybridity. It indicates the simultaneous occupation of the same space by two cultures. It carries both positive and negative meanings. Brinda Mehta with reference to Caribbean writing uses another word '*douglapan*', the word means a number of things – double-faced (can we say Janus-faced?), camouflage and double-sided. According to Mehta, Rosanne Kanhai was the first to use it because it appealed to her as a better term than creole (which indicates a mixture or races or languages)[6], and was expressive of Indian culture. As a term it also reflects upon the two aspects of hybridity. When I first heard it, I felt it was a denigrative term but Mehta explained that the term expressed the two streams of culture which ran side by side. One hopes, at some junction they also intersect and crossover.

The Punjabi diasporic writing presents both the sides, at times separately, at others together. I refer to some of the short stories of Harpreet Singh Sekha, especially in his collection *Baran Buhe*[7] (Twelve Doors). In '*Sura so Pehchanian*' (Recognise the Tunes), is a story where the older generation has adjusted to and adapted to the changed environment and when the Vancouver team wins, they are happy and celebrate the victory in a participatory spirit, just as the Canadians do. But there is another character, Gurjiwan who is unhappy with everything especially with the exploitation resulting from increased technology and capitalism. There are several other stories which also look at the outer world both critically and positively. They discuss the illogicality of transporting the outlived feudalism and the gender roles of the time when they had left their country. Unrealistically, they hope that they can be transplanted on a foreign soil not realising that the old lifestyle will lead to division and conflict. This is a dominant issue in '*Tu Hi Bol*' (Then You Speak). Tarsem's way of thinking is cast in the old patriarchal values and he is adamant at casting his wife and children in the same mould.

Constantly he admonishes his wife from using cosmetics, dressing well and even admiring herself in the mirror. The mirror is a multiple symbol. Tarsem shifts it to the bathroom, within closed doors. As he watches his daughter growing up, he is full of regrets that why did they not go in for a pre-birth test to determine the sex of the unborn child. Through this Sekha indirectly points to the unequal gender ratio in Punjab and conveys a condemnation of the prevalent practice at home as in the narrative the inhumanity of the act stares the reader in the face, framed as it is in a different culture and is about a young girl. Here the story takes on the role of a mirror-reflection for the Punjabi reader back home. Tarsem is not even able to face his own self in the mirror. The reference to female foeticide also draws attention to the negative fallout of superficial modernity and the equally negative employment of science and medicine. The discourse of modernity is multilayered and overloaded with minute shifts in meaning. To be modern at the outset means being open to newness and change. A second aspect is an enhanced use of technology. But these are not necessarily complementary, and are not essential to one another. Gandhi was modern in the sense of an open mind. Dialogicity demands an openness of mind and science requires an awareness of ethical values. Lyotard in his book *The Inhuman: Reflections on Time*[8] has even talked about the separation between body and mind as the computer is taking over the qualities of the human brain. Will then emotions survive? These shifts are largely reflective of power structures and often pay no need to human rights, as they enable imposition of the dominant power on the disadvantaged – be it in terms of international relations, conflict or class.

Tarsem has a schoolmaster friend Jit who advises him to change his way of thinking, to come to grips with the existing reality and move out of the past, which perhaps has also shed some of its rigidities in the home country. Jit's two daughters have studied medicine, are working and with parental consent, and have gone ahead and married men outside their caste, religion race. Jit holds the view that the whole world is one, no one is a stranger, or needs to be treated as inferior or superior. The consciousness of a social self is founded on selfconfidence. But Tarsem wants to recreate his native village on the Canadian soil. A Canadian friend,

Brian asks him, 'what kind of a culture is it, that engages in killing daughters?' (131) Both his friends – one Indian, Jit, the other white, Brian, perform the same role as the mirror hanging on his bathroom wall. Several of Sekha's stories compel, the reader to reflect upon this artificial retention of 'ethnicity' and the manner in which such a dead culture becomes a prison.

But Sekha does not get obsessed with such a portrayal of ethnicity. The objective clearly is to show how redundant it is through the placing together of different perspectives. The story 'Kavita de Paar' (Beyond Poetry), works with an interreligious marriage between a Sikh and a Muslim. Though Deep's parental family stays away, an uncle, his father's younger brother, extends support. He comes to attend a gathering and the silent understanding that Deep can sense between his uncle and his wife strike Deep as rising above differences. Incidentally, 'Kavita' which means poetry is also the name of his wife, a name perhaps bestowed on her after her marriage (Another outdated custom, but here it could mean either that a conversion has taken place, or the name is bestowed on her to soften the cultural difference). The title 'Kavita de Paar' can also mark a shift from romance to everyday life.

In another experimental story, titled 'Chhappar' (Thatched Hut), the writer constantly moves between the interiority of the protagonist's mind and the exteriority of the outer world. Both subjectivity and objectivity keep on entering the narrative voice, which is, for practical purposes the narrator is an observer, distant, invisible and the narrator as participant. Everything in the story has a fluidity about it. Is the time the past, the present or a constant going to and fro? Voices crossover but intermittently they connect. Again, is it the mind's or the soul's voice? The narrative deliberately casts transparent veils that affect the images behind it. This indirect approach to emotional and mental reality represents the confusion and the uncertainty very much like a ghost scene being enacted on a stage. It is a story about unfulfilled desires and desperate longing. There is also the easy surrender to borrowed dreams. But in this process of desperation and surrender, he cuts off his ties with his village at the time of migration itself, in the very beginning. Determined to work for a more dignified position than manual labour, he aspires for an office job. Many an immigrant is sponsored by his relatives who have already arranged some kind of an employment. But Gurjant is conscious of public opinion and at pains to nurture this self-consciousness. For him, life is a continuous compromise between what he desires and what seems good in other people's view.

Storywriting is different from a novel as any other distinctive genre. A story opens up a little patch, an isolated event and builds upon it while a novel creates and encloses a whole world within its narrative. The reader becomes a co-traveller. Harbhajan Hans's novel, *Rishtey* (Relationships),[9] moves to and fro both in memory and space. The novel hovers around a family: Gyan Singh migrates to Canada, hoarding all his dreams. His older brother helps him to the best of his capacity. When he starts earning enough, he starts sending money to the family left behind. But this is not enough. When, on a visit home, he does not accept the matrimonial arrangements his sister-in-law arranges for him with one of her own relatives, he alienates her. The marriage was to be a route to family emigration. And when he goes ahead and marries another girl, who he thinks will adjust better to the life in Canada, the relations are further strained. In the days to come, he disappoints the family by not sponsoring his nephew giving them another reason to feel aggrieved. Thus, feelings of estrangement keep simmering and adding to the distance. The narrative begins almost towards the end, all that has happened is in the past. Gyan Singh now has grown up children, who are also married. The novel opens in a care-centre where the recently bereaved Gyan Singh is an inmate. He suddenly decides to put on his running shoes and sets off for his home. Between this beginning and the end is the story of his life abroad in a foreign land and going back to his youth in India. The narrative expands upon his marriage, his adjustment with his wife, the births of their two children, their social life. But gradually generational differences begin to surface. The young people increasingly adopt western life style and values. Their sense of personal freedom clashes with family claims. Despite this, they go back to India to arrange their son's marriage. The dominant concerns are the carrying forth of tradition and a pure blood lineage. Where daughters are concerned, the same concern is not dominant, they can, and do, step across race. But the male lineage is considered more important.

Gyan Singh does not realise that goodness of behaviour and warmth of relationships have nothing to do with race. The Indian daughter-in-law soon changes her ways, becomes indifferent and grudges the parents everything. Though the house is owned by Gyan Singh, he and his wife move out to a smaller apartment in order to accommodate the young couple's wishes. This also amounts to exile and their expectations of life, happiness and comfort are suddenly put aside by the materialistic and highly individualised desires of the son and his wife. Then one day Gyan Singh's wife collapses and none of the children respond to his calls. The only person who responds is his son-in-law Kevin. Gyan Singh is totally benumbed by the death of his wife and he decides to carry her ashes to India to disperse them in the holy river. At the back of his mind is also the half-expressed wish to go back to India permanently. But here the scene is equally dismal – a displeased nephew, a sister-in-law who blames him for not having done enough. It is only the nephew's wife who shows some concern. Another person is the taxi-driver who drives him around and helps keep alive his sense of being a human being.

The diasporic state tends to be permanent. *Rishtey* makes a clear statement that return is not possible. This is so for various reasons; time does not stand still, the past is only a memory and values back home have also changed. The person who migrates is never alone; the innumerable desires of his family members back home cling to him, hold him as an anchor and are disappointed when that doesn't materialise. It becomes, at times, almost a collective migration with the only difference that it is scattered over a span of time. The drudgery of every day existence overtakes one and, very likely, a clannish feeling develops. Abroad or at home, the routes for dreams and personal freedom have to be found or made. Some past of home automatically transplants itself there but fails to keep pace with the change back home. What happens to the ties of emotions? Gyan Singh begins to realise that relationships need as much care as tender saplings and indifference or pushing them away from a live connection, destroys them. The half-desired hope of a permanent abode in India has to be dismissed. Sad and broken he decides to return to Canada where he is a respected citizen, where his memories of his life with his wife have dwell. Finally, the diaspora comes to live in memory.

When the diaspora writes home, writing in one's own language sharpens both the cultural memories and the presence of the home culture alongwith all its feudalism, ritualism and gender roles in the new transplanted society. Only some develop the strength to change and retain a balance. Others suffer because of the static quality of thought, and still others suffer when they are completely bowled over. Each suffering erodes the very foundation of one's being, one's sense of individuality and of subjectivity. The erasure of a past, the snapping of ties creates a permanent sense of non-belonging; a complete immersion in and absorption of the 'other' culture, becomes a second layer which, however, is never completely grafted. Somewhere or the other both the senses of 'home' – the native home and the created home – need to live together in one's mind. The lingering past will claim its role.

Is this why the diaspora writes home? This writing not only holds up a mirror to us but also to them. But this writing has to remain fluid and possess a linguistic openness, which is present in many a writing. But above all the cultural carriers are values, not rituals; and values are not a cultural or racial monopoly. They are human. We all take them to be axiomatic – goodness, sensitiveness, loyalty, caring, and many more which make us what we are. And the battle for values is always being fought no matter where. Yet, the idea of the word 'homeland' is fascinating for it is the umbilical cord that cannot be shed.

NOTES & REFERENCES

1. Pierre Bourdieu, *The Field of Cultural Production: Essays on Art and Literature* (New York: Columbia University Press, 1993). Bourdieu is of the view that art and culture cannot be delinked from the nature of economic production dominant in a society.
2. Mikhail Bakhtin, 'Discourse in the Novel', in *The Dialogic Imagination: Four Essays*. Ed. Michael Holquist. Trans. Caryl Emerson and Michael Holquist (Austin: Texas Univ. Press, 1987), 259–422.
3. Guru Nanak's 'Udasis' refer to his four major journeys. There was also a fifth journey, but the four towards north, east and Nepal, toward the south and Sri Lanka, Central India and then to Meeca and Medina are the ones that provided him with exposure. These are

discussed at length in my unpublished paper, 'The Dialogicity of Travel: Nanak's Udasis.
4. Refer Salman Rushdie, *'Imaginary Homelands'*, *Imaginary Homelands and Essays and Reviews*. (London: Granta and Penguin, India, 1992), 9–21. Also available in *Creating Theory: Writers on Writing* (Delhi: Pencraft International, 2000), 213–224.
5. Chandra Talpade Mohanty, *Feminism Without Borders: Decolonizing Theory: Practicing Solidarity* (Durham and London: Duke University Press, 2003), 126. Mohanty devotes a long chapter, 'Genealogies of Community, Home, and Nation' to this question and her remark that defining 'home' has political implications is very significant. It comments on the struggle that goes in when non-belonging dominates, when the migrant treats the new home as a temporary abode and multiple fracturing that takes place in his psyche. I also relate it to he political interference, often misguided melitancies and divisionary politics or funding of anti-national activities in the home state. It all amounts to stoking a fire that burns other and the migrant is at a safe distance.
6. Brinda Mehta, *Diasporic (Dis)Locations: Indo-Caribbean Women Writers Negotiate Kalapani* (Jamaica: Univ. of West Indies Press, 2004).
7. Harpreet Singh Sekha, *Baran Buhe* (Ludhiana: Chetna Prakashan, 2013). All the stories referred to are from this collection.
8. Jean-Francois Lyotard, *The Inhuman: Reflections on Time* (1988). Stanford: Stanford University Press) 1991. 8–23.
9. Harbhajan Hans, *Rishtey* (Ludhiana: Chetna Prakashan, 2013).

5

Writing in One's Own Language and the Grounds of *Being*

There is a story by Intizar Husain, 'Letter From India'[1] where a Muslim resident in India is engaged in handing over the reins of the family to his eldest nephew, who lives in Pakistan. The letter is a historical document as it moves in two time-scales: the history of the scattering of the family; and the history of the Muslims and the recurring nature of exodus right from the times of the Prophet. It simultaneously moves through geographical spaces. The writer mentions the scattering of the family. Both his brothers are now dead and sons representing the next generation, are scattered. Some are in Pakistan, others in Bangladesh and still some others in Dubai. This is not simply a letter, conveying news of well-being but an expression of the writer's anguish and feeling of being alone, the attachment to one's land of birth and the painful compulsions of migration as well as the pain of separation from those who have migrated. Even staying back in the land is a moral compulsion and as such whether one migrates or stays back, the burden of pain remain. Those who leave are homeless, face the uncertainty of their future and the challenges of resettlement and those who stay are alone, cut off from the rest of family and live in a changed socio-political scenario. The departure may have been caused by numerous compulsions – political conditions, a state of exile or the need for security or the dream of a new nation and even at times the fascination of success. It is natural for memory and history to surface in such conditions, the roots of being and identity lie in cultures and languages which bind people together as a community. These émigrés, remain refugees or *muhajirs*, the immigrants and clubbed together as diaspora. Despite the reduction of distance brought about by globalisation, the feeling of being uprooted still persists, no matter where one is located. The surface adoption of the host culture does not erase cultural memories. My reference to Husain was to underline the issues related to migration, but I wish to focus on Punjabi diaspora and their writing in their mother tongue. Their writing relates differently to their home culture than the writing in English which loses connection with the dailogicity of the mother tongue and has deeper connections with their culture on account of the linguistic grounding of the expression of their emotional lives, a point I have already made earlier. How then is their identity constructed, and how does their existence shape itself in the process of this transplantation?

It is important to look at the shifting meanings of the term diaspora and the multiple layers it has accumulated through the processes of history. The significance of diasporic literature is also directly related to these changing definitions as it reflects upon the issues of identity and reality. The human being is neither a puppet, nor a non-being that he can be easily relocated. A living being needs to relate to his environment and here both memory and the unconscious come into play in the cultural interaction. Punjabi diaspora is widely spread in different parts of the world. The geographical location of Punjab at the northern border of India has always been an entry point for successive invasions as well as for traders and travellers. As such the community is known for its capacity to face new challenges and is consequently liberal and open in its acceptance of others. There are innumerable recitals of their courage in the face of difficulties, their determination to extract yield from barren land, to fight for their rights (as they did for citizenship in the US), and they have come to be known as a martial race. Even among the diaspora they have made a place for themselves in different fields – Hargobind Khurana, Ujjal Dosanjh, Kalpana Chawla, Vikram Seth, Meera Syal, Gurinder Chadda, Deepa Mehta all hail from the land of five rivers. In the last hundred and fifty years, a large number of shifts have taken place both in India and the general diasporic relationships. A few decades ago, it was the word 'expatriate' which was in currency and this signified a temporary move. The world 'patria' is part of 'expatriate' and this indicates the relationship with one's land.[2] The lives of those who left against their will are also very different from those who went willingly. The first category always clung to the dream of return which for many did not materialise. Also these migrations were largely single-gendered. Vijay Mishra refers to the longing for the homeland as an 'impossible mourning,[3] Edward Said similarly expresses the view that exile is one of the saddest fates'[4]. But exile, émigré, refugee, expatriate – all these categories which signify different things are now clubbed under the general term diaspora erasing all the nuances of difference. The world itself has travelled a great distance from its early meanings of being scattered, or dispersed. This scattering has now reached a stage where it has begun to bear fruit and has absorbed within it concepts of the hybrid, the hyphenated and the translated, adopting them as adjectival terms to describe men and women.[5]

Several others aspects of life such as nation-state, history and memory are now directly affected by these shifts, the relationship with the diaspora and their stay abroad has definitely changed. The lens are now very different. Increasingly the linguistic affiliation is being heightened. Gayatri Spivak defines a nation through language.[6] Earlier, it was said that though time never stays the same, the earth is stable. But now nothing is stable, cartographies are continuously being redrawn. For instance the very map of Punjab has undergone many changes giving birth to other states such as Himachal Pradesh, West Punjab (Pakistan) and Haryana. Similarly the grounds of one's identity and existence also undergo a change. When this happens how does the human being recognise himself, and where is his identity rooted? Culture also can never afford to be stable amidst these shifts. It is constantly moving back and forth and the diasporic culture is markedly different from the home culture

The diaspora, finding itself as a distinctive category working with two cultures occupies a third space, on the periphery of both their host and home cultures; in each their power positions are differently defined. And as such perspectives from different locations will necessarily view them differently. It is questionable whether they provide inspiration by their success models or their wealth represents economic power. Caught between self negation and projections of self importance, they gain an importance which can hardly ever be justified in either aesthetic or economic terms for while abroad they do not necessarily hold any power and their money is equivalent to a normal wage but when on a visit home they gain importance and the exchange rate enhances their capacity to spend. Most writing in English targets the audience of the host culture whose language they are written in and hence dilutes the cultural density. The writing in mother tongues – Marathi, Gujarati, Punjabi, Tamil or Bengali – is likely to escape this dilution as the readership is different. My argument is directed against the dominance of the diaspora writers in their homelands and the uncritical reading they are often favoured with. Their writing occupies a middle ground between us and the west, and as Arun Prabha Mukherjee has argued time and again, comes to occupy a central location. It acts like a window that clouds the vision of the interior and does not allow the outsider to see through its opaqueness. The other culture reader, thus, very often finds the generalised culture of the diaspora narrative (in English) more easily accessible than the writing existing within a country, and hence desists from making the effort to understand the cultural density present in the writing in Indian languages. Is the diaspora a bridge, a buffer or a barrier? Can it ever be truly representative of the home country or does it portray a culture of the third space? These are all serious issues and affect relationships, self-understanding, cultural projection and writerly expression. They also affect the literary canon and the comparative research that goes on in both literature and cultural studies. The moment we acknowledge the difference, all binarisms become irrelevant. The third space is a different category, entered through migration, language and perspective. There is another important issue that of modernity in the home culture. But I propose to address it later. Moreover, the moment we pass on to the second and third generation of the migrants, we need seriously to ask the question how deeply are they rooted either in culture or language. I have often wondered how does dual citizenship work, especially in relation to politics and in times of oppositional crisis between home and host countries, where does the loyalty belong and how effective can the lobbying be, especially now that we are entering the age of the 'selfie'?

Those who migrate and live abroad are of many kinds, and when it is same race to same race such as white to white with similar theological and cultural backgrounds, then the difference is not so sharp. It is often more equal, if not entirely the same for some differences of language and history continue to persist. But the migrations from Asia or Africa have been unequal first on the basis of slavery and indentured labours and then an uneven money value and most of all colour. Benedict Anderson has referred to the nation as an imagined community but we are all aware that geographical boundaries do not confine nationhood. Rushdie has moved even a little further ahead and refers to the immigrant communities where the dream of belonging does not become a reality. In his article, 'The New Empire within Britain', he writes that the English society is based on race where racial inequality prevails, 'even British-born blacks and Asians are thought of a people whose real home is elsewhere.'[7] Those who are of a different race have daily to face this reality. The difference exists not only in colour but in the way thinking processes work – they are positioned on two different sides of a ravine. These differences are of enormous significance where self and identity are involved. Diasporic writing, if of value, finds it in writing about this difference, this gap, the feeling of the unreal amidst their daily reality. It cannot be treated only as an emotional journey to the homeland. The division between the two locations – one physical and the other emotional – comes forth to make its presence felt. This ground reality is directly related to the sincerity and imagination of the writing. How therapeutic is the writing which depicts this division? There is no way writing can be separated from the identity or self-image of the writer, who like a Janus-figure is compelled to negotiate this division in his self. Trilling's work *Sincerity and Authenticity*,[8] can never become dated in the fine distinctions he projects between sincerity, authenticity and the nature of reality. The continuity of culture and a cultural presence works its ways into the in conscious, but one needs to work with its projection in the real.[9] It is here that language gains importance in its reflection on behaviour, on our everyday living. The writing of the diaspora may at times also be bilingual. Most migrants need to transfer their thoughts fully to another language before they can write in it. The Russian poet Joseph Brodsky once confessed that the sound of words was important to him and he did not find the same sounds in English. Language has a dialogicity of its own as Bakhtin has argued in great depth.[10] But the writing, whichever language it may be in, also needs to be published and find a readership.

Meera Syal's *Anita and Me* is the story of a young Punjabi girl who, as she as growing up and has English friends, is keen to belong to both the worlds. All along she unconsciously indulges in comparisons between her own home and the homes of her friends and constantly tries to merge the two.[11] Even her parents feels motivated to follow her example and lower their self-constructed barriers. Syal's film, *Bhaji on the Beach*[12], depicts two generations and the story works with the generational conflict on the one hand and racial conflict on the other, with the younger generation slipping away into a middle ground, where dating and love-relationships are concerned. Several other writers have worked with this theme of generational change and cultural accommodation and interconnections between the home and social culture. This negotiation is greatly facilitated when the writing is in English.

There are also novels about exploitation either by one's own people (as in Sadhu Binning's writing) or by the white employers (as in Farhana Sheikh's *The Red Box*).[13] The economic factor both for survival and for equality can never be far from cultural concerns. This writing is very different from the self-enclosed worlds of Chitra Divakaruni's *The Mistress of Spices* (1997) or *The Palace of Illusions* (2008).[14] But when the writing is in the mother tongue, it seeks also to reach a different category of readership, which perhaps occupies a different space, reality and history. We need to ask, does it function like Intizar Husain's 'A Letter From India' and focus on the social reality in the diasporic home? Does it hold a cultural message, and does it address the problems of cultural adjustment? Jarnail Singh's story, 'Towers'[15], experiments with this negotiation by working through the voice of William who shares his anxiety about their two children with his wife. Their daughter is buried under the debris of 9/11 and their son is missing in the Iraq war. Prior to this he had been fighting in Afghanistan.

For a moment the reader wonders why has it been written in Punjabi, what does it have to say either about India or about the diaspora? In this location in a different totality with characters from a different race and located within the politics of power, trying to convey something through these choices? Does it address the diaspora or is it an attempt to get into the situation of the other? All these questions are valid with reference to its aesthetics. 'Towers' also has another aspect, it seeks to enter the American psyche where alongside power, confidence and arrogance lurk. Hesitation, uncertainty and fear – the need for sacrifice as part of one's loyalty to the nation. Both William and Angela used to be indifferent to the difficulties of people of another race and culture; they never concerned themselves with the worries of Abdul and Jameela. Now they begin to feel for them across race and religion – they all come together on a human level. 'Towers', by focusing on a shared concern and by portraying the white not merely as an 'other' but as one of us, as a human being who feels and thinks like us, creates a world where grief is shared and a community comes into being. This humanistic approach is not to be seen in either the imperial discourse or the writing of the 'empire writes back' kind. As I am discussing 'Towers', Jhumpa Lahiri's *Unaccustomed Earth* (Canada: Knopf, 2009) is constantly in my mind as a work which is somewhat parallel with the crucial difference that the 'white' is not a neighbour but a husband. Love relationships are somewhat different. They work in a one-to-one discourse not merely a social one. Humanist thought or approach should allow us to cross barriers which are constructed by us on our side and they on theirs. If we as individuals and social beings can create them, we can also demolish them and move out into a wider social circle than be limited by the sense of a single community race or language.

There is another story by Jarnail Singh titled *'Paani'* (Water)[16], in which the shifting patterns of behaviour come to be reflected in the changing values and relationships in the family. Sukhjit's son and daughter-in-law wish to sell off the ancestral land, back home in India, in order to build a swimming pool in their new home. The daughter-in-law is an American girl and the land-holding in Punjab has no cultural or emotional memory for her. Sukhjit on the other hand is deeply attached to it and has an emotional attachment to this past. The repeated requests by Raju (her son) and his wife for the land to be disposed of are aggressive in three different ways: one, the indifference to the mother's feelings; second, to consider it his right to make this demand and third, to sell it for personal luxury and status, dismissing cultural values. At this juncture when she gets the news that the water level has further sunk, she realises that before the land's drying up even blood relationships have withered and the eyes are tearless. This shift has resulted in an emotional gap. The poet Gurmet writes:

Question:

Now the young brides also
Would be looking towards the homeward lane?
Waiting for the groom to return home
With longing eyes?

Answer:

No one prays today,
Or watch the path with longing eyes
Rarely does, a blessed one,
Come back home.

('Suneha')[17]

The loose English translation fails to convey the rhythm, the sadness and the longing. The waiting is full of impatience and counting of days, standing on one's toes and watching the road. 'Ausiyan' is a word used for the process of calculating with the help of drawing lines and working out a prediction or foretelling. Punjab is a land of soldiers but the reference here is not only to the warrior husband whose return is anxiously awaited for but includes the reference to an NRI husband who has gone to the foreign lands. The answer to the query works both ways and refers to the changed cultural scenario as well as to the uncertainty of war.

One would not like to generalise and say that the west represents a material culture. That would be both misleading and untrue, but the new immigrant who has struggled to save pennies and is keen to keep up with the Joneses, definitely creates for himself a culture of money. Wealth brings power and the ability to rise in the social scale. The past, the prioritisation of emotions over money, is looked upon as an illusionary romanticism, sketched in imaginary colours. This difference between two ways of thinking and the constant conflict their coming together represents, frequently surfaces in Balbir Kaur Sanghera's writing, especially in the story *Rauna Manah Hai*' (Crying is not Allowed).[18] Sukhbir resents the manner in which his parents are treated by his brother and his wife. When he expresses his resentment, his brother throws him out. Sukhbir then goes to one of his uncles, completes his studies and takes up a job. He goes back to India to fetch a Punjabi daughter-in-law in contrast to his brother's wife who is an American. But Renu, Sukhbir's wife, is equally materialistic. Thus, the rift goes on widening. Sanghera's other stories also reflect on these changing values of the younger generations. She writes about single parents, an exigency that rises not only on account of widowhood but also of divorce and separation. These stories are about man-woman relationships and Sanghera points out that the difference in personal relationships, is not necessarily a matter of culture but also of individual character values. While the virtuous Indian woman suffers in *'Bandi'* (slave), the Irish woman Sylvia Carter has a very caring husband who is an Italian. Both the women possess the same caring nature, similar maternal feelings then why is one happy and the other not? A great deal of Punjabi diasporic writing presents inter-cultural marriages. These mixed marriages generate a mixed culture which is not necessarily bad. In many ways these crossings-over are good and lead to greater understanding between cultures. Individual relationships are the best way to know and love the other. When there is an interaction only at a social level each side attempts to measure the other but personal relationships are more far-reaching in their level of understanding. Identity has several aspects, language being one of them. The writing in the mother tongue by holding on to the language is actually an attempt at preserving that aspect of being. Also emotions, expressions, the traditional metaphors that establish a silent understanding do not require translation. They communicate across space and distance.

There is a significant difference between the language we write and the language we speak and what is finally transferred to another culture's discourse. Bakhtin in his discussion on the presence of a unitary language amidst heteroglossia places it within a single language and the dominance of one 'reigning language' over other languages (Bakhtin 271) but the moment we transfer it to the relationship with imperial governance with its colonies, it ceases to be the dominance of one dialect; instead it becomes a transplantation of a different idiom on the native tongue, one lying outside its own domain and conveniently overlaid. But Bakhtin goes on to observe that 'no living word relates to its object in a *singular* way, between the word and its object, between the word and its speaking subject, there exists an elastic environment of other, alien words about the same object, the same theme. And this is an environment that it is often difficult to penetrate' (Bakhtin 276, emphasis in original). Translation is unable to capture the multilayered formation of the native word, embedded as it is in cultural discourse, the nuances of which the speaker of the same language can capture. The writer who writes in language not his own translates his thoughts and emotions sans this multilayeredness which is loaded with history or histories of political events, personal losses and legendary knowledge and is rich with echoes of the past

Uma Parmeswaran in her essay, 'Dispelling the Spells of Memory: Another Approach to Reading Our Yesteryears', discusses these aspects of life when a person lives abroad. Parameswaran feels the country of adoption at times is one's own. One has a sense of belonging there for one develops friendships, begins to relate to spaces and neighbourhoods and politics. It feels like home. It is memories alone that remain the connecting thread with the past and this is shared only with one's native countrymen. If communication is only with them and in the mother tongue, it leads to exclusion and ghettoisation. The diaspora needs to free itself from this kind of a colonisation and relate to the external social reality of their present. Parameswaran's views raise several other questions and bring to the fore the construction of identity in a contingent world and proceed to acquire a subjectivity and an agency in it. It is there that the 'exile' has to be lived out and a 'homeland' found.[19] Avtar Brah also holds similar views.[20] The example of settler communities in both the US and Australia offers an example. The diaspora is not necessarily a transient traveller.

Freud, in his concept of identity, projects it in three parts: id, ego and super-ego. While Freud went on to consider these aspects time and again but remained consistent in considering id as the unconscious and ego as the conscious, Trilling is of the view that the relationship between id and ego is one of opposition and contention. All the energies that one can connect with the *id* are spontaneous and instinctual, while ego looks outwards though it also is not fully conscious. It works under the flow of some unconscious flow.[21] These oppositional and divisionary aspects find reflection in most diasporic writing where the emotional journeys to and fro between space and time are continuous. The real problem is twofold: how to belong and overcome this invisibility and how to remember and hold on to a valuable past. Memory is an essential part of our very being. Can languages adapt themselves to new cultures and create a self which is not divided?

NOTES & REFERENCES

1. Intizar Husain, 'Letter From India' trans. Vishwamitter Adil and Alok Bhalla. *Stories About the Partition of India*. Ed. Alok Bhalla (New Delhi: Harper Collins 1994), 96–110.
2. The word *patria* has multiple applications: Patria: Native country; patriarchal ruler of the family, clan; patrimony: inherited from one's ancestors; patriot: one who exerts himself to promote the well-being of his country (O.E.D.). Also refer. G.K. Subbaryudi, 'Patria, Expatriacy and the Question of Value', *The Commonwealth Review*. Vol. IV. No. 2 where he says that expatriate is a temporary condition.
3. Vijay Mishra, 'Diasporas and the Art of Impossible Mourning,' *In Diaspora*. Ed. Makarand Paranjpe (New Delhi: Indialog Publication), 2001, 24–51.
4. Edward Said, 'Intellectual Exile: Expatriates and Marginals', 1993 Reith Lecture. *The Edward Said Reader*. Eds Moustafa Bayouiviet et al. (New York: Vintage Books, 2000).
5. Refer my essay 'Rethinking Diaspora: Of Hyphen, Hybridity and Translated Men' in *The Expatriate Indian Writing in English*. Eds. T. Vinoda and P. Shailaja. (New Delhi: Prestige Publishing House 2006), 23–37.

Writing in One's Own Language and the Grounds of *Being* 75

6. See Gayatri Spivak, 'Marginality in the Teaching Machine' where she states that a cultural identity is through language and 'In that sense I am a Bengali' *Outside in The Teaching Machine* (New York: Routledge, 1996), 55. Much before this when she in her Introduction to her translation of Mahasweta Devi's translation of 'Draupadi' had written: 'Any sense of Bengal as a nation is governed by the putative identity of the Bengali language. *In Other Worlds: Essays in Cultural Politics* (New York: Routledge, 1998), 181. I am, however, not in agreement with this.
7. Salman Rushdie, 'Imaginary Homelands' in *Imaginary Homelands: Essays and Criticism 1981-1991* (London: Granta and Penguin India, 1992). 9-21.
8. Lionel Trilling, *Sincerity and Authenticity* (Cambridge, Massachusetts M: Harvard University Press, 1972).
9. Cultural and behavioural patterns are part of a living culture, hence to grow and change is part of their nature. Behaviour besides being a result of culture and upbringing is also a part of response to social and political environment. It cannot be and should not be frozen.
10. See Bakhtin 'Discourse and the Novel,' *The Dialogic Imagination: Four Essays.* Ed. Michael Holquist. Translated by Caryl Emerson and Michael Holquist (Austin: University of Texas Press). 1981. 259-422. Dialogue is discussed more specifically 278-285.
11. Meera Syal, *Anita and Me* (London: New Press, 1997).
12. *Bhaji on the Beach*, is the story of a picnic outside the city, by a busload of women of two generations, actually three the elderly, the middle and the young. The cultural shifts and awareness of emotions is abundantly dear. A film/telefilm: Directed by Gurinder Chadha and story and screenplay by Meera Syal, 1993. The film was done in three languages: English, Punabi, Hindi.
13. Farhana Sheikh, *The Red Box* (New Delhi: Rupa & Co, 1991), and Ravinder Randhawa's *A Wicked Old Woman* (London: The Women's Press, 1993) is the story of a girl who pretends to be old and poor – what she is not.
14. The reference is to Chitra Divakaruni's two novels which represent isolated narratives, self inclusive cultures. *Mistress of Spices* (London: Black Swan, 1997) and *The Palace of Illusion* (London: Picador, 2009).
15. Jarnail Singh, 'Towers' in *Towers* (Punjabi). (Ludhiana: Chetna Prakashan, 2005).
16. Dr. Gurmel, *Shabdan da Safar* (The Travels of Words) Punjabi (Ludhiana: Chetna Prakashan, 2004).

17. *'Suneha'* The original in Punjabi is full of resonances of cultural meaning and reads: *'Aaje vi saj-vihahiyan naran/Ausiyan paoindiyan haungiyan?/Ghar murhde dhole de rahi/nain vichandiyan hongaungiyan? Nan koi ausiyan paonda hai,/Nan koi nain vichandha hai/virla, virla karmawala/murh ke ghar nu aonda hai.'*
18. Balbir Kaur Sanghera, *Thandi Hawa* (Cold Wind). Punjabi (Ludhiana: Chetna Prakashan, 2005).
19. Uma Parameswaran, Dispelling the Spells of Memory: Another Approach to Reading Our Yesterdays,' North Dakota State University, Fargo, Vol. 2.2000. Http://www.ndsu.edu/RRCWL/V2hema. Accessed 4 December 2013. Paraweswaran writes, 'Both exile and home are here' (6).
20. Avtar Brah, *Cartographies of the Diaspora: Contesting Identities* (London: Routledge, 1996). Brah is of the view that this intersection between different communities is a discourse of home, nation, location and culture of borders. Here, there is a confrontation as well as a meeting point. Borders are 'social, cultural and psychic' and they are face to face (198–200).
21. Trilling, 'The energies and intentions of the id are instinctual and libidinal ... . The primary concern of the ego is with the survival of the human organism ...'. Also see 148.

6

The New Parochialism
Homeland in the Writing of the Indian Diaspora

The claims of diasporic writing in terms of critical attention, theoretical formulations and relationships to cultures of origin and adoption are many. These claims may, at times, be contradictory, representing momentary adjustments and impulses and draw attention to the complex nature of diasporic existence and writing. It is not possible to dismiss that complexity as irrelevant. Instead, it forces itself on one's attention and requires a close scrutiny. I would like to address three questions, once we have waded through some preliminary concerns: (i) how does the diasporic writer relate to his homeland and culture of origin; (ii) how far is this relationship valid and aesthetically viable in literary terms; and (iii) what are its implications in terms of power relations and with relation to the culture of the homeland?

The narrative of the diaspora is above all a narrative of the 'self' for the very act of migration implies a 'bodily' lifting out of the familiar and relocation in the new and the unfamiliar.[1] Diasporic presence is a dispersal, a scattering, a flight and has to take root elsewhere, specially if it seeks sustenance and growth. But it continues to depend on the bits and pieces of its origin to hold itself together in the face of the onslaught, rejection or domination by the 'other,' by the world which both frightens and fascinates. Diasporic writing today, whatever mode it adopts, and whatever temporalities it relates to, is still primarily concerned with the contingent of being. The contemporary diasporic writer-intellectual functions quite differently from the diasporas of the past. Migrancy has never been so central as it is now (and perhaps not even as privileged). In the last hundred years or so at least three different phases can be discerned – migrants from one 'white' culture to another where the self was not threatened by the uprooting - Henry James, James Joyce, T.S. Eliot, Joseph Conrad, the refugee intellectuals like Bertolt Brecht, Boris Pasternak, and the rest i.e. the 'unhoused' writers of a later generation who built themselves a 'house of words,' Steiner's extraterritorials.[2] And now the third phase when cultural and intellectual needs are being overlaid by the new economic and political realities with the slave and the labourer being replaced by the info-savvy immigrant very much in demand.[3] Home and homelessness, nation and nationalism, borders and crossing of borders have become uncertain categories.

The word 'home' no longer signifies a 'given,' it does not necessarily connote a sense of belonging, instead it increasingly foregrounds a personal choice which the individual has exercised, and 'home' and 'homeland' are, for all practical purposes, separable units.[4] Recognising this Uma Parameswaran brings in the gender perspective and comments, 'Perhaps women with centuries of indoctrination and expectations are able to adapt more quickly and to accept and love two homes without conflict or ambivalence' (32). But the metaphor does not hold beyond the bare minimum. There are several conflictual areas, and as Edward Said has pointed out, you 'always feel outside in someway' ('On Palestinian Identity' 172),[5] and for Rushdie being Indian outside India is a daily questioning of the self *(Imaginary Homelands* 17). There are also people like Naipaul who travel because they are not-at-home anywhere. And then what about the twice removed – those who have taken several routes? For Vassanji's protagonist Ramji in *Amriika,* home is Africa – where his grandmother is and where he grew up, while homeland is India.[6] In times of conflicts, the acceptance of a dual citizenship is not easy. There may have to be a daily choice as to which side I am on, a conflict between heritage and citizenship, between patriotism and practical considerations. The 'immigrant' or the 'diasporic' self is simultaneously open to at least two epistemologies, two histories and two social realities. There is the history (and the memory) of the colonial past and the racial

The New Parochialism 79

discrimination, which jostles with the native history of resistance and freedom struggle. Two systems of knowledge and two sets of cultural influences construct identity and the socio-economic reality of both the societies confronts the self.

While the word diaspora is increasingly becoming an umbrella term for immigrants of all hues, indicative of large congregations, there is a corresponding move towards fragmentation and specificity. In September (23–25 September 2000),[7] the International Rajasthani Conclave was organised to which Rajasthanis living outside the territorial limits of Rajasthan, whether in India or abroad, were invited thus defining homeland through territorial boundaries and not by nationality or citizenship, narrowing down space to regional concerns. Gayatri Spivak prefers the word nation and defines it in linguistic terms, because she is of the view that cultural identity always presupposes a language and, '[i]n that sense, I suppose I am a Bengali.'[8] In direct contrast to Spivak, is a statement by Mahasweta Devi, a stay-at-home writer and a grassroot activist, some of whose work has been translated by Spivak. Devi, in a conversation with Spivak in 'The Author in Conversation', says, 'I consider myself an Indian writer, not a Bengali writer. I am proud of this' (*Imaginary Maps* xii).[9] Though Spivak identifies herself as a Bengali on the basis of language, it needs to be pointed out that most intellectual activity is often undertaken in languages other than one's own. What import does this have? Rushdie defines the immigrant writer as a translated being (*Imaginary Homelands* 17) and translation has its own politics and manipulations. There is always a sense of loss, and often a recasting in an image acceptable to the 'Other'. Moreover, language does not always hold together a culture; it can also act as an exclusionist and divisionary force. In his 'Introduction' to *Imaginary Homelands*, Rushdie refers to one such incident during the Festival of India when a distinguished novelist expected 'every educated Indian' to understand his Sanskrit sloka thus making the knowledge of language a test of their Indianness.[10] If one is culturally defined by language then entry into or appropriation of another language also implies cultural appropriation and transformation.[11] What about the second and third generations abroad who may have lost the language? And what about those writers who continue to write in the language of their birth while living abroad? Where do the writers writing in Punjabi, Gujarati, Bengali and the rest belong? How do they define their homeland, nation and culture and even more importantly where does their politics rest? The hyphenated identities are difficult to categorise. Very often the hyphen does not exist and sometimes it is twice hyphenated. For instance, Agha Shahid Ali identifies himself as a Kashmiri-American-Kashmiri concerned more with the Kashmiri he has become after the American experience (Shankar and Srikanth 378).[12] The hyphen is problematic whether we are willing to face this fact or not. For it requires an act of balancing which is difficult to sustain at all times; it allows not only a floating identity but also a rotating one, it gets directly linked to visibility (in an alien space) and often to fracturing. The relationship of the hyphen to the homeland is not always one of linkages, it may be one of withdrawal and a withholding of the self.

Recently, at a discussion of Jhumpa Lahiri's short stories, the dominant presence of Bengali characters in her work over-writing the American experience was considered a lack in her work. And she herself has gone out to say that her own experience of India is 'largely that of a tunnel, the tunnel imposed by a single city we ever visited, by the handful of homes we stayed in, by the fact that I was not allowed to explore the city on my own.'[13] Similarly Mistry's concern with Parsi characters and culture has been criticised, a criticism which the writer has responded to in his fine short story 'Swimming Lessons.'[14] A few years ago his novel, *A Fine Balance*, was the centre of a controversy both for its political critiquing and the apparently pessimistic projection of the Indian situation. Not only was his right to write about India under interrogation but the veracity of his knowledge has also been questioned. Was he another of those India-baiters? Did he know enough? And was the realistic mode the right choice?[15] These voices of criticism compel us to explore the extra-literary dimensions of diasporic writing, to ask the question whether aesthetic values are neutral and universal, and where does the literary end and the political begin? How does a writer carry the burden of a whole country/culture on his back?

While the pre-Independence Indian writer abroad worked through nostalgia, memory and a possible dependence on Indian philosophy, creating a mythical past from them or alternatively a return to India and a redefining of the self within the trope of patriotism (Seepersad, Naipaul, Raja Rao, Shantha Rama Rau and the westernised Indian intellectuals like Nehru fall into this category), the writer of the post-independence period works through other constructions which can be broadly categorised as: (i) exotica, (ii) history, (iii) fantasy, (iv) collision and (v) use of a third space. Of these 'exotica' has a long tradition and continues to thrive, feeding stereotypes or re-examining them. This is marked by a variety of different motives, several of which can be suspect, and others which may be very complex. One would expect it to have outlived its utility but it continues to exist, viewing India through a 'seventeen and half hour' flight. Shona Ramaya's novellas put together in *Beloved Mother, Queen of the Night* (1993)[16], Anita Desai's *Journey to Ithaca* (1996), Ruth Jhabvala's *Shards of Memory* (1995)[17] are some which belong to this category. Authenticity may elude exotica, and it may also, as Neil Bissoondath has pointed out, lead to the diasporic writer being perceived as 'exoticism on two legs' (Bissoondath 113).[18] The 'ethnicity' trap is a real danger not only for creative writers, but also for theorists and critics. It spreads its tentacles everywhere back into the homeland because it can disguise itself as a recovery of the past, a fascination with anthropological and mythological studies. It frames the past and encashes its marketability.

A re-visioning of history has also taken place through different modes – historical reconstruction as in Markandaya's *The Golden Honeycomb* (1977), magic realism as in Rushdie's *Midnight's Children*, and also through the realistic mode as in Mistry's *A Fine Balance* (1995). Narratives of personal history, memoirs and recollections also fall within this category, narratives which return to the homeland in many ways as for instance Attia Hosain's *Sunlight on a Broken Column* (1961), Naipaul's *A House for Mr Biswas* (1962) and Mukherjee's *The Tiger's Daughter* (1973). Underlying this historical concern is the need for defining the self and identifying sites of resistance. Fantasy facilitates this search in many ways allowing both self-expression and subversion to work side by side. Salman Rushdie in *Midnight's Children*, Suniti Namjoshi in several of her works including the *Feminist Fables, The Conversations of Cow, Mothers* of *Maya Diip,* Vassanji in *The Book of Secrets,* Amitav Ghosh in *In An Antique Land* and *The Calcutta Chromosome,* Kiran Desai in *Strange Happenings in a Guava Orchard* all resort to this mode. It may or may not be an autonomous or a total construct but it becomes capable of generating new myths and meanings.

Contrasted with this is the novel of culture collision which is often marked by bewilderment, a sense of shock, withdrawal or adaptation. First generation and second generation writers both have written such novels where problems of adjustment and cultural differences are reflected. Farhana Sheikh's *The Red Box* (1991), Meera Syal's *Anita and Me* (1996), Ravinder Randhawa's *A Wicked Old Woman* (1987), Bharati Mukherjee's *Darkness* – works of this nature deconstruct the diasporic world and locate it in a present which throws up its own challenges. These are the narratives of personal choices, of characters growing up and learning to cope with their problems.

Moving away from these anchorings in the homeland is the narrative of a third space which writers like Michael Ondaatje, Amitav Ghosh and Ashis Gupta have resorted to in *The English Patient* (1992), *In An Antique Land* (1992) and *The Toymaker from Weisbaden* (1993), novels which move outside both the culture of origin and that of adoption. But none of these writers is able to sustain this at length. Sooner or later they return to their homeground. At one level this opting out of the two conflicting realities and locating oneself in a third space is not very different from the use of self-contained constructs of fantasy – they both create temporary heterotopias for the self to work out its conflicts, to distance itself and free itself from the necessity of emotional choices. Also these are the narratives of personal recovery and rehabilitation. Where are the narratives of national crisis? Ondaatje's novel *Anil's Ghost* (2000) is about the situation of the civil war in Sri Lanka but even as it reconstructs skeletons and emphasises human rights, it does not reflect or project any such moment where his loyalty to the country of his adoption may dash with the loyalty to the far away homeland. The conscience is moved so far and no further. The flow of power continues to be unidirectional.

None of the above paradigms is exclusive or definitive but they do emphasise the fact that the diasporic writer, like all other writers, has constantly to reinvent himself and work out new strategies to relate to his experience. Also there can be no sustained opting out of origins – they will surface either obliquely or directly as in Dabydeen's *The Wizard Swami* (1987) or Naipaul's *The Mystic Masseur* (1957). These experiences and memories are the writer's raw material. What is of more immediate concern is how do we draw the line between exoticism and ethnicity? Between ghettoisation and self-assertion? And do we evaluate this writing from a purely literary perspective or a cultural one?

The work of a diasporic writer attracts the attention of two different sets of readers – and though both begin with the purpose of assessing how they fare in it, finally the perspectives are different. The culture of adoption wishes to see 'through' the text to the culture of the 'Other'; the culture of origin wants to assess the authenticity of self reflection. However, none of these is a pure motive. The west looks for familiar landmarks, a west-centric vision, while the average Indian reader seeks his own validity. And the writer is trapped between the two. It is here that the writer's perception of himself as anchored in a linguistic culture, a community-based construct, a geographical territory or a nation-state becomes significant. It is here that it begins to intervene with the politics and culture at home.

There is an interesting point here – do we have an Indian diaspora in Pakistan or Bangladesh? One could argue for both sides of the case. There can be a definite 'No.' New countries were carved out of the motherland, new nations born. Often there was no dislocation in terms of physical shifting. In other cases, when people migrated, it was ordinarily a matter of choice. And, memories of the motherland were valid only for the first generation of migrants. But none of these arguments is the final truth or can be sustained fully. The ordinary person was involved only involuntarily in the process of decision-making. People who were dislocated were termed 'refugees.' And territorial dislocation was full of memories and associations, break-up of families and relationships, homesickness, shared cultural myths, legends and history and all these gave rise to questions of identity. The relationship of Pakistani writers of Indian origin with Indian writers, presents its own web of complexity. Besides other things, there is often a shared language be it Urdu, Punjabi, Bengali or Sindhi which offers a challenge to the 'linguistic' framework of Gayatri Spivak.

This problem of a shared culture and language is not applicable to the writers who stay in Canada, England or America and choose to write in the mother tongue. They apparently give little importance to territorial dislocation. They relate to their mother tongue and through it to their mother country and are embroiled in the political situation.[19] Fragmentation and preservation of the culture of origin in its pristine glory also leads to a similar end. Abroad, ghettoisation becomes a side-product of this kind of exercise and back home it becomes a breeding ground of fundamentalism flowing into the fundamentalism rampant in the soil itself. It seeks to view culture as a frozen heritage and denies it the life-breath of change and evolution. It defines cultural realities within narrow spaces transferring the metaphorical division between the home and the world to include expatriation. The preservation of culture, an activity which must go on, is delegated to the mother country and the making of money, a masculine activity is appropriated by the diasporic community. This division is rather unrealistic, self-centred and negative and therefore does not yield any worthwhile literary production. This discourse even as it uses the language of transnationalism, transterritorialism and globalisation, projects its own presence in another country as a justifiable argument.

The writers who choose to write in English are somewhat in a different position. They seek their audiences globally, but are also at the same time engaged in preserving their subjectivity, and their difference, along with their marginality (ref. Spivak *In Other Worlds*).[20] A host of diasporic writers have time and again expressed the view that they write about their homelands in order to preserve their identity, yet the different ways of reception force them into homogenising ethnic identities. But this is a very different position from the one the Indian writer and intellectual adopts, is willing to adopt, or should be concerned with within the larger interests of a cultural stance or cultural freedom. The writer in India has other marginalities to contend with, to project and to foreground. His position vis-à-vis the hegemonic powers abroad is one of resistance (and not acceptance). His subject-position in his own country locates him differently. And he rejects definitions through negatives as the term non-western indicates. His involvement and interpretation of his reality, no matter how fragmentary or selective, has a wider concern than the recovery of a subjectivity or the fear of erasure. The writer in him is continually contending with political realities, dissensions, ideologies and national crises.

Time and again diasporic writers and theorists have been assailed for being inauthentic, for misrepresenting Indian reality, for catering to the market forces and several other reasons of the same kind. Nayantara Sahgal once pointed out that the diasporic writer is not subjected to the daily onslaughts of raw reality. The narratives of the diaspora are framed by memory and distance and motivated by a desire to construct their own reality. For the culture back home their writing fulfils a role similar to that of an 'Introduction' to a translated text. It sets out the parameters and the principles for interpreting the text, for decoding it, and as such it limits the text. It occupies the space between the text and the reader, a space which does not necessarily belong to it. To say the least, the political and literary concerns in India are different from the ones which concern the writer of the diaspora. While the individual's right to his experience and memory is indisputable – the political purpose (and influence) of literature cannot be sidelined. Increasingly the terms which have entered critical discourse are being defined by the west, words such as transnational, hybridity and transborder, fixing us in a slot not of our making. How many of us are willing to accept them uncritically? And how many of us are carried away by their power and surrender to them without sparing a thought as to how they have been constructed?

You may well ask what this has to do with the projection of a 'homeland.' And I may point out that they define the reality of the diaspora – and not my reality. I can forget the western presence if I so desire, consider technology neutral, enter into a linguistically defined world which is not hermetically sealed, which does not clash with my loyalty to a nation-state. I can read Mahasweta Devi and not think of Dopdi or Rudali as people on the margins. For me they project an Indian reality and the narrative can easily be shifted from Bihar to Rajasthan without any corresponding shift or erosion in meaning. I can do all this and much more. And I am constantly exposed in so many different ways to what goes on in the literature of other Indian languages which helps construct my reality.

This freedom does not exist for the diaspora. Several writers themselves have acknowledged the remoteness of a receding memory, the impossibility of recapitulating the lost homeland; critics have critiqued their work on the grounds of their having lost touch with reality, and some immigrants have wondered as to when they'll cease to be aliens and begin to belong. In fact, the diasporic urge to appropriate space at home, and to use it for self-sustenance abroad is partly responsible for their non-acceptance by some societies. Indians abroad have experienced various kinds of marginalisation and rejections, distrust and dislocations and the message should now go home. One needs to strike roots at emotional levels, not merely physical ones.

What is of concern is that literature, which theoretically should have risen above narrow identifications, is anchoring itself in parochial affiliations, a process which begins to smell dangerously of inbreeding. All reflections of the homeland cannot be considered equally valid or invalid. Very often literary evaluations, may be different from cultural and political ones, but this trend towards narrowing of spaces and the myopic vision needs to be watched with care.

NOTES & REFERENCES

1. Several different words have been in use at different periods of history, to emphasise contemporary concerns – expatriate, émigré, immigrant, exile, refugee. But for the purposes of the present essay, the word 'diaspora' is being used as an umbrella term and includes all those who have left their homeland (whether voluntarily or under compulsion is not of significance), and are now living outside India. It is also of no concern as to what citizenships they have acquired, though this directly attacks the concept of patriotism as a unitary whole. Homelands, also in order to lay claim to the wealth of the NRI community, are now enlarging the meaning of NRI to encompass People of Indian Origin. See 'Team Indians,' *The Times of India* 25 August 2000, late city ed. 14.

2. George Steiner, *Extraterritorial: Papers on Literature and the Language Revolution* (Harmondsworth: Penguin, 1972).
3. See Gurmukh Singh, 'The Trillion-Dollar Diaspora: The Empire Strikes Back?,' *The Sunday Times of India* (New Delhi) 13 August 2000, late city ed. In India we have moved away from the early immigrations of indentured labour, political exiles and upper class migrations to that of trained professionals. Today's immigrants are leaving a country which is politically an independent nation-state and very often they also go in for the citizenship of the new homeland. But since September 2000, when this paper was presented at the JNU seminar, and 2001, the employment scene in the west has changed. Everyday there are newspaper reports to that effect, what with IT professionals returning home. See Rajpal.
4. See Parameswaran in *Writers of the Indian Diaspora*. Ed. Jasbir Jain (Jaipur: Rawat, 1998, 2011) 20–39, 38. Also see Kanaganayakam 'Writing Beyond Race: The Politics of Otherness', in *The Toronto Review of Contemporary Writing Abroad*, 12.3 13–14 (1994). I also draw the reader's attention to Rushdie, 'The Location of *Brazil*,' in *Imaginary Homelands* (London: Granta Books, 1991). For Bissoondath, 'even the word "homeland" is problematic,' *Selling Illusions: The Cult of Multiculturalism in Canada* (Toronto: Penguin Books), 119.
5. Salman Rushdie, 'On Palestinian Identity: A Conversation with Edwards Said' in *Imaginary Homelands* (London: Grant Penguin, 1991), 166–186.
6. M.G. Vassanji, *Amriika* (New Delhi: Harper Collins, 1999), 124.
7. This conclave was announced with a lot of fanfare and conducted with great éclat, but the economic results are yet to be seen. The long list of invitees from outside India is outmatched by the longer list of invitees from outside Rajasthan but inside India. *Rajasthan Patrika* has brought out a supplement listing their names and addresses (23 September 2000).
8. See the Foreword to Spivak's translation of Mahasweta Devi's 'Draupadi' She writes, 'Any sense of Bengal as a 'nation' is governed by the putative identity of the Bengali language' *(In Other Worlds: Essays in Cultural Politics*, (New York: Routledge, 1988) 181). Similarly in 'Marginality in The Teaching Machine,' (*Outside in the Teaching Machine*, New York: Routledge, 1996), she is of the view that cultural identity always presupposes a language and writes, 'In that sense, I suppose, I am a Bengali' (55). Contrast this with a text written by a semi-literate nineteenth century Bengali woman Rassundari Devi, *Amar Jiban* (originally published in two parts, Pt. I,

1876, Pt. II, 1906) who begins her autobiography *Amar Jiban* (translated by Enakshi Chatterjee, Kolkata: Writers Workshop, 1999), by stating 'I was born in the month of Chaitra in the years 1218 and I am 88 years old. I have spent such a long time in Bharatvarsha' (21). Here the author is not limited by the limits of her language.

9. Mahasweta Devi, *Imaginary Maps* (Calcutta, Thema, 1991). Also see Mahasweta Sengupta, 'Translation as Manipulation: The Power of Images and the Images of Power', *Between Languages, Cultures and Cross-cultural Texts*. Ed. Anuradha Dingwaney and Carol Maier, (Delhi: OUP, 1996), where she points out how the processes of selection (and omission), rewriting texts, denudes them of their richness, intensity and meaning (160–61). Sengupta proceeds to look at Rabindranath Tagore's autotranslations and observes that he consciously pruned the original and substituted images as the meaning had to be rendered acceptable and intelligible to people of a distant land (170). In a letter to Thomas Stiirge Moore (11 June 1935), Tagore confessed to a sense of futility at the whole process of translation, (Sengupta 171).

10. Introduction, *Imaginary Homelands* 2. Rushdie also points out how the use of the word 'Moghul' for Muslim immediately excluded the Indian Muslims from any claim on their own country and Indian tradition was 'being described in exclusive, and excluding, Hindu terms.'

11. Dingwaney, 'Introduction: Translating Third World Cultures,' *Between Languages*, 3. Dingwaney quotes Fanon, 'To speak a language is to take on a world, a culture,' and goes on to elaborate upon its inference – the importance of contexts. Writers like R. Parthasarthy, *The Rough Passage*, and Bhatt have also responded to the expatriate condition as the loss of a voice. (See Bhatt 'Search for my Tongue' *Daskhat* 1, 1992).

12. Lavena Dhinghra Shankar and Rajini Srikanta, 'South Asian American Literature Off the Turnpike of Asian American', *Postcolonial Theory and the United States*, Eds. Amritjit Singh and Peter Schmidt (Jackson: University Press of Mississippi, 2000).

13. See Jhumpa Lahiri, 'My Intimate Alien,' Spec. issue of *Outlook* (2000): 116–17, where she admits that her own experience of India is 'largely that of a tunnel, the tunnel imposed by a single city we ever visited, by the handful of homes we stayed in, by the fact that I was not allowed to explore this city on my own.'

14. Mistry, 'Swimming Lessons', *Tales for Firozsha Baag* (1987, New Delhi: Rupa, 1993).

15. This discussion took place at a seminar in Jaipur on *Expatriate Writing: Theory and Practice* in December 1996 where some of the speakers also referred to a similar controversy which had taken place in Canada. Also refer Santosh Gupta, 'Balancing Pluralities: Search for Ideology in Rohinton Mistry's *A Fine Balance,*' in *Writers of the Indian Diaspora*, Ed. Jasbir Jain, 1998. and Keki Daruwalla 'Of Parsis and their Literature', *Critical Practice* 7, (2000).
16. See my article, 'Framing Cultural Narratives.' *The Postmodern Indian Novel.* Ed. Vinay Kirpal (Bombay: Allied Publishers, 1996).
17. My initial response to both these novels was that the writers had lost touch with India. Meenakshi Mukherjee's response to Desai's latest collection of short stories, expressed to me in personal correspondence, has been the same. But for a more detailed examination of Desai's *Journey to Ithaca* see the rev. ed. of *Stairs to the Attic: The Novels of Anita Desai* by Jasbir Jain (Jaipur: Printwell, 2000).
18. Bissoondath, He argues for a reduced emphasis on ethnicity and a greater one toward acceptance and a sense of belonging (*Selling Illusions*). Perhaps there a need to create a third category between assimilation and ethnicity which can impart individuality without alienation? Daruwalla in his essay on the Parsi Novel, makes a distinction between multiculturalism and pluralism basing his argument on Fulford's (referred above, 83).
19. My reference here is to a table talk between Punjabi writers who live in North America but continue to write in Punjabi, and writers from India, '*Parwasi Sahitya sambandha Table Talk,* published in the April-June 1994, issue of *Watan* (Punjabi) where Sadhu Binning asserts his claim to a voice in the happenings back home (19). Others also express similar views. Discussants were Sutinder Singh Noor, Mohanjit, Navtej Bharti, Balraj Cheema, Sadhu Binning, Daljit Mehtaand Ravinder Sahraw.
20. See Spivak, 'A Literary Representation of the Subaltern' in *Other Worlds: Essays in Cultural Politics,* (New York: Routledge, 1988), 246.

7

Out of the Colonial Cocoon?
From *The Mimic Men* to *India: A Million Mutinies Now*

> ... one saw the psychological significance of freedom. It does something to a man's way of seeing the world. It is an experience which is not gained by education or money but by an instinctive reevaluation of your place in the world ... . And again one felt the full meaning, the full desecration of human personality which is contained in the word: colonial.
>
> (George Lamming, *Pleasures of Exile*, 65)[1]

Between the colonial experience and that of freedom, lies a whole process of a 're-evaluation' of one's place in the world, an internal transformation of the self from servility to responsibility, from obedience to initiative as well as a changed relationship with the world outside, the once imperial masters, and with the feeling of helplessness and vulnerability. It demands a constant reviewing of history and historical mistakes. Freedom does not imply merely the relocation of power but, in order to be meaningful, it calls for a change in one's attitude to power. The question is not merely can the 'master' adapt himself to a relationship of equality but also can the erstwhile colonial, characterised as inferior, brutal and barbaric, bring about a change in his relationship with (a) himself (b) with the erstwhile master and work outside the categories of exclusion and oppression.

Naipaul has come a long way from the early struggles of a BBC freelancer in London to the present position of a Nobel Laureate, But have the colonial positions been discarded? The post-Babri Masjid pronouncements[2], his affiliation with the Hindutva ideology[3] and the arrogance which he displayed during the Neemrana Conference in 2002, each one of them in its own way connects up with the undercurrents in his India travelogues and those of the Islamic world, his thinly disguised biographical sketch of his father through Mohun Biswas (*A House for Mr Biswas*) the short-lived power-play of *The Mimic Men* and his reading of politics in *Finding the Centre, The Middle Passage* and *In a Free State*. They all add up to the emergence of this racial fascism which is now so openly acknowledged: a need to alienate oneself and to perpetuate fear; a need to retain the static purity of the material self.

In the present paper, I propose to use Lamming's observation on the colonial's experience, Naipaul's correspondence with his family and Bhabha's concept of mimicry in order to work with *The Mimic Men* and *India: A Million Mutinies Now*[4] to enable a conceptualisation of my argument that the Naipaulian vision is firmly located in the idea of a 'self' defined through power and materialist self-interest and a colonial past. Lamming's *Pleasures of Exile* is about several things but the more important ones for my purpose are (i) the master-slave relationship (165–178)[5], the disadvantages of a former colonial subject's education in the country of the erstwhile imperial ruler: the continuity which stunts his growth (23–30) and (iii) the experience of going back to the country of one's origins and the feelings the experience may evoke (33, 36, 46–50, 160–163).

Naipaul came to England in 1950 on a Trinidad government scholarship to study at Oxford, and thus the relationship between coloniser and colonised was but marginally modified. His relationship both to his West Indian background and the British remained the same. This position of being on the periphery has perhaps always been a nagging concern within him and the subtext of all his work. The separateness of being an East Indian (in West Indies) has also been a major pre-occupation with him where identity is concerned. Naipaul's writings, even when they are concerned with the West Indian situation, background or politics, do not convey any sense of belonging to the land or the people. His impatience to leave home and reluctance to go back comes through very clearly in his letters home (*Letters* 8). And Asia was, to him, a primitive manifestation of a long dead culture. He wrote to his sister that India 'was a dead country still running with the momentum of its heyday'[6]

Lamming also observes that while an American can still claim his share in the European past, the West Indian Negro cannot claim a share in his African heritage with the same ease: the relationship is more problematic as his migration to the West Indies was not a 'freely chosen act' (160) and his education has not provided him with knowledge about it. As he had no preconceptions about Africa, when Lamming went there he found himself unprepared for the 'shock of familiarity' (161) Contrasted with this sense of familiarity is Naipaul's search for difference when he lands in Bombay on his first visit to India, the country of his ancestors, an experience he describes in *An Area of Darkness*.[7] And contrasted with the West African Negro's lack of any preconceptions is Naipaul's preparedness for the Indian situation through his reading of books and through the static quality of his own Hindu island culture.

Letters Between a Father and Son tells the reader not only about Naipaul's determination to become a writer but also about his source of inspiration and his way of working. The young Naipaul offers advice to his father and asks him to write a 'straight story.' He advises him to write about West Indies from his observation of others. The narrator, for him, is an observer and stands outside the happenings. While a student at Oxford, he wrote an essay on 'Some Uses of the First Person Singular in English Narrative Fiction' which stressed the role of realistic description. Though he handled the subject humorously (*Letters* 165–167), it relates directly to his advice to his father: tell a straight story. Observation is valued more than experience; a peripheral narrative voice of the outsider rather than the anguished cry of a participant finds its way into almost all his work. Lamming, as early as 1960, commented upon Naipaul's dislike for the West Indian community because it was philistine. Lamming felt that one could not leave it at that for it would condemn the West Indians to a future 'you have already chosen.' Lamming was critical of this attitude specially 'when it comes from a colonial who is nervous both in and away from his native country, I interpret it as a simple confession of a man's inadequacy – inadequacy which must be rationalised since the man himself has come to accept it' (Lamming 30). Standing outside as an observer and passing judgment with a degree of conviction becomes, in the long run, a method of preserving the 'self' as a centre of power. Naipaul prefected that art in his travelogues whether to the Islamic World, the American South or India.

In 2001, when he was selected for the Nobel, he referred to *The Mimic Men* in his Nobel Lecture as a book not about Mimics, 'It was about colonial men mimicking the conditions of manhood, men who had grown to distrust everything about themselves.' It was a book about 'colonial shame and fantasy, ... about how the powerless lie about themselves, since it is their only resource' ('Two Worlds')[8] *The Mimic Men* is also a book of total rejection, a final farewell to West Indies, a country with no sense of history, and one which could never be a power centre and as such it needs to be seen against the West Indian background.[9] Through the manner in which populations were brought there, it emerged as a truly multicultural society but it never integrated as one. Religion, ethnic roots and majority/minority considerations continued to divide it. The histories of origin and of separation from the mother country continued to feature, much more for the Indians than for the Africans, because of the Indians lack of political majority, 'Trinidad in fact teeters on the brink of racial war ... . It is sufficient to state that antipathy exists. The Negro has a deep contempt ... for all that is not white; his values are the values of white imperialism at its most bigoted. The Indian despises the Negro for not being an Indian ...' (*Middle Passage* 86).[10] I do not plan to recount Naipaul's numerous references in his travelogues to India or about his need to belong to something bigger than the island but I would like to draw attention to *The Middle Passage* where he talks about alienation being a source of strength 'Everything which made the Indian alien in the society gave him strength' – religion, ritual, a reproduction of Hindu-Muslim rivalries, family quarrels – all. And yet they saw themselves as superior to the Indians in India (*Middle Passage*, 88–89). But as Cheddi Jagan pointed out to him, the Indians owned more but earned less than the blacks. The energy levels were different. Though alienation was a suitable prelude to escape, it did not feed the urge for freedom. Alienation also kept the Indian away from the centre, the centrality Naipaul has always been in search of. In *Finding the Centre* he confesses his natural inclination towards fiction but struggles with statements of fact (10–11), he talks about the necessity to move to a different world but also realised the need to go back (40).[11] Thus at the centre of Naipaul's role as a writer lies this pull in two different directions – alienation vs. desire for centrality, and escape versus need for history which in fact results in the need to disguise the self with a pose of cynicism: another version of mimicry.

Mimicry is 'the ambivalence of colonial discourse' (Bhabha 85) and is similar to the 'technique of camouflage practised in human warfare' (Lacan, quoted by Bhabha 85).[12] In *The Location of Culture*, Bhabha develops Edward Said's view on the tension between the synchronic panoptical vision of domination and the counterpressure of the diachrony of history that is between identity and difference. In India, we have been through this phase in the early half of the nineteenth century when the desire for sameness pushed the intellectuals towards imitation in morals and manners and the country towards reform and the recognition of difference which resulted in the second half of the century in resistance, a literary bilingualism and militant Hinduism. For Naipaul, in the West Indies, the buffer of a home culture is absent. Unable to identify himself as a West Indian, he talks of Trinidadian Indian community, the extended Hindu family and the brahmanic superiority. The 'self' in his case is constructed first through aloofness and disdain, then through barricading the Hindu in him against other influences. His 'self' is rooted in the past, in Hindu India, and it needs the Muslim as 'Other' in his reading of the past.

But perhaps one needs to move beyond the concept of mimicry (as Bhabha has elucidated it) as a means of disrupting authority, as also a means of appropriation and repetition in pursuit of an authenticity which it fails to arrive at. Bhabha refers to *The Mimic Men* and comments:

> Both Decoud and Singh ... are the parodists of history. Despite their intentions and invocations they inscribe the colonial text

erratically, eccentrically across a body politic that refuses to be representational. The desire to emerge as 'authentic' through mimicry – through a process of writing and repetition – is the final irony of representation. (88)

There may be several possible explanations as to why this happens and how. Bhabha has worked out his thesis along Lacanian and Derridean lines but at a simple level it is the category of power that is absent and which by camouflaging authenticity brings about polarisation between ruler and ruled, the powerful and the powerless, and between the norm and the deviant, reflecting a position of singular fixity. One of the two polarities remains fixed. As and when it can be made to shift, the situation alters. The diagnosis for Naipaul's failed Ralph Singh lies in Lamming's *The Pleasures of Exile* when Lamming analyses the political situation as it prevails in West Indies and compares it with the revolutionary upsurge in Africa. The African has never been wholly 'severed from the cradle of a continuous culture and tradition.' But the West Indians, in contrast, despite the infrastructures of freedom being present in their country are perhaps, 'the only modern community in the world where the desire to be free … is dormant' (Lamming 34–35). Later again, he elaborates upon it, the real difference lies between 'vitality that is more than animal exuberance, and vitality which is truly dynamic. This vitality can only be achieved when the colonial castration of the West Indian sensibility has been healed' (48–49).

The Mimic Men can be read in several ways. At one level it is an archetypal third world story with the political power centres pulling the strings from a distance but at another level it is the story of an individual who fails to find an anchoring, has missed out on a sense of commitment, and has difficulty in belonging. Ralph Singh, a product of a colonial past and a colonial education, is a man whose dislocation is permanent and who, for some reason, has got trapped in a time-warp, this time the warp of mimicry. When he returns home after his marriage to Sandra, he feels that his return in itself is a failure and is overcome by his desire to disown this 'tainted island' (53). The group of people to whom Ralph and Sandra attach themselves is equally rootless and directionless. Ralph Singh recollects 'I lived neutrally … . I always felt separate from what I did'

(63). Their world is, in a sense, temporary and exists on the surface with loyalties only on the surface. It is also a world which generates a sense of fear and a consequent sense of withdrawal. *The Mimic Men* is, despite the statements of withdrawal and separation, a very involved book about Caribbean colonialism and the despair which runs through the country. And as always, Naipaul's style is at its best and seductive as ever. It is difficult to resist the emotion of the moment or to refrain from quoting long passages but because it is not in the nature of a travelogue it reveals more than the writer intended to reveal. There is the recurrent need for escape which in itself is an ongoing need – a certain restlessness, a withdrawal, the incompleteness of a man who wants to be whole (31–32), a politician driven by some little hurt. And for this politician in decay, power is the only thing which can revive him (37–38). But later the dinners in London reduce him in size, and his diplomatic failures strike a death knell.

As Ralph explores his childhood memories, he reflects upon the emergence of a 'self' and the ways of knowing, on the nature of language and the importance of communication. How far are these memories reliable is altogether another question which would need other counter records. But Ralph recalls how, while at a school race, he had decided not to run a race, but he faked his participation by shamming to run and even won praise for it, 'So the reputation as a sportsman not only endured but was enhanced and the day became another of my secrets which I feared I might give away in my sleep or under chloroform, before an operation' (127).

Ramabai Espinet, in an interview given to Frank Birbalsingh, commented upon the invisibility of the Indian Caribbean in the Caribbean discourse, and the persistence of the *Ramayana* pattern of 'struggle, survival and return. 'Part of the survival techniques are identified with hypocrisy, pretence and obsequiousness toward the people in control – all facets of mimicry' (Birbalsingh 162–179). In *The Mimic Men*, the island Isabella, lacks a sense of history. The spaces are artificially managed, and the framing of the life is full of replicas and reproductions with 'English gardens superimposed on our Isabellan villages of mud and grass' (95). And thus:

> Between fear and directionlessness, the colonial missed being himself: We zestfully abolished an order; we never defined our

purpose .... We stood for the dignity of our island, the dignity of our indignity .... We spoke as honest men. But we used borrowed phrases which were part of the escape from thought, from that reality we wanted people to see but could ourselves now scarcely face. (215-216)

In *The Mimic Men* also there is a reference to the *Ramayana* and the primitive sacrificial ritual *Asvamedha* which incidentally comments on Naipaul's views on violence. The whole episode begins with a reference to Tamango, a favourite horse for the Malay Cup race. The African story behind the African name Tamango signified revolt and called back to an event in the past. Then the horse disappeared turning the tide of popularity against its owners. And later it was found dead. The horrifying death with its ritualistic framework and the entrails spilling out filled Ralph with awe and horror and recalled for him *Asvamedha*, 'An ancient sacrifice, in my imagination a thing of beauty, speaking of the youth of the world, of untrodden forests and unsullied streams ...' (150-151). Then he goes on to elaborate the race rivalry in school and the rivalry in politics: 'And I go back to the leader and the deed. The leader intuits the necessary deed.' And an essentially outrageous act becomes a rallying point of 'righteous, underground emotion.' The horse sacrifice also symbolised 'the Aryan ritual of victory and overlordship, a statement of power so daring it was risked only by the truly brave ...' (151-152).

This was in 1967. In 1990, Naipaul wrote *India: A Million Mutinies Now*. This was his third Indian travelogue and one in which he senses a new India as he journeys across from one end of the country to the other – Bombay, Bangalore, Calcutta, Lucknow, Amritsar – each journey providing space for forays into regional histories and interviews with the new rebels. In Bombay, the rise of the Shiv Sena, the 'sons of the soil' movement, Ambedkar and the Dalits, in Bangalore and Madras the southern pasts and the DMK, in Calcutta Charu Majumdar and the Naxalites, in Lucknow the Muslim pasts and the Shah Bano case (which attracted national attention but actually began in Indore), and in Amritsar Bhindranwala and the Punjab militancy. These movements were clamourings for change and called for a decentralised power structure which could accommodate new heroes of a different mould and the voices of the hitherto silent majority. But Naipaul's admiration is not directed necessarily at the above causes; instead it is directed at the generation of fear; the terror that is let loose when individuals and relationships are being sacrificed to a cause. One can also sense the anti-Muslim feeling despite a show of objectivity, as well an element of regret at the erosion of Brahmanic authority.

Fear of anarchy drove many like Papu to the religious fold (10), Sena politics was another facet of religious fervour and the movement had its own hierarchy demanding total obedience (18–19), rituals and superstitions are being firmly replanted (55–57), new leaders step into old frameworks, men are turned into gods and the Shiv Sena openly adopted an Hindutva agenda (63, 81). Periyar and Ambedkar are both hailed as different from Gandhi. The anti-Muslim feeling is present not only in the Shiv Sena, or in the Hindu majority that still ruled in the Brahmanic food code and law of purity, but also in Naipaul when he depends heavily on Russell's book about the 1857 war of independence (392–93) and when he writes 'look back over the 100 years before the Mutiny: right through this period there is an unvarying impression of a helpless, trampled-over country, never itself since the Muslim invasions ...' (396).

Naipaul's view of history is episodic, decontextualised and single-perspective governed. It is almost inevitable that there should be several generalisations. Important questions as to the various initiatives for economic development and the middle class effort in building movements are not asked. Neither does he choose to locate these movements in a continuum of time as to why they have begun and where they may lead us and nor does he examine the continuity of colonial patterns of governance into the present. Naipaul's subsequent interventions through public pronouncements place the *Million Mutinies* firmly within its cover – a text, a mere text, which fails to recognise the monster in its popular disguise. Meena Kandasamy in her article 'Casteist, Communal, Racist. And Now a Nobel Laureate' has commented in detail upon Naipaul's pronouncements about the Indian situation. In November 1999, Naipaul referred to the Hindu militancy as a 'corrective to the history I have been talking about' (15 November 1999, *Outlook*). By repeatedly talking about the Muslims as outsiders not only does he forget his position both in West Indies and England, but he also ignores the Aryan invasions referred to in his other writings. If India is not the homeland for the Muslims born here, a place with which they identify themselves and where they have a sense of belonging then one would like to ask where is their home? Naipaul's meetings with Rashid and Amir testify to this. Turned out of their country (India) through lack of opportunity and non-acceptance they still come back to it. Rashid tells him, 'Lucknow is me. It's not the river or the buildings or anything ... Lucknow is me .... I felt relief to be back here. That sense of belonging, which I had in India, I knew I couldn't find anywhere else' (385–387).[13] As a parallel case it is Naipaul who is homeless. He does not belong to West Indies because he has never identified himself with it. The fact of his birth does not make him a West Indian (if the Muslim in India is not Indian); the fact of his living in England does not make him British, for he was not born there and is an immigrant. And he possibly does not belong to India, because he has looked upon it with disdain. It is only the land of his ancestors, a 'once upon a time,' of which he has always been ashamed.

Naipaul's advocacy of Hindu militancy and his approval of the Babri Masjid demolition ignore the aspirations of the middle class youth who are looking for a future; it ignores the individual Muslim, the individual Dalit and the individual Hindu in his approval of violence, genocide and power. Hitler was an elected leader, he promised nationalism and racial purity against the communist ideology of a stateless and a classless society. The first was a brutal, violent and a materialistic ideology resting itself on power; the second was an idealistic movement which called for sacrifice in the present for a better future. It is 'thought' from below and of the common man and despite its distortions and inadequacies, there was a dream behind it. But Hitler's upturning of Marxist ideals happened at a psychological moment in the histories of nations, especially when the Stalin regime had failed to deliver the goods and a defeated Germany was desperate for power. Naipaul, in line with a colonial's admiration for power, occupies the position of a man who fails to see the contradictions in his own stand as well as the oppositional trend in the many mutinies he describes. They all do not move in the same direction. Shiv Sena and Dalit movements are inspired by different objectives and work for different goals,[14] the middle class youth perceived a certain idealism in the Naxalite movement, which provided him with a rallying point.[15] Movements, like riots, are often manipulated by the power-wielders.[16] The unleashing of terror and the growth of fundamentalism merely give rise to other forms of terror and other fundamentalisms. History does not require only a corrective, it also requires a forgetting, if the future is to go on. One may have to make a distinction between forgetting and forgiving. It may not be possible to forget racial injustices and atrocities. But a continued nursing of grudges and hatred can never lead to any humanistic discourse. Thus, this 'forgetting' is not to be in the nature of historical erasure, but in the nature of a shift in relationships. Naipaul fails to notice the apparent contradiction in his stand on the Babri Masjid demolition and his outburst at Neemrana, where he asked why do the writers keep on harping on the colonial experience. In fact, he advocates a memory of convenience and a lapse into a stage where distant memories exercise a stronger hold on one's mind than the more recent ones. Naipaul's colonial attitude looks at the Indian developments in a non-historical manner. He is unable to trace the undercurrents of history and connect it with the militant Hinduism of the late nineteenth century[17] and the narrow nationalism which surfaced again towards the end of the thirties with the formation of the Hindu Sangathan.[18] Nowhere does Naipaul pause to reflect why mimicry is not able to transcend its limitations and nowhere does he reflect on the misuse of religion for the purposes of appropriating power. Naipaul appears to be approving of casteism, hierarchy and terror, in direct opposition to the non-violence which Gandhi advocated and the fearlessness which both Gandhi and Tagore worked for in different ways. Nehruvian idealism too served a purpose; it worked for the common man's participation in the democratic process. Political moves are a major constituent of history. When and how this process went off the rails and fell into an autocratic mode and an imperial disdain for the 'other' is the issue which needs to be addressed. Naipaul's new found recognition of clan affiliations (refer Kundasamy)[19] draws on the residual Brahman in him, to become an approver of a bigoted policy of narrow nationalism still not out of the colonial cocoon or the feeling of insecurity of the exile.

Four years after *The Mimic Men*, Naipaul published *In a Free State* which is a necessary complement to *The Mimic Men*. 'In a Free State' is the last of the three narratives, each independent in itself but stringed together by a Prologue and an Epilogue. I would like to draw attention to the Prologue and the language, the choice of words which sets the tone in it – 'dingy' little Greek streamer, 'overcrowded,' like a 'refugee' ship, the bar the size of a 'cupboard,' the white American children 'overgrown' (i). And amidst this crowd is a tramp who is repeatedly dislocated from his cabin berth. Either he is locked out deliberately or he locks himself in. As we move on to the next narrative 'One Out of Many' there is again a sense of dislocation with an ominous 'But' at the end of the first paragraph (15). This is a story of an Indian diplomat's Indian servant almost a prisoner of his circumstances, with return almost impossible. The second narrative is 'Tell Me Who to Kill.' As the narrator traces his own genealogies, he begins to sense the fragility and unreliability of all that seems real, there is fear, distrust and hatred and a divided people (62–68). The narrator wishes to board a train which will not stop (58), to be on a ship which does not touch land again (75) to be in a state of protected isolation. Later he finds his strength in money power (81– 83). But it is the third narrative, 'In a Free State', where Naipaul visualises the demon-like strength of the masses. In this African state he talks of the different tribes, who with the coming of independence begin to worry about tribal enmities. In the power game between the King and the President, military strength plays an important role. And as Linda and Bobby, whites both, travel through the land, the reversal of power is evident. They travel in fear of the bush, of the jungle law, oscillate between sympathy, neutrality and fear and wonder whether they should go away or continue to stay? The dilemma continues. Conrad's *Heart of Darkness* lurks in the shadows. Terror is relived again when they stay in a hotel. Bobby is all set for a quick escape when the hotel boy brings him the tea-tray and wishes to extract money. Sitting up in bed, Bobby looked at 'the inflamed African face coming nearer to his, he saw it invaded by such blank and mindless rage that his own anger vanished in terror, terror at something he sensed to be beyond his control, beyond his reason' (196). There are others also who are housebound. The gaps between what they pretend to be and what they feel are getting wider and wider. They only way is to get out. A free state is the reversal of power, and the reversal of freedom. Class and racial warfares are part of this inequality and reversal, and in the power game, hatred and violence become indispensable. Thus the need arises for Brahmanic expatriates to endorse religious warfare, violence and inequality, in order to hold on to their mythical sense of superiority, the only protection they have against a sense of insecurity and rootlessness. This is the colonial heritage – the refusal to imagine a state of affairs where fear is not necessary and violence is not politically sanctioned. Those who confront the reality – like Nayantara Sahgal and Shashi Deshpande – also become self-reflective and self-critical in the process;[20] and those who seek to withdraw behind a make-belief world, fail to do so.

NOTES & REFERENCES

1. George Lamming, *Pleasures of Exile* (London: Michael Joseph), 1960.
2. Refer, *The Times of India*, 18 July 1993. Also <http://postcolonialweb.org/Caribbean.naipaul/meena.html>
3. He has made several public pronouncements and given interviews to the press endorsing it. See *Outlook* (15 November 1999). Also see Mushirul Hasan's 'A Million Mutilations', *The Indian Express* (27 November 1999). His outburst against Shashi Deshpande and Nayantara Sahgal at the Neemrana Conference in 2002, 'Shared Histories: Issues of Colonialism and Relationship with the Past' was also covered by the press. Sandhya Shukla in her work *India Abroad: Diasporic Cultures of Postwar America and England* (Hyderabad: Orient, 2005), has commented on this and compared Naipaul with Jhumpa Lahiri. While Lahiri claims the past Naipaul wishes to step out of it. Shukla observes that in Naipaul's case 'the Anglophilia ... defies all the above', that is the past which needs to be seen through a complex range of perspectives. The concept of 'Indianness' is neither fixed, nor static. The various terms 'Bharatvarsha' and 'Hindustan', also have had a wide range of shifts in their usage and the geographical land mass they evoke. Subaltern histories are myriad, but imperial histories are linear and selective, a single lens narration.
4. *The Mimic Men* (1967, London: Picador) 2002; *India: A Million Mutinies Now* (London: Minerva Paperbacks, 1991).
5. See Lamming, 178: 'Can he change over from master – not to slave – but rather to an ordinary citizen who serves a community by his gifts of experience and skill ... . Prospero must be transformed, rejuvenated and ultimately restored to his original conditions of a man among men.'

6. *Letters Between a Father and Son* (London: Little Brown 1999).
7. *An Area of Darkness* (1964, Harmondsworth: Penguin 1970).
8. This extract has been used as an epigraph for the Picador Edition of *The Mimic Men*, 2002.
9. Refer Frank Birbalsingh *From Pillar to Post: The Indo-Caribbean Diaspora* (Toronto: Tsar, 1997). Birbalsingh through several review articles and interviews has traced a history of East Indians which emphasizes their struggles and aspirations. Comparing Bissoondath's *Digging Up the Mountains* and Naipaul's essay 'Power to the Caribbean People', he comments on the elements of sympathy in Bissoondath's approach which are absent in Naipaul's dismissal of the Caribbean futility (61–62). A question which a serious scholar may well ask is why has the multiculturalism of West Indies not been productive?
10. *The Middle Passage* (1962, Harmondsworth: Penguin, 1967).
11. *Finding the Centre* (1984, Harmandsworth: Penguin, 1985).
12. Homi Bhabha, *The Location of Culture* (London: Routledge, 1994).
13. In this connection, it might be worthwhile to look again at *The Mimic Men* where one of the characters talks about the place of birth: 'But where you are born is a funny thing. My great-grandfather and even my grandfather, they always talked about going back for good. They went. But they came back. *You know, you are born in a place and you grow up there. You get to know the trees and plants: You will never know any other trees and plants like that* ... where you born, man, you born. And this island is a paradise, you will discover' (185, emphasis added). I also draw the reader's attention to the writing of Indian Muslims which discuss this repeatedly, even those who like Intizar Hussain migrated to Pakistan.
14. In an article 'Mass Movement or Elite Conspiracy? The Puzzle of Hindu Nationalism' Amrita Basu discusses this and observes: 'both approaches focus excessive attention on the principal actors ... and neglect the political context. Hindu nationalism has, through RSS and VPH, made inroads into the social networking while the BJP acquires a political role. Political ambitions are behind the agenda. Basu's analyses of the Mandal Commission implementation is that while the BJP could not openly take an anti-caste position, it also could not afford to alienate the upper caste, thus while it formally supported the recommendation at the national level, 'it undermined them locally, its most effective response to Mandal was Hindu nationalism' (Basu 55–58) in *Making India Hindu*. Ed. David Ludden (New Delhi: OUP, 2005).

15. Any study of the extreme poverty of the tribals and peasants would reveal the root cause of such a movement. Again, the middle class youth was in search of a cause. How and when a movement loses balance is often rooted in other political moves.
16. For more details refer Peter van der Veer's paper 'Writing Violence.' Riots are often created artificially through the spread of rumours and management of anti-social elements and by creating a climate of distrust and fear. In *Making India Hindu*, 2005.
17. Refer Bimal Prasad's 'Introduction' and Swami Vivekananda's speeches in the selection edited by Prasad, specially 'Addresses at the Parliament of Religions' (New Delhi: Vikas Publishing House Pvt Ltd., 1994).
18. Refer Veer Savarkar's Presidential Addresses at Karnavati, Nagpur and Calcutta (1937–1939) which reflect a marked shift from his 1907 book *The First War of Independence* wherein he acknowledged Muslim contribution. In his Presidential speeches he shifted the stress from *pitrbhumi* to *punyambhumi*, i.e. from fatherland to holy land.
19. Kundasamy in her article refers to this interview given by Naipaul in August 2001, in *The Literary Review*. This is evident right from *A House for Mr Biswas* (1961) to *Half A Life* (2001). The last is specifically located in India and is concerned with caste and genes, purity and pollution.
20. Sahgal in novel after novel, especially *Rich Like Us* (1985) and *Lesser Breeds* (2002) asks the question about the Indian share in the history of colonialism and several other 'postcolonial' intellectuals are constantly subjecting the past to a critical analysis.

8

Routes of Passage

Identity, Home and Culture through
Dislocations – Dabydeen, Bissoondath and the
Naipaul Inheritance

Such a long title! It reflects the complexity of the multiple dislocations as they work through successive generations and each successive shift. When migrations take place does history remain the same or does it alter? And as the past recedes, what is it that one chooses to remember? In most of the epigraphs selected by writers of the West Indies, the past remains a factor to be considered. George Lamming begins *The Pleasures of Exile* (1960)[1] with a quotation from James Joyce, 'History is a nightmare from which I'm trying to awaken'. Naipaul in *The Middle Passage* (1962)[2] hearkens back to James Anthony Froude and Anthony Trollope, while Cyril Dabydeen, in his work, *My Brahmin Days* (2000),[3] frames it with a quotation from L.P. Hartley, 'The past is a foreign country/They do things differently there' *(The Go Between)*.

Difference becomes a defining category for an immigrant. The difference in his perceptions and remembered pasts from that of the man at home in his surroundings, the difference of colour or language in alien surroundings, the memories of landscape and climate and the association with the flora and fauna. These are the differences which mark him: he merges where he feels different and stands out where he wishes to merge. And as he senses the necessity of recalling a past *(FC 9)*, for blankness does not work, he recognises the inevitability of forgetting.[4]

The immigrant's narrative despite this pull towards or fear of the past is a linear narrative. It contains within it the impossibility of return. There is no going back in time or place (only in memory); there is no possibility of belonging once again even as the past controls the present. How does the writer then construct his narrative and his 'self'? I propose to take up some stories from Neil Bissoondath's *Digging Up the Mountains* (1985)[5] which also happens to be his first collection of short stories (published at age 30) and some from Cyril Dabydeen's collection *My Brahmin Days* (2000). Bissoondath is Naipaul's sister's son, and perhaps is consciously rejecting the Naipaul inheritance – he moved to Canada (at the age of 18) instead of England, studied French instead of English and has rejected multiculturalism because it essentialises and ghettoises the immigrant. His work, *Selling Illusions*[6], critiques the policy of multiculturalism as one which subverts the idea of individual identity. Dabydeen grew up in British Guyana and now lives in Canada. Dabydeen has also, like Bissoondath, explored the meaning and construction of a Canadianness which would include the immigrant. They are both East Indians from West Indies, both have a Brahmin inheritance and memories of recitals from the *Gita* and the *Ramayana*. Thus both of them, as they write their identities, have constantly to negotiate the memories of an inherited past as well their contingent present. A third additional factor which each has to negotiate is the Naipaulian inheritance – how Naipaul has constructed the identity of the East Indian in West Indies and the way he has projected India. They also have to negotiate Naipaul's approach, both the parody and the contempt which underlies his rejection of the past. They have grown up with Naipaul's projections which are likely to affect not only their psyche but also their narrative. One of the tasks I have set myself is to work out the relationship of the immigrant to his narrative as he/she works through the concepts of self and heritage.

Naipaul's *The Middle Passage* (1962) and *Finding the Centre* (1984) are dismissive of the West Indies and see it as a place without a history, as islands where nothing is created, where there is no civilisation and no revolution can take place, a place marked by distrust of the other as well as of one's own self. The island people are defined by sense of contempt which they feel for the 'self' and the hatred which they have for the other. It is depicted as a society where alienness is welcomed by the Indian – everything that made the Indian alien gave him strength, 'it insulated him from the black-white struggle' *(MP 88)*. The Indian was not caught up in a one-to-one opposition, conflict or polarity but a triangular one. The Blacks were not his natural allies, instead they were considered social inferiors (86), while the presence of East Indians' posed a threat to the Blacks. The East Indian in West Indies held on to this 'difference' and got caught up in a culture trapped in a time-warp and frozen at a particular moment in the past. Naipaul goes on to point out in *The Middle Passage* the obsession of the Indians with the mother-country fixation (183) leading them to recreate an India in miniature *(MP 225–226)*. The Indian remained rooted in his own community as opposed to the African's desire to be part of the mainstream *(MP 88)*.

The constant opposition, the sense of 'alienness', used as a protective cover also subtracted from all those human impulses conducive to the growth of a national identity: the individual and the religious identities are prioritised over a common nationhood. Despite the focus on 'houses' and 'homes' in Naipaul's work, there is no emotion of belonging to the land. Instead there is a sense of temporariness, a longing for a future different from the present, and a fear of extinction. In *Finding the Centre* he refers to his father's nervous breakdown caused by his failure to see his reflection in the mirror.

All attempts at defining a self, and the subsequent efforts of the self which is thus defined, are motivated by a need to overcome this fear of extinction. Thus, an exile is born: never at home anywhere as the holding back becomes important to him. Travel as a mode of belonging, cynicism as a way of relating, satire as a way of approaching thus become the landmarks of a writing born out of this sense of alienation. But the fact remains that all alienations are not the same, and this needs to be reckoned with. For Naipaul, the possibility of a dialogic relationship doesn't exist. George Lamming's sense of exile and his need for a dialogic relationship stand in direct contrast to the Naipaulian withholding of self and defining it primarily through difference. The dangers of such a self-definition are many: it encloses rather than expands, it gets anchored in a preconceived expectation rather than allow itself to change or remain flexible, it becomes self-contained and the main point of reference: the tentativeness necessary for a commonalty to surface is placed outside its reach. Insecurity is not always expressed as a hermeneutic surrender, it becomes a holding back. This defines the writer's relationship with his work and characterises a great deal of diasporic writing – whether it is of the mutation variety as in Bharati Mukherjee, or the observer category as in Naipaul, or framed by the need to pick out the exotic, or uncover the isolated event in the past. The holding back of the 'self' does not permit any long-term involvement at a deeper level. The 'self' in this case becomes a resistant 'self'.

Bissoondath in the stories in *Digging Up the Mountains* is concerned with several things. His stories take on fictional constructs. Several of them are written in a female voice, the protagonist is a woman – he projects himself into other cultural situations and landscapes of the mind, identifying himself with them. 'The Cage'[7], a long short story, qualifying itself almost as a novella, is about a Japanese girl and works at several levels of migration, of belonging and alienation – constructing the self bit by bit by being buffeted about rather than defining it through location in the idea of race, an historic past or a notion of the self or through alienation and holding back. The scene of his childhood memories is West Indies, British Guyana – and not India. His concerns are not merely personal, they are political. He does not merely observe political processes as they affect others, but explores their impact upon human relationships and on the nature of flight. In the title story 'Digging up the Mountains'[8], Hari Behary is rooted in his homeland and is reluctant to migrate. Political unrest, murders of his friends, fear stalking the streets, state of emergency, the sense of being encircled and confined in his home, finally push him to take the decision to migrate. And as he plans to leave, he is informed that if he does not return within six months, his property will be confiscated. All along images of insecurity are contrasted with Hari Behary's pride in his possessions, and his need to root himself in this present. His plan for planting the lawn – which never really gets done – is highly significant and works at a metaphoric level expressing the need to belong. India for him exists only in the remote past, 'dipped into darkness' (2), his identification is with the present, 'This is my land and my house' (4).

The other side of this flight is projected in another story titled 'Insecurity'[9] in which Alistair Ramgoolam has a deep realisation that he will need to escape and hence he carefully goes on building up a bank balance in the United States, smuggling money through business deals. The island of his birth, 'on which he had grown up and where he had made his fortune, was transformed by a process of mind into a temporary home. Its history ceased to be important, its presence turned into a fluid holding pattern which would eventually give way. The confusion had been prepared for ... . He could hope for death here but his grandchildren, may be even his children, would continue the emigration which his grandfather had started in India, and during which the island had proved, in the end, to be nothing more than a stopover' (72); a 'way-station, a point at which to pause for a brief respite from the larger scare' (81).

But as observed earlier, the diasporic narrative is a linear one, despite its engagement with the past in so many ways. It is impossible to return. In the same volume, there is another story titled symbolically 'There are Lots of Ways to Die'[10], which is about the homecoming of Joseph Heaven from Canada to his island home with the noble sentiments of doing something for his people. But he realises that his memory had betrayed him – he had forgotten how 'sticky the island could be when it rained, ... The morning rain wasn't as refreshing as he'd recalled it and the steam had left his memory altogether. How could he have sworn that the island experienced no humidity' (79). And now the nostalgia is reversed, he imagines himself on Bloor Street, he could even conjure up the sounds of a Toronto summer: 'the cars, the voices, the rumble of the subway under the feet as it swiftly glided towards downtown' (80). He seems to be hallucinating all the time about the life in Canada. He begins to mistrust his memory, is unable to talk about it to his wife, walks around in search of the past – in search of the dreams which could have been realised and materialised. Joseph's house is on Pacheto Street named after an old mansion on the street, a house said to belong to a general, and one which had led to the island's mention in a book other than a history text – outside the context of slavery. This house becomes the central symbol of the nature of reality – It 'was like a dying man who could hear his heart ticking to a stop' (87). Finally he seeks a childhood friend and finds that there is nothing to be said or shared, Frankie used to be his best friend. He was the most intelligent person Joseph had ever known. But now he works in a bank having given up his dreams of a university job. Frankie tells him 'why did you come back? A big mistake' (90). Several of their friends are dead. Frankie tells him `You mean to tell me you had the courage to leave and the stupidity to come back?' (91). Overcome by uncertainties Joseph finds his way to Pacheto House, and it is here that the idealist in him crumbles – it is very different from what he had imagined it to be. Doubts assay him 'Might it not have been always a big, open, empty house ... with a facade that promised mystery but an interior that took away all hope?' He feels confined – 'a man in an island on an island' (95) – a final signal for him to leave.

Contrasted with Bissoondath, Dabydeen has chosen different ways to shake off the Naipaulian inheritance. Not marked by rejection, his work is also not overtly located in the self. Memory, landscape and history coalesce into a continuity. The jumps are not into a historic past. But the questions of identity bother him – where does one belong? How does one root oneself? His colour, his memories of religious texts, the gods who appear in his dream project an identity he is unable to relate to. There is a story titled 'Jet Lag'[11] which is a narrative about travelling to India in a Lufthansa flight. The Naipaulian fear of India, the distrust and uncertainty, the preconceived notions of loss and of being defrauded by Indians surface in his memory. His anxieties are reflected in a recurring nightmare he has wherein, 'my luggage was quickly lost ... a cab driver kept running away with it despite my frantic efforts to hold on to what was mine.' The writer-protagonist feels 'I was not an Indian and may be Canada had done this to me', compelling him to approach India as a stranger. He asks himself the question, 'Why go to India? We were West Indians. Then Canada, also far away, sounded like Xanadu. All shifting grounds' (76–77). There is then a disowning of India. 'India seemed no longer the land of my ancestors', and as he shakes off this almost mythical past he acknowledges to himself that he was in fact a Canadian with all earlier identities shaken off, 'I was a Canadian entering a foreign land. This was no mere defence mechanism. History dispensed with, Kala Pani vanished. The flux of time and change only, I was a Canadian I was indeed a Canadian in a vast new land' (82–83). Ironically and meaningfully, this new found confidence is refuted by the officer at the airport who includes him in the sweeping remark 'we are all Indians here'.

Again and again, the Indianness surfaces. In his 1988 novel, *The Wizard Swami*, the opening sentence 'Devan slowly postured himself, folding his legs Buddha-style' (5), immediately harks back to the culture of South Asia. *The Wizard Swami*[12] is, at one level, a reworking of Naipaul's *The Mystic Masseur*[13], and one way of getting rid of the Naipaulian presence. Devan assumes the role of a scholar-preacher as he talks about Hinduism to the village people, reminding the reader faintly of Murthy in Raja Rao's *Kanthapura* (1938) and Raju in R.K. Narayan's *Guide* (1958). The role of a swami comes naturally to him as it does to Naipaul's hero in *The Mystic Masseur* (1957). Religion, language, myth and legend work their way into the present as the writer constructs a 'self'. Even in *The Dark Swirl*[14] (1988) which is entirely located in the islands, the Hindu family reflects a mixed tradition. The father Ghulam has a wife called Savitri and a son called Josh. In social terms, however, there are only two divisions, the white and the coloured, with Ghulam identifying himself with the Africans, which never really happens with Naipaul. As Ghulam walks along he wills himself to be one with everything:

> The insects, reptiles, animals and plants ... . It was then he felt himself to be truly Hindu and yet something else. Most times he scarcely thought about his people's origin in that distant subcontinent. Here, in this isolated part of the Guyanese coastland ... they – Indians, Africans – lived in a strange harmony ... . Whatever they had been, he sensed they were becoming something else ... . (39)

Ghulam has a sense of belonging to the land and against outsiders the people project a oneness (72). At the end of the novel as he looks for the white stranger and cannot find him, he remembers his face and their common search for the massacouraman. The present, uncannily, turns into memory before one can control it – memory like 'an ancient, primordial imaging that surpassed the places where they had come from – Africa, India, Europe – or where they secretly yearned to return when the soil no longer accepted them' (92), but for the moment the soil claims them.

In the short story 'My Brahmin Days',[15] the author records a visit to India when the host family immediately opens out to him an India of the past. As the young son of the family accompanies him to Agra and converses about the west, the realisation comes to him that they – he, as a person living in Canada, and Amit, as an Indian who has never travelled abroad – relate to each other's background through media projected stereotypes and static memories. The Indian from abroad has to wrestle with his 'outsider-insider' status, discover the meaning of language in a different cultural context – origins, caste, family – across a varied experience while the Indian at home is lost in dreams of a distant land. India was 'homeland' to the expatriate, and Canada suddenly seemed like another planet. In between was the Caribbean background (13). The self, for Dabydeen, is rooted in all of them, not a single segment is irrelevant or dispensable. 'My Brahmin Days' is not the simple, humourous experience which it appears at first sight. It addresses questions of power as well of identity, the 'littleness' of South Asians in a white country, the ego-projections of the Indians through travel abroad, a sense of apology at being Indians going hand in hand with need to identify with and be proud of the diaspora on part of the stay-at-home Indians. Amit and the visiting writer meet through opposing visions even as they share a common inheritance. The visitor, even as he acknowledges his Brahmin origins, uses a few words of Hindi 'picked up a long time ago, from a grandmother who'd come from a part of India I'd never know' (25) realises that he doesn't belong. There is no past he can return to. In a companion story, 'Short Story Seminar' he clearly states, 'yes, diaspora was at the heart of everything I wrote ...' (124).[16]

In both Bissoondath and Dabydeen, it is clear that history is transmuted through the remembrance of selected events. The past impacts the 'self' through this remembrance which exists in a rootless present and which is isolated and distanced from the culture or origin both through acts willed or otherwise. Working through familial frameworks, and parodies of the past, the writers create a new self based on intertextualities. As successive generations interact with inherited frameworks, the moulds either change or crack. This is a mysterious process in itself where traces of the past linger in the subconscious and have a tendency to surface either through recognition or memory or collectivity. Holding on to the self becomes important in an alien environment, preventing a natural growth, identification and constructive relationships. But how long can or should this alienness persist and if it does so, is it able to expand the idea of self or not? How does memory relate to the intervening accumulation of details? How does one define the whole process of relating to a tradition? It is important to note the wedge which Naipaul has created for the West Indian East Indian towards the West Indian segment and the definition of the self which he has projected through resistance. This intertextual presence has to be realised. Then the question arises, is pastiche born out of this process of defining the self through difference or is it a defence mechanism, the result of a location on an island, a narrowing of space or falling in line with the western position? What kind of an aesthetics is promised by a resistant self and what kind of an aesthetics is possible?

The role of imagination is also a crucial one in the whole process of creating a 'self'. Aritha van Herk, in her essay 'In Visible Ink'[17], writes about the double narrative of the immigrant story. There is the overt story which relates outwards, reflects a worldly 'making of the self' as it confronts or adapts itself to the contingent forces, as it yields to the seductions of success and recognition in its search for both identity and opportunity. The second narrative is the covert one which hides in crevices and surfaces every now and then through conscious or unconscious memory. Religion or language or both may have a great deal to do with its construction. There is also, at times, a third story, the absent story which does not connect either with memory or reality but hovers between the two as a lost possibility. It is difficult to say whether the absent story has come into being or not. And if and when it is written whether it will have fantasy as a dominant mode or incline toward dystopianism.

Diasporic writers have worked variously with their material. Ondaatje has moved from culture to culture, absorbing and adopting different cultural myths, several others have accepted the Janus-faced hyphenated self, choosing to locate themselves in the hyphen, yet others like Bharati Mukherjee have shed their pasts, if not as material, at least as professions about it. And there are still others like Rohinton Mistry who, like the Jews, wishes to locate the 'self' in a sense of community. Even as he writes about India, his cultural projection is of the Parsi life right from *Such a Long Journey* to *Family Matters*. Mistry's writing draws attention to an important facet of the diasporic self – the need to relate to a community.

Culture, history and memory interact anew for every generation. With second and third generation immigrants appearing on the literary scene, the need to explore the multiple dimensions of location and dislocation as they contribute to the making of the 'self' has become important. Even as the immigrant's narrative is linear, his relationship to the past is not in one straight line. It has many breaks, twists and paths. There can be no clean break with the past but the relationship of the 'self' towards a 'sense of belonging' can be differently governed. The 'self' may remain in constant need of an 'other' and thus adopt a resistant attitude, or it may progress from a resistant to a dialogic self, willing to give and belong, willing to transcend the ego.

NOTES & REFERENCES

1. George Lamming, *The Pleasure of Exile* (London: Michael Joseph, 1960).
2. Naipaul, *The Middle Passage* (1962) (Harmondsworth: Penguin), 1985. The two epigraphs are from James Anthony Froude from his work *The English in West Indies (1887)*. Both are damaging to the enslaved people. The first ends with the sentence, 'There are no people there in the true sense of the word, with a character and a purpose of their own'; and the second contrasts the affluence of imperial powers with the financial ruins of the islands. The reference to Trollope is also to a passage dated 1860 and gives an additional evidence of Naipaul's remaining locked up in the imperial past and his heavy dependence on western perspectives. Trollope's passage praises Demerara as the Elysium of the tropics, the one 'true and actual utopia of the Caribbean seas' (*MP* 92).
3. *My Brahmin Days and Other Stories* (Toronto: Tsar Publications, 2000).

4. Naipaul, *Finding the Centre: Two Narratives.* (Harmondsworth Penguin, 1985). Naipaul's successive engagements with different cultures – both in the islands and during his travels were ways of negotiating his 'many-sided background' (9). Travel, despite the demands it made, 'broadened my world view, it showed me a changing world and took me out of my own colonial self; it because the substitute for the mature social experience – the deepening knowledge of a society – which my background and the nature of my life denied me' (11). But one may well ask how could this actually become possible with the critical (and cynical) observer's eye and can social interaction be fruitful if entered upon through unequal positions?
5. *Digging Up the Mountains: Selected Stories* (Toronto: Macmillan, 1985).
6. *Selling Illusions: The Cult of Multiculturalism in Canada* (Toronto: Penguin, 1994).
7. In *Digging Up the Mountains*. 39–57.
8. Ibid., 1–20.
9. Ibid., 68–77.
10. Ibid., 78–97.
11. 'Jet Lag', *My Brahmin Days and Other Stories*, 73–82.
12. *The Wizard Swami* (Leeds: Peepal Tree Press, 1989).
13. *The Mystic Masseur* (London: Andre Deutsch, 1958).
14. *The Dark Swirl* (Leeds: Peepal Tree Press, 1989).
15. 'My Brahmin Days' in *My Brahmin Days and Other Stories*, 11–25.
16. 'Short-Story Seminar', *My Brahmin Days*, 114–125.
17. *In Visible Ink* (Edmonton: Newest Press, 1991).

9

A Bit of India
Under African Skies

The Afrindian diaspora is both varied and distinct from other diasporas in the way it has spread to different parts of Africa, often crossing borders in the political strife that has possessed the continent. Again, migrations have been of different kinds: slavery, indenture, trade, employment, farming and industry. Also fortune hunting. Its constituent populations make a wide-ranging mix from Vassanji's Dhanji Govindji to Govender's Cato Manor. Another difference is that several who were born there have moved on while others are more territory bound. The varied kinds of migration from Kerala, Tamil Nadu, Gujarat and other parts of India was brought home to Gandhi through the signatures and thumb impressions on the petition the Indians prepared against the marriage law.[1]

I propose to discuss four writers – Ronnie Govender, the progeny of indentured ancestors; Farida Karodia who was later to move to Canada when she ran the risk of having her passport impounded, came from a trading family; M.G. Vassanji, who too is a third or fourth generation migrant from the Shamsi community of Gujarat and who also like Karodia moved to Canada, and Abraham Verghese, the child of a Malayalee couple, who were teaching in Addis Adaba. Verghese was born there but returned home to the medical college in Chennai (then Madras) and moved further afield to the States. Whether settled in parts of Africa or having moved away to any of the western countries, these writers are seriously engaged with the past. Both Govender and Vassanji prefix their semi-autobiographical works, *Cato Manor* and *The Gunny Sack* with maps or charts. Govender provides the territorial layout of the community colony which was later shifted from the edge of Durban to a lesser developed area on account of the Group Areas Act (1950), and Vassanji prefaces his novel with a chart of family descent and the varied composition of its extended family. These define their ongoing concerns with history and geography and the markers of the Indian past that linger there. The Afrindian diaspora also reflect a triangular encounter between cultures, histories and races. Pallavi Rastogi, commenting upon this has observed that this encounter 'unsettles that paradigm of racial interaction and focuses instead on how different non-white constituencies interact with each other in non-western geographies'.[2] Rastogi is pointedly speaking about her own work on Afrindian writing but it is an observation equally applicable to many other non-western situations. A similar situation prevailed in West Indies and the different power relations are amply reflected in the writings of Arnold Itwaru, V.S. Naipaul and Neil Bissoondath, to name only a few. In the Caribbean, the Blacks exercise more power than the Indians, while in South Africa it is, or was, the reverse.

At the Edge and Other Cato Manor Stories has a long history. Govendar in his Introduction to the collection writes, 'I began writing these stories after my family moved from Cato Manor in the fifties, when the district became the first victim of the National Party's notorious Group Areas Act.'[3] The diaspora, especially the one racially and economically weaker was always at the receiving end. The community was made to relocate, after they had spent more than two decades on building, with their own effort, the infrastructure required for development 'its own schools, shops and bazaars, temples, churches and mosques,' and set up welfare institutions such as 'homes for orphans and the aged' (*ibid.* 11).

Both *Cato Manor* and *The Gunny Sack* replicate the multi-religious nature of India and are enthused and sustained by the sense of community and the way it signifies belonging. At the same time, the involvement in the Afrindian struggles and political histories is a considered choice. Ami Nanackchand specifically refers to the stand he took against apartheid.[4] For Vassanji, the many coups and mutinies both interrupt and divert the paths that Dhanji Govindji's family wants to travel. Another thing in common between Vassanji and Govender is the oral storytelling. Vassanji returns to this time and again, while Govender says at the very beginning, 'Listen my friends, listen to the voices of Cato Manor District Six and Sophiatown as we struggle to fashion a new life – a life free from the contradictions that prevent us from seeing good in Everyman'.[5] And then follow the stories where languages flow from one to another, creating space cultural representation and the rooting of the migrant self. 'Poobathie' and 'At the Edge' are two very powerful stories. The collection is titled *At the Edge* after the second story. Govender's language is beautiful, sensitive and frames the landscape. As Vellamma (grandmother) said her prayers, her voice from deep within her, ... rising gently to caress the quilt of leaves, that covered the syringa tree and avoiding the 'patch-work of thoughts that sought to disturb the evenness of the mind as it delved deep into her soul to catch the words that started somewhere inside' (61).[6]

Vellamma's story is the history of the family – her journey from India, an almost child marriage to a man much older than her and thus she was to become mother of eleven children. Over the years, there were losses in the family. First, two sons died, then her husband, 'And she was at the edge.' The edge of her reason and peace. It is at such a time as this, that the community comes to their help. She turns her anger against the gods to prayer and it is this strength which enables her to heal a woman who had turned hysterical under stress. Together they then sing the Hindu prayer *'Hari aum naameshivaya'* (Hari Om Namoshiva) (64).

Govender is perhaps one of the few writers who are truly Afrindian for two reasons; one, he has not moved away from the land of his birth and second, his work in its representation of an Indian past weaves in with the Indian present in Africa. He reflects on what makes a culture and also critiques the discriminatory baggage it carries on account of the caste system. The transformation to another, more liberal system, fails to take place as there is a second layer of discrimination enveloping it with the natives resenting them and the whites containing them. Are there ways to surmount this discrimination? One is power, and if it cannot be money power, it has to be physical power. In his novel *Black Chin, White Chin*[7], Govender has a character Jack who is a boxer and fearless for he realises that alone is the way to push ahead. Similarly in Vassanji's *The Gunny Sack*, the character of Shivji, who pushes his way through is also similarly empowered. But there are also other strengths available to the human being – spiritual strength of moral truthfulness.

Cultures survive through a process of sifting and carrying forth the essence. One of the first stories that I read and which introduced Govender's work to me was 'Poobathie', apparently a slight distortion of Parvati. The dark Tamilian outcaste girl has the protective cover of an upper caste elderly woman. The story, despite its brevity, captures a multitude of things: culture, religion, language, myth, caste discrimination, conversion, resistance to intercaste marriages, all are reflected. The story opens with a description of her dark colour 'She was almost as black as the ace of spades ...' . And to top it, her father's conversion to Christianity sent out a clear signal as to their low status; 'And if your father's name was not Pillay, Reddy, Singh, Maharaj or even Mohammed, you didn't feature much in the consciousness of the people, except perhaps when they strenuously avoided social contact with you. They didn't eat at your place.' And thus there is also a reflection on the ugliness of the cultural signifiers. Yet, her grandmother had noticed a change due to the locational shift, 'she had said it wasn't as bad as it was in India. There they wouldn't allow you into the temples and in some districts you had to step out of the way to prevent your shadow falling over a passing Brahmin' (25).[8] It is this temple which becomes the centre of her being as well as of the story. Despite her father's conversion, Poobathie remains a Hindu, refusing to change her name and the picture of hell, the preacher paints, refuses to shake her determination and she does not budge a bit, 'she would not change because there was a temple she could go to' (26). A temple that belonged to an old woman, she had visited it secretly since she was nine-year old, and thus a relationship had developed between the old woman, Vellama and Poobathie despite the caste difference.

But the social discrimination and her black complexion hurt her, damage her sense of self-image. When she looked into the mirror, she hated herself. And it hurt more when friends pointed out towards this. Then there was gender discrimination as it is bound to be amongst the economically under-privileged. There was no escape through education, she was not a boy. Fortunately, there are good people around. Mrs Rasool, the wife of a factory owner takes her in for housework, then sends her to the factory so she can earn more. The significance of Mrs Rasool being a Muslim is not missed. Islam, besides being more liberal for, as Mrs Rasool points out, the practice of religion lies in the goodness with which it is practiced, 'Being a good Muslim does not only mean you must go to Mecca. You must also be good to people' (29). Mrs Rasool's presence in Cato Manor, further brings in the mixed and harmonious relationship of the community as she distinguishes between act and ritual, and faith and ritualistic practice. Economically somewhat independent, Poobathie's peace is disturbed when her friend Selvarane, the granddaughter of Vellamma, the temple owner, falls in love with Poobathie's Christian brother Charles who is not only not a Hindu but also a low caste. How are these two hurdles to be crossed? The young couple want to keep their relationship a secret until the actual rites, but Poobathie insists and takes it upon herself to approach the grandmother.

Vellamma (grandmother), is shocked at this sacrilege and feels her trust in Poobathie betrayed. The unasked question which lingers in Poobathie's mind is, 'why did god choose to treat people differently?' (34). Or was it the misled human beings who were responsible for these divisions and discrimination. The marriage takes place, the anger and the anguish persist, the little crack in Poobathie's relationship with Vellamma haunts her until one day, determined to heal this rupture, she takes an oath in the temple that she had nothing at all to do with it. It fact, she had tried to stop them. The old woman relents and expresses the hope, 'Maybe in the next generation I will have a daughter like you' (35). 'Poobathie' deals with a number of issues in this short narrative – the history of past, the carry over baggage, conversion, religion, faith, trust and inter-communal relationships – each one of the relates to India, critiques it and points out its chains. The use of Tamil words further contributes to the cultural negotiations.

Discriminating in his use of the past, Govinder does problematise the relationship between mother tongue and the being of man. In 'The Incomplete Human Being',[9] the story begins with the fact of death's finality and the narrative is interspersed with Sathie's experiences, Sathie as a ten-year-old had witnessed the death of a neighbour; he is also obsessed with the Tamil school; it also ends with the sixty-year Sathie, now retired, recall a warning of a Tamil teacher about the connection between language and culture. One is justified in asking in what way are the facts of the story connected? But they are. One does not live only in the present; the past and family histories have their own relevance. They construct identity and link death, time and life. Sathie's delicate health had made it difficult for him to cope with load of the double schooling of learning both English and Tamil. His mother was initially keen because Tamil would enable the children to understand their prayer. Mr Thaver would expound on the merits of the mother tongue. It teaches more about life than a foreign language which locates one in an economically competitive culture geared towards power. But Chellamma objects to the harsh discipline and withdraws her son from the Tamil school, not that the teachers who taught English were kinder. The result is that Sathie develops a complex about both, his lack of fluency in Tamil and his fragile health. He had little connection with the myths of Sita and Savitri and a whole world was closed to him. Older and wiser, a retired school principal, Sathie reflects on his life and regretted 'not just his own halting Tamil, but that none of his children or grandchildren could speak their own tongue ... *the world's oldest living language*' (94).

The diasporic representation of the home culture has many facets and Ronnie Govender makes it amply clear not only in his short stories but also his other writing that folklore, myths, languages are an integral past of human society, despite migrations. The past, or its remnants, travel invisibly and weightlessly and require no packaging. But time and environment compel one to shift and adjust. His novel *Black Chin, White Chin*, takes us deep into the urban business world, far away from the somewhat enclosed community of *Cato Manor*. *Black Chin, White Chin*, a family history, is a collaborative recollection of the past and the nation which is now their own, as they compete, choose, make space for themselves and also suffer setbacks. It is a kind of a memorial to the memory of his uncle. Beginning in 1930, it takes the narrative across space and time. While Jack takes on the responsibility of the household after his father's death, it is Chin who seeks new pastures. First book-keeping, then hoteliering, where he begins as a waiter and works his way through to a bar manager's job, and then manager of the hotel. Chin is also involved in an affair with the proprietress Greta. There are hiccups about both – the affair and the management. But the way Chin handles authority and power is mature, sensitive and just. The resentment of the Blacks is natural; he has to learn to discipline them gently and win over their respect. The incident with Michael demonstrates this. The Black staff at the hotel was elated to see for the first time a non-white holding a position of power. The doorman greeted him on his arrival, 'Mr. Chin, new you're a big man – now I must call you baas'. Chin is sensitive to the irony underlying the greeting and replies, 'Thanks, Michael, but I am not your baas. See my skin, its the same as yours. Don't you ever call me baas' (93). In turn Michael becomes a friend and a gentle adviser. When another employee Sam is caught cheating, Michael steps in. He advises a gentler handling rather than outright dismissal (94–95).

Black Chin, White Chin needs a longer and more detailed discussion, which may not be possible here, but the significant thing, about this novel, which follows a family biography outline, is the way the Cato Manor people have made their way into the world. Their cultural bonding, their holding on to family values, the sense of responsibility they are trained to feel, perhaps because of the hierarchical family patterns, help them fight their way through. The bond which Chin is able to build with the Reddys, who too are protective towards him, and the respect he is able to get from people of other races, makes him bold enough to step outside the rules that hold the race back and thwart progress.

Govender's work occupies a very significant place amongst Afrindian writers, primarily because he shows a way to survive and to come up to the top, a portrait with a sufficient base in life and thus acceptable. He provides a contrast to Farida Karodia's work but it must be conceded that Karodia brings forth the gender dimension of the immigrant's life, Govender's focus is on men and the community. Vassanji, similarly focuses on the masculine perspective and community life. The role of the community is of great importance in groups that need to hold together and carry forth the past with them. In this there is recognition of both the family nurturing and the organic environment; the community contributes the most, character strengths emerge from that.

M.G. Vassanji's *The Gunny Sack*[10] shares with Govender's Cato Manor stories several factors; it is also a family saga, moving across three generations, and working with matriarchal family heads but there are differences as well. His story is about the 'passenger Indians', the Gujarati and Muslim traders 'who had followed the Tamil and Hindi speaking indentured labourers to South Africa' (*Black Chin, White Chin* 51). The passenger Indians are more independent and occupy a better economic status. Both Vassanji and Govender use the storytelling tradition the way grandmothers tell stories. But Vassanji enters the world of Arabian Nights by using the gunny sack as the holder of the past and using the name Shehrbanoo. His Shehrazade is the sack and the three diaries in it, properly locked with a padlock and with 'two faded inscriptions in gold, wriggling in opposite directions: one in Arabic-looking hand, the other indecipherable, supposedly in a secret script (3). A proper atmosphere for the opening of the sack is prepared before the story begins.

The Gunny Sack takes up several of the issues which Govender has foregrounded and most of all the cultural baggage, not only of the family but also of migration, the Shamsi community and the political history of Ethopia, Tanzania and the rest of them resulting in more migrations. The complexity is multiplied as time and histories flow into each other and the complex lives of the Dhanji Govindji and his family flow into extended relationships. One central stability is provided by Kala, who is the inheritor of the sack, at the other end are the diaries which provide a peg to hang the memories on. Vassanji provides the map of Africa and the family tree to guide the reader through this narrative.

The novel opens with Kala thinking about Ji Bai, who now is dead, 'Memory, Ji Bai would say, is that old sack here, this poor dear that nobody has any use for any more ... . In would plunge her hand through the gaping hole of a mouth, and she would rummage inside'. As she explored through bits and places, the remnants of time gone by, she would gravely say, 'He who opens it will suffer the consequences' (3). Ji Bai is the legitimate descendant of Dhanji Govindji and his wife Fatima while Kala happens to be the grandson of Huseini, born of Dhanji's union with Tarantibu. Thus she is related to him through the great grandfather. Like Shehrazade's storytelling sessions as a survival strategy, the sack sits beside him as a life sustainer. There is no way and no time when the past can be dismissed; it is an important reality that the winged diaspora needs to remember. It also acts as a provocation to enter into personal pasts, return to origins, the coming of the Shamsis.

Memory also sends Kala back to the past he has not lived and the land which his ancestors had abandoned; it sends him to other continents and geographical locations, to Juanpur in India, to the mixed Hindu and Muslim origins, to Vishnu and the possibility of harmony which provides a basis for life in a multicultural society. Migration too is framed not merely as a necessity but also as adventure. Travel was not merely a one-way journey but traders and merchants did come home laden with riches. These success stories had nurtured Govindji's dreams of an unknown land and attracted him to it. Not only is migration differently viewed but Africa is also rescued from being merely the dark continent, it is also a place of hope (9). History is not necessarily all present in the diaries but they evoke the past and call for supplementary recollections. Abroad, the community is held together by the guiding hand of the 'mukhi', the head of the sect. Swahili, Sindhi and Urdu words are used freely, without resorting to explanatory glossaries. In this respect, these writers are very different from the ones located in western societies, where the kind of language, which reflects a confidence in one's culture, is not to be seen.

Govindji's story is a mix of contradictory forces and ongoings. Kala refers to the curve of family history, a 'crazy dance' (11). Would history have progressed differently if the racial mix between tribals (Huseini's mother) and the Islamic affiliations of his father continued? But this intermixture of slaves and free men was protested against, marking difference and exclusion (13). The beginnings are important because they create two parallel lines, one laden with unused opportunities and possibilities, the other the actual course it took deviating under social pressures and personal desires. Amidst all this Huseini goes missing and Govindji's single-minded devotion to money-making is sadly interrupted. He spends his fortune looking for his absent son, uses community money and is thus marked forever with this act for which he suffers.

A strange line of half magic, half superstition, of make-belief, of good and evil, separates this world from the wars, the international struggle of power, for many of which Africa itself serves as the ground. This history is recorded in ruins and losses, violence invades cities. The first part ends with Govindji's murder and the narrative passes on to Kulsum, a daughter-in-law of Huseini's family and the mother of Kala. There is a leap from one generation to the third (Huseini's and Ji Bai's generation lives through interspersed narratives). It also shifts to Kala's parents, Juma and Kulsum and is located in Nairobi 'Beautiful, beautiful Nairobi. But all is not well in this Eden,' there is the Mau Mau violence in 1952, then war, followed by a temporary peace, fear and massacres. The gunny, as Kala fears, would like to 'throw out one more bad memory' (89). And that is his father's death (92–93), which comes not through violence but a sudden illness. This is followed by a shift to Mombasa by Kulsum and her family and further to Dar-es-Salaam, another sea journey, another beginning. The shifts in the location, whether real life or fictional, all come together to delineate geographical and human terrains and at the same time weave the political history of the turmoil in Africa into the family history. The land and the people are peculiarly welded in a mysterious union. None can run away from the other, just as the past cannot be erased or forgotten. And dreams take birth, 'There were three dreams in this town that aspired to Baghdad once and New York afterwards. The European dream stayed near the seashore' (97). And then there is also the dream of adulthood, of growing up.

How does one grow up? Through independence, employment, enforced discipline or love? All of them happen almost simultaneously to Kala as he serves his period of compulsory military service, tests his strength and falls in love with Amina, much against the rules of his religion and his family. The third part of the novel is devoted to this growing up and the tragedy it unveils. This is the time when religious identities become a matter of strife (241), as it also the time for defiance and resistance, for changing loyalties and simply surviving. The Africans are at the lowest rung of power and their struggle is for the recovery of self-respect (242).

And thus the past connects. Troubles within the Shamsi community catch up with them and splintering of the Indian community follows the pattern (253). Where are then the dreams of the home country – 'Bharat Desh! The Old country!' (193). Instead the realisation, as Kulsum states it, is that they have no home outside their present one, 'But we have nowhere to go ... we were all born here' (189). Where then is home?

Life goes on, some members of the family seek other shores, moving away from troubled Africa, protected by their British citizenship. Love may not die, but separation is inevitable. Amina and Kala don't get married. And the storytellers whisper together – Shehrbanoo and the memory of Ji Bai, Kulsum's many stories including tales from the *Mahabharata* and remembered fragments all come together,

> Sweet knowledge. Ji Bai spoke and I listened.
>
> Who go to their graves not knowing where they came from ... who hurtled into the future even as the present was not yet over ... for whom history was a contemptible record of a shameful past. In short, those who closed their ears when the old men and women spoke. But the future will demand a reckoning. We will not forgive those who forgot ... .' (154)

The past is etched in our lives and there is no clear breaking away from it. *The Gunny Sack* works with this pull of time in the two directions, the past and the future, turning its face alternately towards each.

As contrasted to Govender and Vassanji, Farida Karodia presents a woman's voice amongst these immigrant narratives and that too of a Muslim family. *Daughters of the Twilight*[11] like *The Gunny Sack* works with a three generation family. The idea of kinship and community life prevalent back home is carried forth to the new society. Yasmin and Meena, the 'daughters' of the title live with their parents and maternal grandmother. The two sisters, one beautiful and ambitious the other withdrawn and observant, are different. Yasmin dreams dreams of success while Meena is more rooted in reality. Their house and the family shop happen to be the only Indians in a dominantly Afrikaan community. Constantly humiliated and subjected to indignity, they really have no other option but to live with it.

Daughters of the Twilight is Karodia's first novel and works within an autobiographical frame. The two girls get an early taste of power when it enters their lives at a very young age both positively and negatively. Meena, just five, gets a doll as her birthday present, a much-longed for doll which is snatched by the local MP's son, the local bully Cobus Stayn, and quickly dismembered. The struggle which takes place between Baboo and Cobus is symbolical of 'the hit and snatch and get what you can', the way things work in the adult world. The dismemberment of the doll, a haunting image in itself, is also metaphorical in the way the immigrant is dismantled and required to dislocate himself culturally.

As a result of this incident Baboo is sent away in order to escape reprisals with violence disrupting even the adult world. The family is also broken up. Baboo is an orphaned second cousin and has to move to another relative who is much harsher than his present adoptive family. The sacrifice extracted by this move is Baboo's dream of becoming a cricketeer. Later, in the novel, we once again meet Baboo who now is living alone by himself. Though his love for the family in which he grew up has survived, his spirit is shattered. Cobus also surfaces again in the novel, this time even more aggressive and predatory. He rapes Yasmin, once again forcing the family to rearrange its priorities.

Parallel to the shrinking of space which works at the social level as they are pushed into pre-defined spaces, like the ghettoes away from the mixed population, and into schools for coloured people and wildernesses where the economic prospects are bleak, runs the course of the two girls' lives as they grow up intelligent and ambitious, desirous of a mainstream life. These two parallel forces run in opposite directions. While the oppressed want to come up for air the oppressor wants to push them down. Yasmin is sent to an expensive English boarding school, takes riding lessons with Europeans and falls in love with a white man. But the course of love is compelled to face, negotiate and cross many an obstruction which take their toll of creative energy. The interracial interaction meets only with disapproval. Personal and social relationships all come under the purview of apartheid, segregating people and distorting human relationships reducing men and women to pawns. It breeds hatred both for the self and the other, leads to camouflage and pretence, and enforces almost a double life. At no point do the exterior and the interior worlds meet, the girls' mother Della pretends to have separated from her husband, mainly to get her younger daughter Meena admitted to a school. In every way, they are hedged in and compelled to be false unto themselves.

Other hurdles are caused when there is no possibility of inter-racial marriage. Yasmin is not able to marry the European, then she is raped, reminding the reader of the dismemberment of Meena's doll. And she leaves the child of the rape with her parents. Every little action, right from Baboo's resistance to love and happiness, has long-term consequences. Society is determined to corner and punish the Indian immigrants. This oppressed population includes the Africans – subordinated in their own country – the tribals and the Indians. Apartheid pushes them all to the margins. The Indians lose their language and are locked into nothingness. It is the female body which becomes the site of violence, interaction and bargaining. The bully Cobus's father makes advances towards Della, cornering them still further. The naked display of power is a constant source of fear and leads to social tension. The attack of this naked aggression is on the human being different in colour and race cutting off the individual self from its cultural roots. The younger sister, Meena, turns to an underground resistance movement as a desperate strategy for survival. *Daughters of the Twilight* (1986), surfaces again in Karodia's writing especially in her novel *Other Secrets* (2000)[12], where the two sisters' lives are placed amidst a four generation novel and woman to woman relationships worked out. As critics have observed, there is hardly a male voice in the novel. In one of her interviews quoted generously by Rajendra Chetty, she observes that she could not have given any more strength to the father of the two girls. It was the women who held the family together at home even in an hostile social environment. 'The kitchen was a site of comfort, it created a feeling being at ease and it was a familiar site. The power was in the house.'[13]

Abraham Verghese's diasporic presence in Africa is not in the spirit of the early migrations but his parents' stay there and the fact that he was born there. His attitude to both the Indian past and the

African present in his novel *Cutting for Stone*[14] is bound to be different. India is present in many ways. It is the place from where the journey begins and a young nun, a trained nurse, travels to Addis Ababa to join a hospital, it is also the place where she was trained and had met Thomas Stone. The novel is located in the Missing (Mission) Hospital in Addis Ababa where the twins are born. The father confused, goes missing and the mother dies on the delivery bed as the operation goes wrong. The adoptive parents, Hema and Ghosh are both Indians and the Missing Hospital is home. As the narrative progresses through its meandering events, recording the political upheavals in Ethopia, one of the twins journeys to the US where he comes across his father, for whom he has only harboured hate. The years in the US do not end in a permanent exile. There is a homecoming to the hospital. In his own past, Verghese's birth in Ethopia did not take him directly westwards. He came back to India for his medical studies. Hence, the nature of his diasporic experience is different yet the beauty of the landscape, the political coups and rebellions find their place alongside the Indian inheritance and the Indian home of Hema and Ghosh. The hospital constitutes a community in itself with the matron, the doctors, the probationers, the workers and the staff quarters in one compound and the many violent interludes disrupting their peace and harmony. Verghese's other novels, *Tennis Partner* and *My Own Country* are also novels located in hospital communities but not in Africa and the environmental forces work differently. Location goes a long way in creating the community environments and bonding.

Cutting for Stone begins with the birth of the twins, Shiva and Marion, supposedly identical but a mirror image of each other and differently talented. but that is yet to prove itself. Their birth represents a double crisis – the mystery of their origin and the death of their mother. Another crisis that adds to this is Hema, the gynaecologist's being away in India, Ghosh another medical man out and Thomas Stone, the surgeon, taken wholly unaware by the nun's pregnancy and never having delivered a baby, totally helpless and confused. The young probationer is a slow learner and as such no help at all. The nun's pregnancy is a shock to everyone for it had been well camouflaged all these months and was a violation of the nun's oath. Later, we learn that Thomas stone is the father but he too is totally unaware of the pregnancy. The letter, Sister Mary Joseph Praise, had written to Stone goes missing and is found only years later – too late.

The narrator for most part of the novel is Marion. He is the older of the twins and could easily have been the younger, if the mother did not have to undergo a caesarean. Suddenly things begin to fall in place. Hema arrives with thoughts of marriage in her mind, but realising the situation, gets straight to work. What does this conjunction of crises signify? How many systems are shaken by it? Medical knowledge, God's discipline, the visibility of the body, the almost unannounced and unexpected birth? Was it the immaculate conception? Another case of Mary and Joseph?

Shiva, who was almost on the verge of being hammered by his father, is unable to breathe properly and needs constant watching. With Dr Thomas Stone disappearing, Ghosh and Hema take them into their care, marrying in the process – a marriage which otherwise may have taken its own time. Even as the twins separate one set of parents, they bring another couple together.

The novel beings with the event of their birth on the twentieth of September in the year 1954, 'we took our first breaths at an elevation of eight thousand feet in the thin air of Addis Ababa, Capital city of Ethopia' (3). The reader realises that located in Ethopia as they are, none of their two sets of parents belong there either by birth or education – only by their choice of working there. Suddenly events begin to reflect a new set of problems which the diasporic consciousness has to negotiate. Belonging is one of them. Where does one belong – the land of birth, or the nationality, or relationships? Genealogies cannot be traced back; for the two boys they begin here.

Verghese's sensitivity to the landscape in almost absent in his other novels, but in *Cutting for Stone* there is a constant reminder of the location, of the season, of rain or storm. As the rattling of the rain on the roofs stopped, 'Overnight, in that hushed silent, the *meskel* flowers bloomed, turning the hillsides of Addis Ababa into gold' (3). Sumathi Ramaswamy in her Foreword 'Thinking Territory: Some reflections' to a volume of the same title writes, 'territory is not merely a predetermined area ... it is a complex outcome of discursive mediations and everyday mediation, an a structure of sentiment produced through imagination, memorialisation, recollection and visualisation.'[15]

The beauty of the landscape is captured intermittently in the narrative, registering the seasonal changes as well as the locational shifts. India travels to this enclosed community. Hema calls in a Maharastrian pundit to read the children's fortunes, and Ghosh tells them stories. One of these is Abu Kasem's story about the man's desire to get red of a pair of shoes, now much repaired, heavy and ugly. But they inevitably keep coming back to him (286). Stories travel from one land to another, one generation to another. Ghosh narrates it to his co-prisoners in the prison; he also narrates it to the boys.

Political moves, underground movements, coups, power struggles affect their lives. Someone gets killed someone hanged and someone imprisoned. Genet, Rosana's daughter, joins the underground movement; Marion has to flee the country as he is suspected of being a terrorist. He goes to the States and does meet his father, but has nothing for him except hostility and a need to punish him for being absent throughout their childhood. Gradually the anger is spent. Genet, his first love whom he had promised his virginity, cheats on him with his brother Shiva. Shiva also cheats him of his association with the probationer. Their look alikeness is deceptive; it is also life-giving as well as death-giving.

Marion falls seriously ill with a liver infection. Hema and Shiva rush to the States to be with him and in order to save Marion, Shiva donates part of his liver which is also not risk-free. Shiva is partly motivated by a need to make amends for his betrayals and partly out of genuine concern and hope that both may come out of it. But it doesn't happen; Shiva dies, leaving behind a part of himself. Now it is Marion and Hema who return to the Mission Hospital and to a drastically changed world, both politically and personally. A father found, a brother lost, the past now seen differently, the gaps in the story of their birth filled and Ghosh ill but determined to fight it alone. On the way to this stage of their lives, they have lost much. But finally with the missing letter surfacing, found behind a painting the realisation dawns that their father is not as guilty as believed. Marion reaches out to his now eighty-year old father and makes a call to the US. *Cutting for Stone* closely weaves in biblical tales (the titles of the chapters reflect this), it also brings in constant reference to the hospital in Madras, to the Indian background and works as much with the past as with the present. A sad and an intense novel, it reflects upon the essential diasporic self where relationships are simultaneously tenuous and strong, where the beginnings are veiled in mystery but the bonds assert themselves unconsciously. It is a world which present men like Ghosh who give without reserve, one who understands the biological urges and the psychological states of mind of his adopted sons. It also is a world where forgiveness is difficult but it comes in the end as the only way out to live with oneself.

The mysterious combination and constituents of culture are always elusive. No definition either of culture or of belonging can adequately convey the whole truth. Each of the four writers discussed above relates differently to the land of origin. And almost all of them admit the possibility of more homes than one. 'Where does one belong?', is a query which needs to work with 'how does one belong?' Through participation, political action, love or bonding and memories of the environment? Despite their difference, these writers represent a little bit of India and that too with love. There is no vituperative anger here against the home country and perhaps no exploitation of its political situation. Instead there is an anchoring in the culture that has survived around them. Communities, landscapes, memories have a history there. India survives in them in its scattered surfacings. The land of origin does not possess their writing as a past which beckons them but allows them to move forward.

NOTES & REFERENCES

1. See Giriraj Kishore's novel *Pahla Girmitiya (The First Coutractee)*, based on Gandhi's South African experience (New Delhi: Jnanpeeth, 1999). Kishore works through Gandhi's questionings and doubts – his silent inquiry, why the Muslims call themselves Arabs and the Christians form a separate category. Are they not Indians, i.e. word that Kishore constantly uses is '*humwatani*', people of the same land.

Also see Gandhi's autobiography. *An Autobiography: The Story of My Experiments with Truth* (Ahmedabad: Navjivan Press, 1927, 1997).

2. Pallavi Rastogi, *Afrindian Fictions: Diaspora, Race and National Desire* (Ohio: Ohio State University Press, 2008). She asks the question, 'Are Indian Africans too, or when does a subcontinental become a citizen', thus seeking to define citizenship as more than a formal passport. Rastogi comments, 'The impact of Gandhi on South African Indians, particularly in their response to political oppression, should not be underestimated ... . The South African Gandhi opened up a space of political awareness among the Indian community ... .' She goes on to observe that the frequent surfacing of Gandhi is one things that distinguishes South African diasporic fiction from the one in the west. Indian diaspora in South Africa has attracted attention both in African and Western scholarship such as Mariam Pirbhai, Ronit Frenkel and Devakrishnam Govender but in the Indian scene it yet has to make a visible appearance.

3. *At the Edge and Other Cato Manor Stories* (Pretoria: Manx, 1996). Introduction 11–14, 11.

4. Ami Nanackchand, Foreword *At the Edge and Other Cato Manor Stories*, 13–14, 13.

5. Prologue, *Cato Manor Stories*, 15–16, 16.

6. 'At the Edge' in *Cato Manor Stories*.

7. *Black Chin, White Chin* (New Delhi: Harper Collins, 2007).

8. 'Poobathie' in *Cato Manor Stories*, 25–35, 25

9. 'The Incomplete Human Being' in *Cato Manor Stories* 83–94.

10. M.G. Vassanji, *The Gunny Sack* (New Delhi: Penguin, 2009). First published by Anchor (Canada) 2005.

11. *Daughters of the Twilight* (London: Women's Press, 1986).

12. *Other Secrets* (South Africa: Penguin, 2000).

13. Rajendra Chetty, 'Farida Karodia's *Other Secrets*'. Chetty's article is based on an interview, he conducted at Karodia's home in Gautang in South Africa when *Other Secrets* was launched. internet reference. see Samyukta info 13 November 2009. Accessed 27 August 2014.

14. *Cutting for Stone* (New Delhi: Harper Collins, 2009).

15. Sumathi Ramaswamy in *Thinking Territory: Some Reflections*. Eds B.P. Giri and Prafulla C. Kar (Delhi: Pencraft International, 2009) 9–15. 11.

10

In Search of Nationhood Across Borders

Rabindranath Tagore's 1916 novel *Ghare-Baire*[1] translated into English as the *Home and the World* is a novel about a revolution, about the 1905 partition of Bengal, the impoverished Muslim population and the conjunction of gender and modernity. Bimala is caught up in her own complexes and is unmoved by her husband's gentle nature. Longing for the masculine hero, she is inspired by Sandip's rhetoric, flamboyance and flirtatious nature. As the magic works, she steps into the image of a modern day Kali, the benefactress and the one demanding sacrifice. It is at her altar that her husband's life is sacrificed. But more significant are the political issues which pervade the novel, the partition, the resistance and the Swadeshi movement. Was the partition an honest administrative gesture as many historians believe?[2] Or was it a territorial division along population lines? It attacked the idea of an integrated community by recognising, and perhaps sharpening the inequality persisting along the margins. Bhabha in his essay 'Dissemination: time, narrative, and the margins of the modern nation' focuses on the locality of culture and defines it as such:

> This locality is more *around* temporality than *about* historicity: a form of living that is more complex than 'community'; more symbolic than 'society'; more connotative than 'country'; less patriotic than *patrie*; more rhetorical than the reason of state;

more mythological than ideology; less homogenous than hegemony; less centred than the citizen; more collective than the 'subject', more psychic than civility; more hybrid in the articulation of cultural differences and identifications, gender, race or class than can be represented in any hierarchical or binary structuring of social antagonism.[3]

Issues that Bhabha was to raise in 1990, Tagore had raised as early as 1916 in *Home and the World*, where gender, religion, economic status and margins had been placed in a complex network. But Bhabha's perspective suits me comfortably to make the connection between the two diasporic writers I wish to focus on, the questions of identity they raise with reference to culture, gender, religion and racism, one in East Pakistan and other in London. Tahmima Anam's *A Golden Age* (2007) is the narrative of the painful and violent birth of Bangladesh and its struggle for survival. The central question is nationhood and belonging. Monica Ali in *Brick Lane* (2003) works with the Muslim community's concentration in one neighbourhood and the mounting hostility towards the community in the aftermath of 9/11. Gender is central to both.

Monica Ali and Tahmima Anam both live abroad. Their memories of home, despite an overriding similarity of concerns with violence and conflict, are also very different in their territorial and cultural foci. Beginning in 1959, *A Golden Age*[4] places the beginning in loss: 'Dear Husband, I lost our children today.' She has lost the legal battle for the custody of her own children, now that her husband is dead and the times are troubled. Her communication is with Iqbal's grave, which is her confidant and she takes the children there to say goodbye to their father. Her husband's brother Faiz and his wife Parveen, a childless couple, are taking the children to Lahore. Separation thus begins the novel, a falling apart as if heralding the future.

1959 marks the political turmoil. It is at this time when Gen. Yahya Khan is the President, that East Pakistan pushes forward its demands for an equal representation in the army and civil services as well as linguistic rights. West Pakistan, population-wise is in a minority, yet Urdu is the language of the nation. The resentment is also on the unfair share of the economic resources. Early in the novel, the young Sohail is worked up on this issue: 'If you know anything about the country, you would know that West Pakistan is bleeding us out. We earn most of the foreign exchange. We make the rice, we make the jute, and yet we get nothing – no schools, no hospitals, no army. We can't even speak our own bloody language!' (29). The Bhasha Andolan has begun and shifts the concept of nationhood from religion to language and culture – the nebulous thing which Bhabha has been at such pains to describe. The need is felt to compel those in authority to acknowledge the relationship between language and culture. The country is already heading towards a confrontation between its two parts and the division of the nation.

The next point of time, the narrator arrives at, is March 1971 and the reader is transferred into an entirely different world – of gardens and rose bushes, of a community of women representing a secular gathering and a new annexe that Rehana Haque has built called Shona. Homes have multiplied: two gates, two houses, two driveways. Shona has been built to 'save her children' (16), now back from West Pakistan, aged nineteen and seventeen. In between the preparation for the day and the visit to her husband's grave, the information about the elections is slipped in. She tells her husband that they are waiting for Mujib to be declared Prime Minister (20).

The main strands of the narrative are all carefully laid out, Silvi's betrothal to Sabeer, the groom's army background and Sohail's silent heartache for Silvi (24). But at the moment politics and at that confrontational politics get a priority over affairs of the heart. Soon the riots break out. The assembly is postponed and the Bengalis are left out in the cold. Bangladesh flags come up and Mujib is hailed as their leader (42–50). But countries are not won in the streets; battles have to be fought. And the oppressor doesn't easily hand over power. The Pakistan army lands in Dhaka, bullets are fired, the people are coerced and made to take down Bangla flags and war breaks out. All these happenings follow each other at a bewildering pace in the month of March 1971 – a short span of time but it changes their complete world, upsetting routines, separating families, leading to many Hindus moving across the border to India and the surfacing of secret underground non-military groups. Both Maya and Sohail participate in different ways as Dhaka is now transformed into an occupied city by hostile forces, a government that has lost its mandate and is unwilling to negotiate or concede any rights. Is this a civil war, being fought against enemies or a war between two nations, where borders of power are in question? The city soon adjusts to its silences, curfews and the soldiers marching the streets. Almost all the young people are now involved – Joy, Aref, Sohail, Partho, Maya – all of them except Sharmeen who goes missing and is in enemy custody; genocide has become a reality: 'The deaths, the arrests. The children with no parents. The mothers with empty laps' and all those who simply vanished (85).

But the question of reaching out to safety doesn't arise. One doesn't leave one's own country. Pakistan is now another country, a foreign land. Soon the housewives join in, preparing clothes, collecting sarees, stitching quilts for the homeless and the refugees. All the card-playing women join in and the task is endless as the numbers of those seeking safety and protection from tyranny mounts (98–99). It is now that the house Sohna also acquires a role and serves as a hideaway for an underground horde of weapons, and for injured soldiers. And amidst this Faiz and Parveen, Rehana's brother-in-law and his wife are posted to Dhaka with the government's instructions to get rid of the Hindus, the Communists and the separatists (106). But the Bengalis think otherwise. It is a Hindu doctor who attends to the wounded Major now sheltered in Shona. Amidst this slaughter that General Tikka Khan has unleashed, the house turns into a nursing home and Rehana has a severely injured Major in her care. It is during this that an emotional connection is made between the two, and the incompleteness of her own marriage dawns on Rehana (137). But as the war heightens and the torture conducted on the prisoners comes to light through the broken mind and body of Sabeer, there is no time to mourn lost loves. Rehana moves to Calcutta to join Maya and her journalistic friends and again ends up with nursing responsibilities. Rehana's nursing is an experience that transforms her whole being. The return home promises no peace as by now danger is their reality and a constant alertness is required. Weapons that are buried in Shona need to be dug out before the authorities find that cache. The year from March to December is full of crises, losses, deaths and casualties; the past is over and beyond recovery, even the women's gatherings are different with many members missing or absent or alienated. Anam traces the history of the birth of Bangladesh through the history of a family and its neighbourhood. It is from here that we get a view of the larger changes taking place in politics and the human experience. The central character is the human heart with its capacity to endure, to bear loss, to muster courage, to cross boundaries. Rehana discovers in her relationship with the Major, a man she had not liked at the beginning, a new strength and a new facet of her own feelings as she begins to understand his silent strength. There is a gentle critiquing of marriages where it is expected that love will follow. Instead the love that reaches out of its own accord is the love which holds meaning.

Lahore and Karachi, where part of Rehana's family lives, are just mentioned. West Pakistan is now another country. The journeys that are made outside the territory of East Pakistan/Bangladesh are journeys to India. But there are voices of disagreement. Silvi is totally estranged from the world outside, her husband's capture, torture and death have totally alienated her. She is in favour of national unity (248). Thus it is not just the birth of a country but the partition of Pakistan, with its own guilt, its own loss and prisoners of war and violation of Human Rights. No birth can take place without blood and pain. Anam records a slice of history through looking back home. Others too, from different locations – diasporic locations – have written about this period. Sara Suleri in her memoirs writes about her brother-in-law, her sister Ifat's husband, who was taken a prisoner and his changed character ever since.[5] And then her sister's death through a hit and run accident. Accident or murder?[6] And Ashis Gupta, a writer of Indian origin, living in Canada has his novel *Dying Traditions* which revolves around Mukti Bahini and the shared Tagore heritage.[7] Gupta writes about a family of three generations so that cultural histories can be traced. But it is the Pakistani diasporic writer Sorayya Khan, who looks homewards to present a different side of the war – rescue, compassion and lifelong support – in her novel *Noor*.[8] A young Pakistani soldier rescues and then adopts a young girl child, orphaned in the cyclonic storm and brings her home to Pakistan. He brings her up as his own daughter, stays unmarried and has this mixed family of colour and language – he, the child and his mother – an odd family.

Sajida, the child grows up, is married and her husband also now lives with them and thus they bring up a fourth generation. It is the birth of Sajida's daughter, her third child, Noor, which brings the past alive. The child is a different kind of child – possessive, slow and non-communicative – but has an uncanny sense of underground memories. Her drawings draw upon her mother's experiences, the cyclonic weather, the swaying trees – a past she has not experienced and nobody has discussed with her. It is as if, right from her mother's womb, she has stolen her mother's unconscious memories. The past comes to confront them.

As she watches Sajida, 'Nanijaan admitted to herself that her son had died in the war. The one that had come home was different. He didn't pray. Every so often, she would watch as his face was gently transformed, and she knew ... that it was the weight of remembering' (143). She refuses to invade his privacy but wonders, ' what does it feel like, to kill someone? How do you live with that knowledge, the guilt and the responsibility?' (151). He had watched death, witnessed rape, molested bodies all in the name of nationalistic fervour. And he was forced to rape an almost lifeless body (154). Why can't war be clean violence? But is violence ever clean? He had to kill and the memory haunts him; war is war, no victors are different, they always torture the captured (199). Khan captures the essential violence of war and the inroads it makes into the human psyche. Nation and identity, why do the two have to go together, overriding all human concerns? Why is it that there is no place for difference along with equality?

Monica Ali, in her debut novel *Brick Lane*, seeks to place identity in the self and that too in the gendered self. Married at age sixteen to a much older (and overweight) man she is taken to London. *Brick Lane*[9] begins in 1965. Home is remembered through a parallel narrative traced through the life of her sister Hasina who had eloped at a young age. These letters are written in pidgin English and mark her gradual slide in social status: from wife to a prostitute and then a housemaid. Does it provide her any choice or any more freedom than Nazneen, who lives in London? Does a marriage of her own choice give her any more satisfaction? Ali's narrative closely focuses on the Muslim community in *Brick Lane*, Nazneen's life, her children, the death of her son, her husband's frustrated hopes for promotion, the unsuccessful attempt at seeking favours. But through the effort of socialising in self interest, another character, Dr Azad enters the narrative.

Nazneen too, like Rehana in *A Golden Age*, has a community of women friends, occupied in various ways. This group is a support structure in a foreign land. Sukhdev Sandhu in a review in *The London Review of Books*, 'Come hungry, leave edgy' comments upon on both the history of the area, which was one upon a time (in the eighteenth century) a cemetery, a land for the dead. It is on these ruins that now there is a gathering of immigrants. While commenting on the novel, he also remarks, 'How strange then that this novel, part of it set in 1985, has so little to say about the campaign of violence and intimidation that marked the lives of every Bangladeshi ... .'[10]

But Monica Ali locates the Muslim community in its diasporic space. Nazneen is not obsessed by any dream of going back home; instead at one point she is keen to bring her sister Haseena to London. Despite the fact that she is not an independent earner, she takes on some assignments and is able to save some money. As Nazneen Ahmed in her essay 'Doing Double Duty: Long Distance Nationalism amongst Bengali Migrants in Britain'[11] has pointed out, 'Bangladeshi migrants use the public sphere within their new home, *bidesh* ... to further their support for the homeland ... through public protests, petitions and political lobbying due to the stress, helplessness and guilt that is caused by observing the homeland sliding from afar.'[12] And Nazneen in *Brick Lane* is very much part of it. It is through this activism that she meets Karim and is attracted towards him. Nazneen's memories of home are kept flowing by her sister Hasina's letters, letters which she answers in short notes and which do not awaken in her a desire to go back there. Karim is just the opposite of her husband Chanu whose manners are not polished and whose stomach, as he pats it, is oft-mentioned, and whose recurring references to his degrees and the quotations from Shakespeare distance him from the almost illiterate Nazneen. Karim is handsome, smartly dressed and a leader of the protest movement. The Palestinian prisoners, the Iraqis and the 9/11 come together in this discourse. The community is not only of the women's circle that Nazneen lives in but the meaning of community is enlarged to include the battle which Huntington had triggered with his *Clash of Civilizations*. The community is a religious community before it is pushed together by a civilisational hostility. Dispersed in different lands, it is held together not as much by rituals as by the sense of being at the receiving end of western aggression.

Chanu's decision to leave England and go back home holds no solution for Nazneen and her children, she decides to stay back in England. There is nothing to go back to – no choice, no freedom – and through this Ali raises the issue of a woman's need for freedom over and above political freedom. The borders she wants to cross are societal restrictions, religious impositions and the confines of orthodoxy. There is no prosperity in England but there is breathing space. She refuses to attach herself to Karim. Her personal space now withstands no encroachment.

Beginning with a brief introduction to the life in East Pakistan in the sixties and Nazneen's home, the cyclonic weather of the region and the proposal of a marriage which Nazneen accepts docilely, we, along with the narrative are transferred to Tower Hamlets in England in 1985. The in-between years have changed the national identity of the inhabitants back home, a country has been divided and a nation has been born. And Nazneen, as she had watched the paddy fields in her homeland, after the havoc rendered by a cyclone, her attention is caught by a hut standing askew, saved amongst the disaster but self-conscious about its own awryness, had also perhaps unconsciously realised that agency lay with the men, who even though not powerful had certain strengths, which women did not have. Her first friendship in England is a waving relationship with a woman, the tattoo lady, living in the block across the street, a home which had no curtains. Between cooking meals she examines her forced exile and wonders what she would wish for. But the reality is too stark for her as she is constantly reminded of Chanu's puffy face and his lips parting indignantly (18). The longing to make friends, to knock at someone's door with an offering of samosas, somehow to crack the barrier of her loneliness, is fraught with sadness. She is held back by her timidity and lives one day at a time, testing her own endurance. The Qur'an features early in the novel and one thing, free of nation and territory, that holds the community together.

The picture of her own domestic life is drawn very vividly as the objectification of her own features and body surface in her memory, reminding her of her husband's assessment. And the sorrows of a childless marriage are thrust on her through the gossip about a woman jumping to her death. Nazneen is thankful that she has so far not been beaten by Chanu. She hardly ever goes out, 'why should you go out?' her husband asked. Chanu vacillates between purdah and modernity. For every little decision he falls back on philosophy and comparisons with the life back home. He is generous, he can get her all that she wants and he is westernised but if she had been in Bangladesh she would not have gone out. So why here? Thus goes the convoluted reasoning (45).

The opening chapters lay the ground for Nazneen's decision towards the end. Her life is closed in, barricaded as if it were. She has been transplanted but is not allowed to adapt in order to survive. The crowded little apartment is all the space that she has and an observer's status goes with it. Once she goes on an exploration, walks into unknown streets and loses her way. Hasina is lost in their hometown and Nazneen feels abandoned here. Her suggestion to help Hasina is rejected outright and Nazneen responds in her own way, a somewhat childish and comical: 'Nazneen dropped the promotion from her prayers. The next day she chopped two fiery red chillies and placed them, like hand grenades, in Chanu's sandwiches. Unwashed socks were paired and put back in the drawer'. Almost all things are deliberately done the wrong way, 'All her chores, peasants in his princely kingdom, rebelled in turn. Small insurrection, designed to destroy the state from within' (63).

The gender question dominates all her thoughts and her recollections of the past – her mother and her mother's sister, her aunt talking to each other, unable to act but willing to suffer. Women were helpless against fate. All that they can do is weep over their lives (101–103). In England, Dr Azad puts his finger on the tensions that exist in the migrant community. The tragedy of their lives is the cultural clash and the resulting struggle between the need to assimilate on one hand and preserve one's identity and heritage on the other. The doctor's wife is more practical. She feels that in the west they should not be afraid to embrace the western values. In the outside world one has to be like them, they can preserve their culture in their homes, 'The society is racist. The society is all wrong. Everything should change for them. They don't have to change one thing, that ... is the tragedy' (113–114).

It is only in the seventh chapter that the locale shifts to Dhaka. Hasina's letters register her sister's sorrow, the loss of her son. The letters ranging over a period of nearly fifteen years from 1988 to 2001, record her life as well as Nazneen's. Time moves on, families grow and troubles too mount up. The computer arrives in their flat. Chanu changes his job and Karim enters their life and it is this attraction that pushes Nazneen into the movement to save Islam. A countermovement to curb their extremist activities also starts. But amidst this an affair is afoot between Karim and Nazneen (299, 343). Gradually the overfat Chanu, frustrated with his life and his thirty years of stay in London, which doesn't seem to be leading anywhere, is more and more inclined to return to Bangladesh, a haven as it were while Nazneen is unhappy about the closed door of Hasina's life. Amidst this confusion, plans are being made to go home, Nazneen tries to imagine what life would be in Dhaka, 'would we sit like this and would it feel just the same' (372)

The resistance movement, meanwhile, is hardening itself into extremist positions, becoming fundamentalist – religious zealots all. Yet Nazneen is undecided. Here or there? Chanu or Karim? All the while the winding up of the London home is in full swing and more suitcases are purchased. Days are counted both by Chanu and Nazneen but for entirely different reasons; Chanu is eager now to get back home, while Nazneen feels threatened as the day of departure approaches. In her mind she has decided, she'll not board the plane, she'll not go. And she decides that Karim is not the solution she is looking for; Chanu and Nazneen come even in the final assessment (459). Strangely enough Chanu's liberal views come to his aid and he agrees to leave his family behind, telling himself, they'll follow later. Chanu back in Dhaka traces Hasina only to lose track of her once again ... and Nazneen and the girls prepare to go skating, as it is by living alone and thinking about her economic needs, Nazneen is on thin ice. Women changed from saris to jeans and had the freedom of body – 'you can do whatever you like' (492).

Brick Lane problematises home and homelessness as the violence and conflict surrounding religion and race involve the immigrant community. The freedom of movement does not promise them much beyond a little more space. But Nazneen feels she is better off than Hasina whose struggle for survival has taken many forms. Does one have to live with ruins – ruins of Brick Lane, the ruins of the past and of broken dreams or a little bit of air is compensation enough?

Tahmima Anam and Monica Ali write about home in different ways. While Anam recalls a period in history, Ali looks at the tragedies of life. *A Golden Age* is deceptive in its title, even though it captures the golden whiff of freedom of Shonar Bangla, but it is tale full of losses, deaths and suffering, of building anew on ruins. *Brick Lane* on the other hand allows the past to invade the present as letters cross the seas to make Nazneen live two lives, one her own and the second Hasina's, who never really makes an appearance. Her presence is a ghost presence. Rehana's (*A Golden Age*) space shrinks and expands in turns. Maya's room in Calcutta, the life in the hospital, the narrow prison cells, confined spaces, but Shona is an extension and the house is spacious and communication itself opens out spaces. Nazneen, on the other hand in *Brick Lane* has to measure carefully the distance between chair and sofa. Does a writer from a young country carry a mixed baggage? Are conflictual memories far too near to be safely remembered or its history as Nazneen realises, a history of the present? Their memories are of their own lives and do not go much beyond their ownselves. Nazneen at least recalls her mother and aunt, but Rehana, only her dead husband and the immediate present. But both the writers raise very important issues related to nation formation. Are nations only constructed through power, or through language and religion? Is nationhood a territorial affiliation? Or the individual has a role in the nation? Both the writers locate gender in the formation of national identities, else woman will remain a gender without a sense of nation. This is an important issue where national belonging is concerned for women all over the world, as to the share they have in the nation. Revolutions and resistance movements, tend to involve women on the fringes but whether they promise any space within it, remains a matter of concern. Both

Rehana and Maya (*A Golden Age*) demonstrate that there are other ways of growing into freedom than Hasina's (*Brick Lane*), but the reader cannot ignore the fact of access to education and a degree of economic independence necessary for this freedom. Marriage and communication are also relevant where freedom is concerned. True, the memories of Anam and Ali do not go very far into the past, their fictional narratives have a short-distance look backwards, yet now located abroad they write the homeland through gender issues and ideological positions. Mukti Bahani or Karim's resistance movement: how much do they promise, and how much hold back?

NOTES & REFERENCES

1. Tagore, *Home and the World*. Trans. Surendranath Tagore (Madras: Macmillan, 1916). I have given a brief account here of the main narrative but the novel's complexity is unending in its multiple resonances. for a more detailed discussion refer my essay 'Evolving Traditions, Retrealing Modernities: Women and the Gendered Social Reality,' in *Feminism, Tradition and Modernity*. Ed. Chandrakala Padia. (Shimla: Indian Institute of Advanced Study, 2002), 289–302.
2. See Michael Edwardes, *British India 1772–1947* (Calcutta: Rupa & Co. 1967, 1993). 196–208. But there are several other perspectives including a separate interpretation of the history of Pakistan. East Bengal had a Muslim majority and the 1905 is seen as part of the British divide and rule policy, the authorities had been encouraging community-based political parties. But the 1905 partition, on account of popular resentment was rescinded in 1911. Nevertheless the seeds of a future partition had been sown.
3. Homi Bhabha, 'Dissemination: time, narrative and the margins of the nation,' in *Nation and Narration*. Ed. Homi Bhabha (London: Routledge, 1990), 291–322, 291–292.
4. Tahmina Anam, *A Golden Age* (New Delhi: Harper Perrienal, 2009.)
5. Sara Suleri, *Meatless Days: A Memoir* (London: Flamingo, 1991),.
6. *Ibid.*, 125.
7. Ashis Gupta, *Dying Tradition* (New Delhi: Spantech Publishers, 1992).
8. Sorayya Khan, *Noor* (New Delhi: Penguin, 2003).
9. Monica Ali, *Brick Lane* (New York: Scribner, 2003).

10. Sukhdev Sandhu, 'Come hungry, leave edgy,' *London Review of Books*. Vol 29, No. 19. 9 October 2003. internet reference LBR9... wwww. bb.co.uk/u25/come-hungry-leave-edgy. Accessed 24 October 2014.
11. See Nazneen Ahmed, 'Doing Double Duty: Long Distance Nationalism amongst Bengali Migrants in Britain', internet ref. www.surrey.uk.cronen/racialised difference/files/conf2010 papers/ Ahmed.pdf. Accessed 24 October 2014.
12. Ahmed responds here to Benedict Anderson and Rajagopal Radhakrishnan. Anderson's view that migrants do not participate in the political life of their new location and Radhakrishnan's entirely different position that they cannot think of their new location as not home, instead they relate to both and do double duty (see Radhakrishnan, *Diasporic Mediation Between Home and Location*. London: Univ. of Minnesota Press, 1996). Where employment and its intersection with education and ethnicity are concerned, Avtar Brah's analysis of the Asian, community in *Cartographies of Diaspora* (London: Routledge, 1996) and the LSE economic survey of Bangladeshi women are highly informative as they comment as the discrimination against Bengali migrants. Bangladeshi women have hardly any representation, they mostly work from home while Pakistani women have a minimal representation. Indian women, however, have made a breakthrough in the job market (see Kulwant Bhopal's essay in Sociological Research Online, Vol. 3 No. 3. internet ref. <http://www.socres online. org.uk/3/3/3 6 html.) accessed 24 October 2014.

11

Mid-Air Tragedy
The *Emperor Kanishka* Crash

23 June 1985 in the early hours of the morning, Air India Flight 182 crashed in mid-air near the Irish Coast in which the passengers and the crew – 329 people – all perished. There was not a single survivor. As the morning news carried the news of this tragedy, waves of shock flowed across the world. How did it come to happen? Neither a natural disaster, nor a technical failure but, as it was to come to light, it was a dastardly terrorist attack which brought the plane down; later the ocean threw up shrapnels of the plane, bloated bodies, reflecting the impact of the fall on their limbs, faces swollen or distorted beyond recognition and, at times, no bodies at all. It was a collective burial at sea. Very little has been written about this tragedy. Human grief is difficult to talk about; human destructiveness even more so. The arrow pointed at the terrorists sympathetic to the Khalistan cause and the crash came just a year after Operation Bluestar, which had taken place in June 1984, when the army had been ordered to march into the Golden Temple in Amritsar, and almost eight months after the 1984 Delhi riots which had occurred in the aftermath of Indira Gandhi's assassination. But the whole sequence of events was not a matter of simple cause-and-effect; there were a series of causes and a multitude of issues involved in the before and after of this tragedy, across time, across space and across geographical boundaries.

Two years later, in 1987, Clark Blaise and Bharati Mukherjee collaboratively brought out a book *The Sorrow and the Terror*, about this happening from both human and political perspectives and looked into the many factors that brought it about. Bharati Mukherjee has also written a short story about the bereaved victims coping with their sense of loss and the process of putting together their broken lives in and the process of 'The Management of Grief' (*The Middleman and Other Stories*)[1], but *The Sorrow and the Terror*[2] is an investigative work and has several layers. The title of the work itself encapsulates the earliest recordings of the 'tragedy'. For one, the Aristotelian processes of catharsis comes to mind: the pity and the terror, the reaching toward the sufferers and the simultaneous withdrawal from them. The substitution of the word pity by sorrow indicates a much deeper involvement and drawing toward the victims. It also indicates sadness felt on the circumstances that brought it about. The title also reminds one of Greek tragedies with their inevitable endings as the action moves forward, despite all human interventions aimed at averting it. But Blaise and Mukherjee do not go that far. The happening distributes its own share of guilt and responsibility to its many players. The writers structure the work more closely in accordance with the Shakespearian five-act play. In fact, the work presents its own difficulty. How does one read it?

In order to properly understand, interpret, evaluate and judge, the reader – like the book itself – has to take many roads. The text demands a contrapuntal reading. The Air India crash went much beyond personal loss and bereavement; it raised complex questions about the sovereignty of a nation state, rights of citizenship, shared community feelings across racial boundaries, laws of immigration, the Canadian state's initiative embodied in the Multicultural Act, the rise of terrorism and its spread across national borders, economic conditions of unemployment, and the games played by the big powers. The tale of personal loss and bereavement is dwarfed against this background; it seems extremely difficult to stem it against such odds. Yet, in its tragic dimensions, it centre stages the human – the sense of deprivation, vengeance and revenge, the refusal to yield to any kind of hegemony; the human need for a cause that supplies a reason for living; the 'longing', as Timothy Brennan puts it, for a 'national form' (45).[3] Then there is the human interplay of terrorism, dark, somewhat sinister. The other more close to our positive feelings is the writers' capturing of the 'living' energy of the passengers as they make their way to India, their ancestral homeland during the summer holidays; their many artistic pursuits, and later their unfulfilled ambitions, inspirations and interrupted lives – all hit the reader. The immense human effort that went into the rescue operations, the recovery of the bodies, of the plane parts, the black box – the doctors, counsellors, divers, and the coming together of technical expertise and machinery at an international level, all converging together to show the better part of being human. Then, there are the ordinary people who offer hospitality, put up strangers, offer their sympathy and resources – each one of these brings forth a human spirit that rises much above the power games and the politics of revenge and far surpasses the solidarity which was evident amongst the conspirators.

The Sorrow and the Terror engages with history and the processes of history, moving frequently between the staged events and the green room lights and analysing the roles that minor characters play. Bharati Mukherjee has used contemporary history in some of her novels, especially *Jasmine* where it is the Punjab militancy which forms the background. Some of the issues present in the work are part of the raw material of her novel *Jasmine*[4], to be published in 1989. There too she worked with the issues of illegal immigration, unfulfilled economic dreams, social compromises in search of employment, and a total transformation of values and cultural codes in an alien world. But as the novel focuses on the plain village girl Jassi turned Jasmine, the socio-economic issues are absorbed into her life story, perhaps a little artificially framed with the sati and the Goddess Kali narratives which lend themselves so easily both to tales of victimisation and revenge and the exoticisation of a culture for western consumption.

Later, in another novel – *Desirable Daughters* (2002) – Mukherjee again weaves together history, fiction and mystery as a family narrative. But *The Sorrow and the Terror*, in its confrontation with bare facts and the sharp analytical approach put together in a 'concerned' narrative, rises much above the fictional engagement with history and the compulsions fiction may have. Let me explain the word 'concerned', a word I have used in preference to realistic or authentic or even 'interested'. The concern with private dreams, with international frames of power, discrimination and domination, and with the existential facts of loneliness, mortality and grief transcend all other concerns across race and religion. It is not like telling only one side of the story – either of the dead or the survivors, or of the aggrieved and the violent – but a moving beyond that to the encompassing narratives of connivance, interference and indifference to all that is human. Moreover, sympathy does not go overboard. The right degree of objectivity essential for interrogating the before and after of the crash is sustained.

Beginning with three short sections forming a kind of a prologue, the work proceeds to work with five major parts almost like a five-act play. It moves non-linearly, to and fro in time and centrifugally branching off into different directions. The first short section is a one-page account of the facts as to what happened. The second, titled 'Introduction' builds an outer conceptual frame enlisting the issues that the crash has raised which happen to be more than political and legal; they have social and psychological moorings. Moral issues of guilt and responsibility also raise their head. The third section switches to the Indian political scenario, provides the background to the Sikh religion, an account which depends in the main on Khushwant Singh's *History of the Sikhs* (1953), but with some personal observations on the Hindu-Sikh relations interspersed. Every Sikh may or may not agree with these but they still do not do any damage and do not create an imbalance. The views of the writers are rooted in a contemporary non-Sikh reaction. Not at all strange in itself. Sikh opinion about Sikhism and its essentials is today divided along political ideologies. This section also fulfils the two writers' own need to understand the issues and principles involved and their attention to the non-Sikh, non-Indian reader. A brief history of the surfacing or re-surfacing of the demand for Khalistan in the early 70s and its appeal alike to the Sikh leadership, as to the Sikh diaspora especially the one which finds itself displaced and unemployed follows. The idea of a homeland has both its visionary and emotional appeal to the excluded. At one point in the 'Introduction', the writers state: 'The final question that guided our investigation was this: Could this entire tragedy have been avoided? Were there warnings?' (xix). By asking this Blaise and Mukherjee definitely give an indication of their larger concerns, going much beyond any simple interpretation of history or a study of the wayward diaspora.

What follows is the main body of the book divided into five parts. The first part begins with the adherents of the Khalistan movement dancing in the streets of New York as the news of Indira Gandhi's assassination spread. In itself a macabre moment of death juxtaposed with merriment and expressing long-distance oneness with the like-minded ones back home. The horror is all the more sinister and it is followed by the Delhi riots as madness and violence are let loose. In short dramatic shifts, the narrative moves across time and space, back and forth, tracing the course of the events and the conspiracy which culminated in the tragedy about. The various people, agencies and ideologies that fanned it, gradually crowd the scene. The big players are Jagjit Singh Chauhan, Gurpartap Singh Birk, Sukhwinder Singh while the small players are many.

The second part, brings us to 23 June, the day of the crash and its immediate aftermath, when suddenly a host of agencies, individuals, institutions had to step in and join in the mammoth (and heart breaking) rescue operation. Non-involved strangers help, hospital patients are shifted, neighbours open their homes to strangers and, amidst this public effort all attempts at salvaging human dignity and the privacy of grief continue to be made. The immensity of the tragedy is matched only by the immensity of the coping machine. Death is never silent or invisible. It cannot efface itself. In fact, it is another beginning – one of shock, mourning and bereavement; and of incomprehension and smell of decay, of form-filling and photograph-matching. Death by drowning had its own additional burden of bloated bodies and torn limbs.

Part three finds us amongst the bereaved relatives, the hope that some may have managed to survive, unknown fears, fresh shocks and renewed disappointment, longings and homage to the beloved ones, and suddenly the reader is sharing this private space of grief. These families are truncated and incomplete with either one partner gone or whole families having disappeared or the children having perished leaving behind a solitary survivor to mourn the dead. As they reach across, at times to others equally bereaved, a new kind of family, one that has shared grief comes into being. They have all been baptised by the 'ultimate tragedy a man or a woman ... can suffer' (89).

Alternating between happenings and processes, entrusted with the task of collecting evidence to find out what actually happened. It is an effort at reconstructing the crash as divers dive deep into the ocean for the black box, all the time fighting against time and the flowing currents. The private habits, friendships, ideologies, loyalties and equations of the crew are closely examined in an attempt to find out if the bombing was an inside act of sabotage or not, whether there were two bombs or one, and commissions of inquiry are floated. Then, all at once, the focus which was like a self-contained balloon with its inner layers is suddenly expanded. Part five, once again steps into a larger world, like the three-section prologue. It moves quickly into a large array of concerns, intra-group rivalries of the various Sikh groups, their associational adherence, Punjabi migrants to Canada attracted by dreams of material success, the immigration laws and the policy of multiculturalism before moving on to international external agencies which fanned terrorism. From amongst the diaspora, many remained 'untouched by their Canadian experience' limited as they were by their lack of English, for others it was a comedown in terms of caste and status while all along the claims from the family back home continued to build up a constant pressure. For people who feel caught between non-belonging and non-acceptance (read immigration and economic failure), there is no real Punjab to return to, 'To return as poor as they'd left is intolerable for any immigrant, especially for a proud Jat Sikh male'. What follows is a one-line independent statement, all by itself, almost like a tight-fisted blow; 'They are time-bombs, ripe for conversion' (177). Thus trouble brews in different ways and circumstances, not all of them necessarily religious or even political, many were personal and familial, and Khalistan became a way of accommodating failed dreams and ambitions, a diversion from the forked existence in which they had been caught. The reader is bound to ask 'who was responsible?' and 'whose responsibility were they?' – which nation, which country, which society and people? And can one cope with terrorist activity or potential terrorism without looking into the multitude causes which feed it?

Again, with migration from one country to another, cultural codes are shifted to another society which does not value them or understand them. In actual terms there is a deep schism between the location of the immigrant's physical location and the mindset, especially if bridging processes like education and modernity are absent or have failed to work. The substitution of a failed dream – economic progress – by the visionary (and divisionary) dream of Khalistan was not as difficult as one would like to believe. Rituals, a sense of being the chosen pure, the observance of identity markers both build up a sense of community and restore self-respect. The Sikh turned Khalistan worker, the writers comment, thus experiences a sense of belonging somewhere. This is the, 'Portrait of a terrorist, Canada, in the 1980s' (179).

Once again the reader is brought back to India and to the 1951 Government of India Census, when Punjabi Hindus who spoke Punjabi but went on to claim Hindi as their mother tongue thus dividing the Punjabi literary, linguistic and cultural heritage on lines of religion. This tiny seed was strong enough to develop into what is known as Punjab militancy which was almost a state of civil war, unleashing violence on both sides – the State as well as the Sikhs. This connected India and Canada; the diaspora was generous with funding and turned its own sense of alienation into the movement's strength as self-exiled leaders carved out a role for themselves. Suddenly there was a mushrooming of newspapers (in Canada) and full-colour blow-ups of the Delhi riots found a place in the Khalistani homes in North America (185). The whole movement, culminating in the crash, is not merely a tale of two lands, but one flamed and fanned by a multitude of external forces including Pakistan, United States and Soviet Union among others. The rivalries of the big powers alike are carried on the South Asian region, converting what appear to be internal and nationalistic concerns to serve their own purpose. Blaise and Mukherjee refer to a speech credited to Jeane Kirkpatrick but actually having been proxy-written by the Soviet Union.[5] Once again the difficulty arises of pinning guilt. Following the writers' research and line of inquiry one is overwhelmed by the complexity of the conspiracy and the sheer enormity of the problem. One begins to look suspiciously at almost everything. It is obvious that no movement solely directed towards fanaticism can sustain itself for long, if not indirectly or directly supported by other interested parties. In contrast to Blaise and Mukherjee's researches we also have inside stories about the leaders of the movement located in India, stories which give their version of the facts, which is factually correct. I refer here to Manraj Grewal's *Dreams After Darkness: A Search for Life Ordinary under the Shadow of 1984* (1987), where an analysis is made of the retaliatory Sikh militancy.[6] Amitav Ghosh, himself a diasporic writer, also comments on this in his essay, 'The Ghosts of Mrs Gandhi' (*Imam and the Indian*), where he records the horrifying experience of the massacre in Delhi in the aftermath of Mrs Gandhi's death. Such happenings when death is easy and terror stalks the land raise questions not only regarding the responsibility of the state but also of its citizens.[7]

A fictionalised version which focuses on individual lives and examines closely the processes of alienation of a community within a native context as well as its parallels in immigrant situations is Anita Rau Badami's well-researched novel, *Can You Hear the Nightbird Call?*[8] It is about the rising Punjab militancy, the alienation which loyalist Sikhs are made to feel and the thoughtless identification of an act with a whole community, as it happened after Indira Gandhi's assassination in 1984, an instant method to deal out reprisals. Part of the narrative is also an exploration of the Sikh psyche as political power forces whole sections of population to move from one area to another resulting in emotional dislocations and unsatisfactory rehabilitation schemes. The memory of the Partition trauma is firmly etched in the community's subconscious. It gets a treatment similar to the one meted out to *muhajirs* in Pakistan. Furthermore, the 'refugee' label attacks its sense of self-respect. The issues raised within the country are similar to the ones raised in diaspora locations. How does one belong and when does one belong? Again, the formation of a nation is neither a political process nor a territorial one: it calls for recognition of belonging on the basis of equal rights and participation.

Jasbeer, the young Sikh boy, is taken to Canada by his mother's aunt Bibiji, as a gesture of compensation for the wrongs she may have done to her elder sister. Sharanjit Kaur, now addressed as Bibiji, harbours a feeling of guilt at having stolen her sister's fiancé much before Partition. Bibiji and her husband, Paji, run Delhi Junction Café in Toronto which is a popular meeting place for the South Asian diaspora. Their house, Taj Mahal, offers open hospitality and has a floating population as new immigrants make it their transit home. These places of community get-togethers, like the gurudwaras, are places of linkages with the past, with the homeland and the politics back home.

In 1965, the Indo-Pak war was also present in Delhi Junction when the seating maps of the customers altered, and 'Hafeez and Alibhai moved defensively over to a separate table' (66–67). Leela, when she first arrived in Canada, doesn't want to shop with Mrs Wu because of the Sino-Indian clash of 1962. It is strange how porous the borders become when trouble has to go through from one to the other. But houses remain opaque. The struggle for connections, social status and recognition seems to be unending. Leela wonders as to when the sense of not-belonging will yield to sense of belonging: 'How long would she remain foreign? Would she eventually become a woman of meaning here ... or would she remain without context, tied to a past that meant nothing to anyone except herself. A past, that would, if they lived long enough, become irrelevant to her children?' (129). Bibiji tells her that a bad memory was necessary for a person wishing to settle in to become one of the crowd, to become 'an invisible minority' (136–137).

Badami's novel expounds on the many issues involved in the immigrant's place in the host society. The novel is prefaced by a series of epigraphs – in fact, three – which point out towards its concerns. The first is from Agha Shahid Ali's poem 'Farewell', a single line – 'My memory keeps getting in the way of your history', while the other two are about the '84 Delhi riots and the Kanishka crash. The quote from Agha Shahid Ali points towards the complexity and the need for multiple memories as well as histories. No single narrative or version is capable of presenting the whole truth. Truth is fragmented, personal and with historical roots even as it is simultaneously reflected in dates, facts and interactions. It is best reflected in personal narratives. It also points toward the imposition of hegemonic narratives over personal truths and problematises dislocation as a necessary discontinuity.

Can You Hear the Nightbird Call? is a sensitive portrayal of individual histories, community and national narratives as they get embroiled with each other. And histories have a long past; they also have an uncanny habit of invading other spaces. As for the sense of being alienated or being an outsider, it is connected not only with law, employment, economic justice but it also a fall-out of difference, of identity constructs and non-recognition. Canada's Multiculturalism Act comes in for its own share of critiquing both in *The Sorrow and the Terror* and in *Can You Hear the Nightbird Call?* Immigrants are referred to as a 'visible' minority, but in actual social space they are a contradiction in terms; they are an invisible (insignificant) visible (people of colour) minority, the Sikhs even more so with their identity-markers sticking out. The Multiculturism Act, rather than reconcile this contradiction, makes way for ethnicity but not for equality. Indian immigrants have commented upon its ineffectuality and its underlying strategy. Chelva Kanaganayakam, in 'Writing About Race', takes up both the aspects of multiculturalism, its non-assimilationist agenda and its tendency to treat people as representatives of a group, ways of seeing which lead to ghettoisation and enforced 'homogeneity'[9] (11). Multiculturalism appears to be a policy of accommodation of difference but in actuality it denies individuality as well as the freedom which accompanies distinctiveness by pushing all identities into stereotypes – in short it becomes an easy solution to the problem of understanding the 'Others', a mental laziness as it were. Other voices critical of the policy of multiculturalism and its implementation are those of Himani Bannerjee and Neil Bissoondath. Bannerjee considers the policy as originating as a preventive measure of deterring the separatist tendencies of Canada's own French and Native population, notionally extended to take in the visible minorities. Her work *The Dark Side of the Nation*[10] is an indepth study of the underside of the Act. Neil Bissoondath on the other hand in *Selling Illusions: The Cult of Multiculturalism in Canada*[11], critiques it with reference to his own identity. Despite his full allegiance to the country of his adoption, the colour of his skin and the country/ies of his origin fracture his Canadianness. The visible difference marks him out. Both Bharati Mukherjee and Anita Rau Badami are sensitive to the limitations and shortcomings of the Act. Mukherjee in *The Sorrow and the Terror* is critical of Canada's lack of responsibility for its own people. The majority of the Indians travelling in *Emperor Kanishka* were Canadian citizens. 'Three hundred and seven passengers and twenty two crew members were killed. Over ninety per cent of the passengers ... were Canadian citizens' (vii). But, the authors point out, Canadian officials hung back and this angered the relatives of the dead. They felt that they had been abandoned, shunned even in their moment of grief by their adoptive country (67). The Canadian Prime Minister himself was slow to wake up to this. A phone call to his Indian counterpart appeared to him to be enough. The security lapses at the Canadian airports were not given enough weightage, sufficient and timely evidence was not put together – and moreover the nation did not share the Indian community's sense of loss. Badami works through Jasbeer's experiences in school, where he is always bullied and is consequently uncomfortable. His grand-aunt Bibiji wonders whether he was 'teased or bullied at school for the colour of his skin or because he wore his hair in a topknot like all good Sikhs? Was he required that he have his hair cut in order to blend in?' (197). It is this being pushed to the margins that throws him, in his growing years, into terrorism.

Back in India, things are no better. Economic and political issues are relocated within religious differences as linguistic and territorial claims are made and vote-gathering is prioritised over justice and equality. In Badami's novel, Nimmo, a fervent admirer of Mrs Gandhi, finds herself trapped in her Sikh identity in the aftermath of the assassination as the Partition riots are reenacted and Operation Bluestar is a carryover of the colonial mentality in the close similarity it has with Jallianwala Bagh. Amitav Ghosh's 'The Ghosts of Mrs Gandhi' is an analysis alike of lawlessness and injustice, with the state resorting to indifference and the people joining in the brutal violence. Shonali Bose in the film *Amu* examines the psychological affect on the psyche of the victim, even if these are faint, childhood memories as well as on those caught between their conscience and loyalties on the one hand and greed and fear on the other.[12]

The issues are not merely of law and justice, or of equality and citizenship, or even of guilt and responsibility but are even more wide-ranging as civilisations and their constructs are placed under the scanner. Jasbeer's journey (*Can You Hear the Nightbird Call?*) from innocence to a die-hard terrorist is matched by Nimmo's withdrawal into madness, a journey which is also traced by Gulzar in his film *Maachis*.[13] Who is a terrorist? How does he come into being? And can a reverse journey be undertaken back into ordinary life? The brutalisation of human emotions so evident in the careful planning and its aftermath, on part of the Khalistani's is not only singular to them. It is evident in the State as well as the people and relationships in both national and international politics. Actually if its history can be traced back to the holocaust, it can also be traced back to the bombs on Hiroshima and Nagasaki, events providing ample proof or the total indifference to the human. Modern day power politics is far more barbaric than the wars of the past. Even as the world is now playing the game of forgiveness by trying publicly to apologise for the deeds of the past and the wrongs done in history by bygone generations, the death of conscience is written large on the inhuman acts of humanity.

While reading *The Sorrow and the Terror*, one experiences a series of different emotions as one responds to the sense of solidarity reflected in the conspiracy on one hand and the sheer brutality and callousness of it all even as it rots the insides of the guilty. It interrogates the Fanonian position. Is violence ever justified as Fanon seems to suggest? Can violence bring equality, freedom or peace? Can violence help to erase differences and is it the right kind of power to be desired? Resistance can take other forms than violence. Yet, the postcolonial world, in its theory and practice, seems to have opted for power both as a controlling medium and an instrument for decolonisation. Fanon attributes the idea of non-violence as having been floated by the colonialist bourgeoisie (Fanon 48)[14], a point of view which continues to be questioned by men like Gandhi, Luther, Mandela and many others. Except that violence is more immediate and more visible. It kills the conscience. Non-violence addresses, evokes and probes the conscience. Perhaps the time has come not to enter into debates on the death of God but on the death of the human conscience. As long as power, desire, domination and retaliation/resistance work through violence and revenge, the intervention of the past in our present will persist and cultures will run parallel rather than converge.

It is difficult to give the credit to any single author of this two-member team for the research, the findings and the organisation of *The Sorrow and the Terror*. But one must acknowledge that the organisation of the material, the laying out of the scenario, the focusing on the crash, intensifies our concern with the issue of meaningless, inhuman violence. It makes us sit up and think twice about the politics of migration; it evokes our emotional responses and provokes our critical judgment as we join the writers in their journey into different histories, different pasts, led by them into asking questions pertaining to several very significant issues if mankind is to survive and peace have a chance. The work is no romantic engagement with history or a projection of a culture; it is a thought-provoking, issue-raising work splintering off into multiple directions. And it was one of the first books on the crash. Returning to its five-part structure, and its title, let me ask the question does it in any way fulfil the cathartic effect or is tragedy truly dead? Blaise and Mukherjee write, 'The Air India disaster was a Canadian tragedy, from the beginning, growing in part from a national character flaw: the comfortable myth of instructive goodness. The bedrock certainty of "it can't happen here", which translates into complacent airport security, yields only slightly to a partial revision: "Sad as it is, it's not really our problem" ' (203). Roland de Corneille, a member of the Parliament pointed out 'Not enough Canadians are deeply touched. Not too many realize it was Canadians who were killed. There still remains racism, a separatism, the loss affected them, not us' (quoted by Blaise and Mukherjee 203). The same could apply to 1984 anti-Sikh riots, and the Gujarat genocide in 2002. How many of us, as Indians, and members of a nation, reached out to the victims and felt for them? The real tragedy lies outside the crash: and it is this which leaves the reader with both a sense of bewildered helplessness and a surge of sympathy which seeks transformation both within and without – in our mindsets, policies, hatreds and revenge as also in the flow of histories. The past, strangely enough, needs both to be remembered and forgotten. The future will anchor itself on our selections of the past which we choose to remember and build upon.

NOTES & REFERENCES

1. In 'The Management of Grief', Mrs Bhave is at the centre, a bereaved mother and wife. It is her whole relationship with the counselor, Judith Templeton, who is appointed to help her. Judith's interaction with Mrs Bhave is an effort to puncture her silence, understand her cultural attitudes and together they share memories, hopes, dreams of the dead and the blanket of loneliness gives way to communication. See *The Middleman and Other Stories* (New Delhi: Prentice Hall, India Private Limited, 1990).

2. Blaise and Mukerjee, *The Sorrow and the Terror* (London: Penguin Books, 1987)

3. Refer Timothy Brennan who, in his essay, offers a complex analysis of the concept of nationalism. Locating it within power on one hand and powerlessness on the other, he comments that while in the first it led to hegemonic control over others, in the second it was a reclaiming of a collectivity, lost earlier by conceding to the terms of the former rulers. Timothy Brennan. 'The national longing for form'. *Nation and Narration*. Ed. Homi Bhabha (London and New York. Routledge, 1990). 44–70, 57–58.

4. In fact, Jasmine the protagonist of the novel *Jasmine* (New York: Grove Press, 1989), goes through several transformations and gradually the past, her cultural codes, her values all dissolve through this process. Some of the passages are too melodramatic to be real as they frame murders and rapes and women being depicted hanging out their tongues like the blood-soaked one of the Goddess Kali.

5. See *The Sorrow and the Terror*, 193 when the writers refer to a speech titled 'Operation Balkanisation of India' (included in *The Agony of Punjab* and credited as a reprint from 'the leftist *Link* magazine'. The speech had apparently been delivered before 1300 delegates at the Mayflower Hotel in Washington, on 27 February 1982, before the convention of the Conservative Political Action Conference and ascribed to the then U.N. Ambassador Jeane Kirkpatrick. Though, it gave all internal evidence of Kirkpatrick's style, careful research, revealed that the speech had been 'concocted in Moscow, and leaked to an Indian Communist paper' to be further disseminated (193–194).

6. Obviously sympathetic, it follows the biographies of the leaders. In this reference also see http:\\www.khalistan.net/sjs_bhindranwale.html, an article by Ranbir Singh Sandhu which looks more closely at the speeches, events, action and counter action of the period, and analysing the role of the State, both at central and State levels.

Manraj Grewal's book, *Dreams After Darkness A Search for Life Ordinary under the Shadow of 1984* (New Delhi: Rupa, 2004). See also. Ranbir Singh Sandhu, 'Sant Jarnail Singh Bhindranwala: Life, Mission and Martyrdom'. internet reference http:\\www.khalistan.net/sjs_bhindranwala.html. accessesd 25/1/2009.

7. Amitav Ghosh locates the aftermath of Mrs Gandhi's death in his personal experience of being in Delhi at the time and comments that when the state did not act, right-thinking people acted. They took out a march in defiance of the attacking crowds, pointing to this collective response necessary to living together in a multi-ethnic and multi-religious society. These protests, Ghosh writes, 'are the weapons with which society asserts itself against a state that runs criminally amok, as this one did in Delhi in November, 1984' (59). See 'The Ghosts of Mrs Gandhi', *The Imam and the Indian: Prose Pieces* (Delhi: Ravi Dayal Publisher and Permanent Black, 2002) 46–63. The same volume also has an essay on 'Diaspora in Indian Culture' and 'The Fundamentalist Challenge', which dwell on the political environment.

8. Anita Rau Badami, *Can You Hear the Nightbird Call?* (New Delhi: Viking/Penguin, 2006).

9. Chelva Kanaganayakam, 'Writing Beyond Race: The Politics of Otherness', *The Toronto Review Contemporary Writing Abroad: Race and Writing*. Vol.12, No.3. 7–17.

10. Himani Bannerjee, *The Dark Side of the Nation: Essays on Multiculturalism in Canada*. (Toronto: Canadian Scholars Press Inc., 2000).

11. Neil Bissoondath, *Selling Illusions: The Cult of Multiculturalism in Canada* (Penguin: 1987).

12. Bose's film works through the life of a young child orphaned in the Delhi riots and her gradual unraveling of her memories and the trauma experienced at that time through direct confrontation with the memories of the guilty ... *Amu*. Director/Writer Shonali Bose; Performers: Konkana Sen Sharma, Ankur Khanna, Brinda Karat, 2005.

13. Gulzar's film *Maachis* (also scripted as a novel), works through two Sikh families in rural Punjab, pushed into fear, terrorism and retaliation through police brutality. Once branded as terrorist, there is no coming back. The only viable option is death, in or outside prison, almost always self-inflicted. *Maachis*: Director/Writer: Gulzar, Performers: Om Puri, Tabu, Chandrachud Singh, Kulbhushan Kharbanda, Jimmy Shergill, 1996.

14. Frantz Fanon, *The Wretched of the Earth*, 1961, translated by Constance Farrington (Harmondsworth: Penguin, 1967, 1976).

12

Call of the Homeland
The Civil War in Sri Lanka

'This isn't just "another job"! I decided to come back. I wanted to come back'[1]

'Their marriages, their careers on the borderland of civil war among governments and terrorists and insurgents'[2]

'She Tamil. That's enough. They take our land, our jobs. If we let them, they'll take the whole country'.
... 'Look at her, she's a Sinhala girl. Only a little dark. You goondas can't even tell the difference?[3]

'No more the school?' she asked. 'Not the same way. I think I will specialize in history lessons. That in itself is becoming a battlefield.'[4]

The diaspora turns to the homeland to reflect upon childhood memories and cultural histories. Selvadurai's first four novels are all about growing up where the dominant factors are the sea coast and the gradual realisation of his homosexuality. Gunesekera moves from Sri Lanka to Britain and works with mixed themes. Ondaatje, after his early autobiographical narrative in *Running in the Family* turned to other locations other myths and fables until suddenly in 2000, he published *Anil's Ghost*. As Anil says that she simply had to come back.[5] Many subcontinental writers living abroad return to home turf either prompted by nostalgia, childhood memories, seascapes or cityscapes. The two Indian writers, Salman Rushdie and Rohinton Mistry, return to India and more specifically to Bombay, now Mumbai. One could go on listing the various locations and the reasons the diaspora writes about the homeland – the violence, the strife, the policies, the culture – but my concern here is with some novels about the civil war in Sri Lanka. Ondaatje's *Anil's Ghost* is one of the earliest. And suddenly in 2013–2014, we have several more novels: Shyam Selvadurai's *The Hungry Ghosts*, Romesh Gunesekera's *Noontide Toll* and Nayomi Munaweera's *Island of a Thousand Mirrors*. The war too had multiple reflections. And as Selvadurai has observed, though the war has ended, the conflict has not. Himself a Tamil-Sinhalese mixed background, he is perhaps the right person to know it.[6] Each writer explores a different dimension and looks at it from a different lens. But no matter how different they maybe the ruined remains of the social fabric stare one in the eye as individual tragedies mount. It is difficult to forget the last part of *Anil's Ghost* when Sarath's body is being cleaned and bandaged by his brother Gamini. But bodies don't mend and souls too remain scarred.

Anil's Ghost is a complex novel and its true meaning reveals itself only in a second reading for by then one can read the clues present in the first few pages. They almost foretell the end like Marquez's *Chronicle of a Death Foretold*.[7] There is an uncanny feeling of all that is going to happen and a silent prayer that it should not. This is unnerving. Ondaatje's brief note to the book talks about the 'three essential groups: the government, the antigovernment insurgents in the south and the separatist guerrillas in the north' (Author's Note). This is further substantiated by Anil's reflections (27)[8]. The legal and anti-legal official acts are also placed side by side. Anil has been away for sixteen years and now she has come home as a forensic expert. So far she had felt detached, 'the island no longer held her by the past', and had learnt to interpret Sri Lanka with a long distance gaze. The novel is interspersed with italicised passages which constantly refer to the past, to archaeology, history and culture. There is an early reference to Bodhisattvas about loss and survival. This is also a reference to Palipana, the archaeologist, though he enters the novel later as a participant character (11–12). The first body that Anil examines, she finds the bones in both the arms are broken, an indication that it has been tortured, something that is later going to happen to Sarath.

Where is the future for this country engaged in fratricide, where bodies are disposed off, buried and reburied? Anil thinks of it as another hundred years' war but with 'modern weaponry', a war sponsored by gun and drug-runners. Ondaatje quotes from Orwell's *Nineteen Eighty-Four*, from the Inner Party's *Manifesto*, 'The reason for war was war' (43).[9] As if a counter civilisation was under way.

The diaspora's right to speak is questioned, (a self-questioning by Ondaatje?). Sarath tells her Anil: 'you know, I'd believe your arguments more if you lived here... you can't just slip in, make a discovery and leave.' This happens to be the truth though Anil discovers for herself only in the end that the 'law is on the side of power not truth' (44). In contrast to the fact of unleashed power and unthinking violence are the archaeological finds which bear testimony to the origins of the ancient civilisation – as old 'as any in India', and a site which ironically is used to dump the bodies of political victims. It is when Anil and Sarath find a skeleton, not more than four or six years old on this government site, that Anil is motivated to trace the responsibility. The clues abound: the soil is different and the skeleton is not of the hoary past. Someone who had gone missing was in fact killed and buried. Distrust is easy to brew in this tension-filled atmosphere. Anil, an outsider and in untested waters, is unsure of Sarath's loyalty – on which side is he? Every skeleton tells a story, Tectonic slips and brutal human violence 'provided random time-capsules of unhistorical lives' (55). The civil war story unveils itself through the government's victims – the skeleton found amongst ancient ruins and Palipana moved gracelessly out of the establishment, his research labelled fiction. History, knowledge, science and the human being – all become victims of the political turmoil, the power game which aims not at peace but at holding power, at not sharing it. And this in the land of the Buddha! These little biographies both of men and the country, come together in these times of violence. And dead bodies help trace the agents of death (88–89).

Fairly early in the novel, the ceremony of painting the eyes is mentioned (99) a ceremony half-sacred half-ritual and whose actual enactment is to follow towards the end (305–307). It is a ceremony carried out in the early hours of the morning, the hour when Buddha attained Enlightenment. Palipana is blind but he tells

Anil, 'without the eyes there is not just blindness, there is nothing. There is no existence'; the eyes he refers to are not merely the physical eyes, the ability to see but the ones that represent an inner vision, intuition, sensitivity and the ability to sense truth behind the apparent reality. Palipana though blind has developed these inner eyes, his world is not reduced to nothingness. His life spells out some home truths, the importance of the past, of vision and of relationships. There can be no present without a past. Without this continuity, all is reduced to a wilderness. Hence, human responsibility goes beyond the temporal. Anil's visit home, her obsession with the skeleton, her realisation of knowledge beyond science, and the multitude ways of drowning one's sorrow. As Anil and Sarath travel from one site to another, always in search of something or someone, personal and national histories weave a pattern. Anil Tissera, Sarath, Palipana, the girl Lakma, the artist now a drunk, grieving for his wife, people from different worlds all come together in pursuit of the unknown. Is it truth, history or knowledge?

No one can remain outside the violence of this war, there is no place that is safe. From skeletons and civilisation, the reader is taken to hospitals, overflowing with victims of bomb explosions, 'intentional violence', hospitals that have run short of painkillers, and to the newly-sprung habitations coming up near hospitals and doctors. Archaeologists, detectives and forensic experts have learnt to be suspicious of everything and everyone with this disconnection between truth and reality. Sarath's brother Gamini is a surgeon. Seeing the pain, his ears full of the cries and the shrinking male population, he 'stopped believing in man's role on earth. He turned away from every person who stood up for war' (119). The violence of war spared none, not even children; even knowledge is harnessed for the purposes of war. Palipana is in search of the meaning of history, Anil for truth and accuracy and Gamini for the hidden routes of psychological and physical damage to the nerve bundle called amygdala, a part of the brain where fear and perhaps anger is housed. It is the dark aspect of the brain, the place where fearful memories are located (134–35).

While violence destroys, kills, injures, the task of healing the injuries, reconstructing the body, the mind and the habitation, all have to go on, no matter how futile it maybe. Ananda has been called to help them trace the unknown victim and is asked to reconstruct the skeleton. Very likely it will lead them to another wrong. Yet Anil persists in her need to prevent further loss of life. She weeps for interrupted lives, lost loves and broken bodies and decides to fight this injustice. But the conspiracies are much too strong for her to get through the hostile barriers. She manages to escape with her life but Sarath has to sacrifice his. *Anil's Ghost* conveys to the reader a world badly entangled in violence, where human life has no value, where power moves forward relentlessly indifferent to all else, where another Buddha is needed for peace to be attained. *Anil's Ghost* is a sad, intense novel where the diasporic agency is ineffective and the human loss immeasurable. There is desolation all around. Anil has to go back because there is no place for her in Sri Lanka. She is an outsider and speaks in another voice. The novel is suffused by a Buddhist discourse, which is home-grown, native and centuries' old; this also no longer works. Is it that violence closes doors and windows, frightens and creates barriers or does it override the human in search for power? But then who is to push these closed doors open? Men like Sarath who know how to give or Ananda who drowns in his world of sorrow? *Anil's Ghost* is a grim novel all the way through offering no other solution except the human will to sacrifice and struggle. This is what the present tells us and this what histories of the past reveal.[10]

Nayomi Munaweera in *Island of a Thousand Mirrors* compresses the beginnings of history and the end, locates them in a family's self-exile to the States, both included in the story of a family and a house. The house owned by a Sinhala family has no difficulty (only some hesitation), in making space for a Tamil family. Their children play together and later fall in love. But war disrupts their lives as it enters as an external enemy, through a racial consciousness which pervades the environment; it comes as suspicion, distrust and dislike, and violence. Beginning in 1948, the novel has its own share of history – the British rule and the Buddhist inheritance. The English, at their departure, contemplate the meaning of 'home' and realise that the vision that possesses them is the Sri Lankan landscape.[11] The other important aspect of home is belonging, a sense of place and environment, which enters even a migrant's psyche. One could read Munaweera's novel also as an exposition of 'home' where the meaning ranges from house and dwelling in the Heideggerian sense through memory, landscape, peace, belonging and security. Heidegger in his closely argued essay, 'Building Dwelling Thinking'[12], makes a point by not punctuating the title in any way and establishes the point that they are interlinked. He moves from the external to the inner mind and the negotiation takes place between building and thinking through the process of 'dwelling', a lived-in, an at-home experience. The essay is crucial to the concept of the human being's relation to space and gives priority to memory.

Houses are not merely enclosures, they have windows. The relationship with the outside locale still persists when we are inside and reflect on ourselves. Heidegger goes so far as to say that dwelling 'is the *basic* character of Being, in keeping with which mortals exists' (254). At the other end is thinking. Houses hold memories and define human beings. They hold our essence and our past struggles. It could also mean love – not only a fulfilling love but a lost love and shared grief. Even the distant transient home in the States can become home! The hierarchical caste-oriented society is described through a doctor's change of family name and Beatrice Muriel's diatribes against her husband (14–15). The social and caste segregation is the dividing factor; later it is census, where the figures of majority and minority is showcased, the greed for political power and the enactment of unfair laws all add up to sharpen the divisionary forces. The country soon becomes a house divided.

Short snippets follow each other in quick succession to unravel histories of the past and open doors to other houses, courtyards and 'soldiers marching in the streets', short, quick movements in time. From Beatrice Muriel's house, we shift to the yet unborn Visaka's house and the dream house which Visaka's mother, Sylvia Sunethra, dreams of – a house full of children and grandchildren (32), a dream that persists but materialises only tentatively. The third person narration, the constant references to names all build up quick steps of the narrative. Unlike Ondaatje, who has Anil Tissera enter a war-torn world and who explores the past through this entry point, Munaweera uses this snippet strategy for constantly looking over the shoulder and filling the reader in on past histories, past spaces and mindscapes and simultaneously moving through birth, childhood and schooling, all the time preparing the background and emotionally relating herself to her country of origin (as well of her birth).

The constant factor in the family is the presence of Alice – friend, maid, counsellor and housekeeper. The third generation arrives on the scene, children grow up as destinies take shape amidst the shadow of strife. Sylvia Sunethra's family lives on the ground floor and the Shivalingams on the first. The rioters, when they come to harm them, create fear and uncertainty and lead to exodus. The Sinhalese family moves to America, the Shivalingams pack up a few belongings and leave. As the Shivalingams leave, it is not only the house that is empty but the divisions in the country are more sharply marked. The Sinhalese hunt for the Tamils and the Tamils hunt for volunteers as a fighting force are two movements, one outwardly directed towards the Other and the other inwardly towards the community. Educational institutions are invaded and the process of living is now geared to protection, evasion, hiding and either exodus or violence. The real disruption is in relationships. Shiva is in love with Yasodhara's younger sister, Sri Lanka. They have played together as children as they shared the two floors of the same house. Later, Shiva's sister, Saraswathi, is compelled to join the Tigers in a post abduction scenario and has to transform herself into a weapon-carrying body. As Saraswathi trains to become a suicide bomber, Sri Lanka restless in America, comes home to her country. The final encounter between Saraswathi and Sri Lanka takes place in a bus – the former the suicide bomber and the latter a co-traveller, recognised by Saraswathi a little too late. Right in the middle of the novel, Yasodhara had wondered at the makings of a suicide bomber (117–118), and now she is left to face the death of her sister, torn into fragments and her broken body in the mortuary, awaiting identification and her playmate's younger sister the agent of this dastardly act!

The suicide bomber's psychology is worked out from the Tamil perspective: the search for identity, the need to surmount the social inferiority and the political marginalisation thrust on them, to be recognised and become hero. It is a refusal to be hated and denigrated to a cipher. A violent response to a violent existence. But the repercussions are felt in personal tragedies – Sri Lanka's death – her name acquiring an added symbolical resonance – and Yasodhara's relationship to Shiva – a wounded relationship seeking solitude and comfort in a house in faraway California. Where is home? The histories of homes and houses unveil the country's history and the dreams that are shattered, the exiles that are thrust on people. A shadowy, secretive refuge is what they build together as traditional hatreds are crossed hesitatingly and with love but the homeland lies in pieces. The pattern of everyday living, the network of relationships, political affiliations, dreams and hopes – all go awry. The violence leaves behind scars and the need to put aside memories of innocence and happiness. It is a scary world without open laughter and the past in dark shadows.

Romesh Gunesekera's *Noontide Toll* takes up the site of these ravages when a whole country lies desolate and stumbles into a slow process of reconstruction, ironically enough, directed towards tourist traffic and foreign investors. Gunesekera works through a van-driver and his different passengers. This strategy enables him to travel to different parts of their island and study the foreigners' response, take the reader through the breadth and length of the country and its war-torn areas, bombarded buildings and Tiger strongholds – all of them. The war as Ondaatje had put it, is a triangular one and Gunesekera, in taking an account of the price the country has paid also works in the losses in terms of culture, monuments and emotional loss. *Noontide Toll* is the toll that has to be paid at this moment of putting things together – 'noontide', with the dawn having been obscured by the cloud of violence.

Divided into two main parts, north and south, it reflects the geographical division along political lines. Space, as David Harvey has observed, expresses not only political divisions and social relationships but also reacts back on them.[13] Edward Soja refers to space in a different context, but the dialectic between space and social psychologies is in particular relevant to the demarcated social spaces caused by violence and caste or colour discrimination. Even political enmity, maps and boundaries play a similar role in power politics as in the Empire and its colonies, borders of conflict and underground movements.[14] The very fact that houses can be shared, as in Munaweera's novel, by those whom politics is going to cast in oppositional roles or the fact that the soil on Sailor's body

(*Anil's Ghost*) is different from the soil of the place where his body is found, all provide abundant proof of the intricacies of space formations. When Romesh Gunesekera works with a concept of fluid space – as each trip is a separate one – and enclosed territories that mark the movement of history with its buildings and monuments, he works with a retrospective vision. The house in the woods which has escaped bombardment because of the heavy forest growth around it holds a history of time, of families and their lineage. This works through a space-time continuum as two streams of time, one of the travel, the other of history, interact with each other. The journey is located in a short duration of time, history is spread over a much longer period encompassing past, present and a possible future. Soja distinguishes between contextually given space and socially based spatiality (79). But this aspect is in adherence to Marxist definitions of class and economic production. A terrorist or militant hideout is clearly a demarcated space as much as any other concentration of population, and is a constant challenge to peace and equality.

Of the modern theorists, Foucault's concern with space is far-reaching as is Bakhtin's. Foucault in his essays, 'Of Other Spaces' and 'The Eye of Power'[15], works with these complex relationships and comments on his own position in an interview with the editors of the *Herodote*.[16] Foucault acknowledges his dependence on several disciplines and points out that no historical work 'that has political meaning, utility and effectiveness,' can be done without an involvement with the struggles taking place in the area in question (64). Foucault goes ahead and relates his own obsession with space to a study of power: 'Once knowledge can be analysed in terms of region, domain, implantation, displacement, transposition, one is able to capture the process by which knowledge functions as a form of power and disseminates the effects of power' (69). In 'The Eye of Power', Foucault takes an example from medical methods of diagnosis. They take account of local conditions, co-existences, residences and their environment and displacement ('The Eye of Power' 150–151). Doctors, Foucault writes, were along with the military, 'the first managers of collective space' (151).

Space is of importance in all war novels, except that the location of perspective is different in each case. Gunesekera's strategy is the driver's perspective, a person always on the move, engaged in travelling from one place to another and often coming back and forth on the same route. The opening sentence is, 'Every time I drive across the causeway to Jaffna, I feel I am entering another country' (1). One feels compelled to ask, why? Is it that the land has been out of bounds for long, or that the changes are occurring too rapidly or is it that his co-passengers provide a new perspective? We look to others in order to assess that we have become. They act as mirror reflections.

There are other stray references capturing the past, the multiplicity of hospitals, one could say 'that we have all been a little damaged by the last few decades' (3). It is a wounded country, 'buildings are relined, moats run dry, trees have been chopped, even the grass has been beaten to the dust' by the marching soldiers of the two confronting armies (15). Roads too are ruined. And restrictions of movement still prevail. War, as Adorno expressed it, damages the fibre of human life. He referred to his generation as a damaged generation. But internal strife is worse. It raises ecological problems of both the natural and the emotional world. The Empire still lingers on in the remnants of ruined colonial forts. History is thus recorded and often reconstructed. But the people know it is not the original. In between these trips, the narrator recollects his own experiences and recalls his father who had diagnosed the main trouble with this country as religion, 'It puts demons in their heads'. And he, a man of little learning, had realised the past is unforgiving (19). And yet people are born in these times of trouble, to be handed over to an uncertain future. The ways of man are contradictory, we love but do not worry about the consequences.

The passengers are always of a different category: foreigners, tourists, former colonials, men of religion. Once on his way to Jaffna, he wonders whether monuments celebrating victory are a healthy reminder for a country coming out of a civil war, do they remind one of loss or only of humiliation? Our histories are also flawed. There is no place for emotions in history. This journey is to an army camp in Jaffna, perfectly rehabilitated with every sign of comfort, with an orchard surrounding the camp. In the new humanitarian effort they are now required to make peace, not war, and help in restoring the health of the mind. But don't they err? His passengers, a man named Patrick and a priest are investigating a case where a woman was beaten and left to die, and the suspect is the Major whom they have come to meet. But the first shocks wear off and nobody bothers any more, you don't look twice and don't measure the loss of life or limbs. Almost a static situation continues. Despite the losses, hatred and animosity continue to persist. Normalcy in the aftermath is still a faraway dream though there appears to be a feverish intervention of capitalistic interests.

The travellers' eye provides an overview. It may not be very sympathetic but it is perhaps keener in its comparisons with the outside world than the natives. Those who have always lived here are bound to place the present in both historical and personal memories. It is interesting to see the difference from these two points of view as compared to the diasporic returnee. The person who has lived abroad makes an arc – the past, the time abroad and the return – and places the experience abroad between the two ends, past and return. A serious and a heart-rending question is: can the past ever come back, can it be restored and can the losses be evaluated dispassionately? Restoration does not involve only buildings and monuments, it requires men and emotions, feelings, the act of living together, relating to the environment and ecological shifts.

Fairly early in the novel a doctor from England comes home to visit his country and the house in which he had lived. Dr Ponnampalam comes home after the war along with his young son to visit his childhood home. The house was enormous, 'It rose like a giant beast through the tangle of overgrown ferns and bushes and trees' (58). This visit has materialised after several interruptions, his wife's illness and then the war and now when they come it has become a guest house. As they go over the house from room to room, Vasantha, the van driver, is cautious and tests every wooden step, a lesson that the war had taught him but the doctor slipped into a reverie as if he was now receiving his childhood memories (68). The present owner has also come back from Canada with the idea of doing some rehabilitation work. Lost in the past, the doctor is unable to locate himself in this new geography, 'he was clutching at fragments in the slow motion explosion that had been his life'

(73). His son wants to come back and stay in the house but the father feels there is no possibility of recovering lost ground. Far too much water has flown over the bridge. And several of them have literally collapsed. 'Thirty years of war, sixty-five years of independence, three hundred years of colonialism, two thousand five hundred years of Buddhism ...' (80). Finally, which one of these remains?

The south is no different. The country is fast trying to catch up with the world and its entrepreneur skills. Instructors come fully laden with full equipment remodelling both themselves as saleable images as well as the country. Mr Weerokon is one such, jiggling and bouncing and lecturing. In this crazy mess, one actor is also the Indian Peace Keeping Force. Vasantha's frequent trips bring him a varied experience as the range of his clients includes capitalists, tourists, returning diaspori as, army men, and religious and political men from different nations representing different ideologies, Vasantha realises that there can be no clear cut division between the mistakes of the past and the promise of the future, 'To go from one to the other, you need a road. And a road is nothing if it doesn't connect' (207). The actual war may be over but all is not yet right with the world as many little wars have yet to be fought.

The multiple perspectives of Gunesekera create several different roads for the reader, some through ruins, some through the woods and some through water, each of which is a mysterious power in itself. The 'noontide' of the title has an association with solar tides. Sri Lanka is surrounded by water and it is the strength of this water which has imparted it a separate identity, separated from the land mass of India. The war also had risen to a spiralling high point, which by its destructive strength pushed the politicians and people to finally arrive at some solution no matter how fragile the peace. Vasantha's journey north and south, with the variety of observers contributing their views, becomes an assessment alike of the price the war has extracted and the modernity descending on it.

In contrast to *Noontide Toll*, Shyam Selvadurai chooses a storytelling approach linked together by a personal family narrative in which he uses his own real life double inheritance as a powerful symbol of both the family and the nation's conflict. His preceding works have already defined some of the intervening forces – one the class background in *Cinnamon Gardens* and the other homosexuality which is acknowledged in *Funny Boy* and *Cinnamon Gardens*. Selvadurai's novels so far have always carried a fair amount of autobiographical element and *The Hungry Ghosts*[17] also traces the earlier riot situations 1965, 1983, and the others in-between. It was the 1983 riots that finally decided their emigration.

Two beliefs, one in the theory of karma, of destiny connected with one's past acts, a belief which Shivan's grandmother emphatically believes in and blames all ill-luck to someone's karma, ruling out all social and political factors of oppression, correction or of responsibility. And the second is the myth of the *peréthayas* – the hungry ghosts – who are driven to a certain restlessness on account of their ambitions. But later Buddhism and Boddhisatva, the essential Sinhalese belief, come in forcefully in Shivan's mother turning to it. It is this belief which transforms the mother-daughter relationship from strife to tolerance and forgiveness. The last is important even for the thirty years' war which has brought about a certain bitterness.

While Romesh Gunesekera works with a narrative strategy which branches out in multiple directions from one centre, like the rays of the sun, Shyam Selvadurai works with a to-and-fro time flow interwoven with storytelling as in the traditional epic narratives and religious texts. There is a story to illustrate every human experience or to elucidate on the sources of these stories, which again are several: Shivan's grandmother, at times his mother Hema and the stories from Bodhisattvas. They connect with each other as they run through the narrative as the main strand and tie together the various locations and times. Beginning at the end, he takes us back to an earlier visit home to Sri Lanka when his grandmother had suffered her first stroke. He goes home for a short visit but stays on at her persuasion. By this gesture he is also freed of the debt he has incurred and his grandmother offers to repay his loan. This material foundation of the family relationship is another running theme, right from his childhood when he is introduced to his grandmother's numerous properties.

His stay in Sri Lanka, his involvement with the Human Rights Group and the young worker Mili also has an autobiographical input. His work *Write to Reconcile* has come out of his engagement with this.[18] But in the novel, the experience at Kantha is centred on his relationship with Mili, a Sinhalese boy and his intense relationship with him, which because of the Tamil-Sinhalese conflict and the surveillance activities mounted also by his grandmother result in Mili's murder, camouflaged as drowning. This is to mark his relationship with his family and himself, forever. Unable to forgive either himself or his grandmother, he returns to Vancouver, estranged and unhappy, frozen, withdrawn and isolated.

A partial restoration takes place through his relationship with Michael and the resurfacing of Buddhist discourses in his life. The sustenance has to come from love and forgiveness and not hate. His grandmother's successive strokes, Hema's visit home to her mother, her acquiring finally the power of attorney and adopting more generous policies towards the tenants, release Shivan from being the family's pawn in the relationship between mother and daughter. Each life has had its bitter struggle, its tragedy; his grandmother had an unhappy marriage and found compensation in money and building up an empire, his mother sought freedom from her own mother's possessive grasp and married a Tamil Christian. Later, when she returns to her mother's place she is a widow and with two children, and limited resources. There is no communication between mother and daughter.

There is an early reference to the story of the *peréthayas*, the hungry ghost whose hunger can never be satisfied, awaiting release. A dream, a story, a myth all come together in this. It calls for a relay action, a connectivity of performing good deeds and passing on the credit to those who are in pain, those whose sins are not yet forgiven. The '*peréthayas* that appear to us are always our ancestors, and it is our duty to free them with from their suffering by feeding the Buddhist monks and transferring the merit of that deed to our dead relatives' (25). These stories are supplemented by his grandmother and form a recurring narrative thrust as are dreams about longing and dissatisfaction. As one cannot go back to make amends, one can only go onwards, is the message that the story of King Nandaka gives us (25). The story of the *peréthaya* resurfaces every now and them, especially towards the end (77, 255, 335, 368) just as the mentions of the recurring riots 1965, 1977 and so on. It is the 1973 riots that lead to their emigration in the first place. Mili had once asked him 'what choice do most Tamils have?' And Shivan has responded, 'If we are abandoning Sri Lanka, it's because Sri Lanka abandoned us first' (75). Like their Sinhalese grandmother who rejects her daughter for her choice, not realising that she had pushed her into this escape.

Are they refugees or immigrants? The question of identity at all levels, personal, national and locational, is a multilayered one and includes sexual identity. The fact that homosexuality in Sri Lanka was a punishable offence, a rejection of Mili's sexuality is an added reason for his death. And both, Shivan's own homosexuality and the guilt he harbours for Mili's death push him to eternal exile. Our release from our bonds, like the *peréthayas*, has to be worked through other agencies, the merit of the deeds of others, faith, belief and trust and above all, forgiveness. Forgiveness is another refrain, like the 'rain soaking a parched land', an expression which Selvadurai uses for the dedication, which his grandmother uses for him, which is used by many more people and in different contexts – that is what Sri Lanka needs: forgiveness like rain to extinguish hatred, to release the *peréthaya*, to rebuild.

Sri Lankan diaspora has responded well to the call of the homeland and realised that no home can be abandoned, even if it rejects you. Connections have to be established no matter who you are and where you are:

NOTES & REFERENCES

1. Michael Ondaatje, *Anil's Ghost* (New York: Random House, 2000), 200.
2. *Ibid.*, 289.
3. Nayomi Munaweera, *Island of a Thousand Mirrors* (New Delhi: Hachette India, 2014), 29.
4. Romesh Gunesekera, *Noontide Toll* (New Delhi: Penguin, 2014), 71.
5. Ondaatje, 200.
6. See internet reference, 'Shyam Selvadurai: Both here and there'/National Post:arts.nationalpost.com 2013/04/12. Accessed 26 August 2014. internet reference.
7. Gabrial Garcia Marquez, *Chronicle of a Death Foretold*. Translated by Gregor Rabassa (London: Picador, 1983).

8. Ondaatje, *Anil's Ghost*, 27.
9. For details of the Inner Party's Manifesto see George Orwell, *Nineteen Eighty-Four*, 1949 (Harmondsworth: Penguin, 1962). 150–161, 162–173.
10. This novel has also been discussed in another of my papers, 'Terrorism at the feet of Buddha', included in *Crossing Borders: Post 1980 Subcontinental Writing in English*. Edited by Jasbir Jain (Jaipur: Rawat Publications, 2009) 23–37.
11. Nayomi Munaweera, *Island of a Thousand Mirrors* (New Delhi: Hachette India, 2013), 9.
12. Martin Heidegger, 'Building, Dwelling, Thinking', *Basic Writings*, Ed. David Farrell Krell (London: Routledge, 2011), 239–256.
13. Quoted by Edward Soja, *Postmodern Geographies: The Reassertion of Space in Social Theory* (Jaipur: Rawat Publications, 1997). 76–93, 76. David Harvey had discussed this with reference to Henri Lebevre's Marxist theory's emphasis on space.
14. Michael Foucault, 'Of Other Spaces', Translated Jay Mokowiec. *Diacritics* 16, 22–27.
15. See Michael Foucault, 'The Eye of Power', *Power/Knowledge: Selected Interviews and Other Writings 1972–1977*. Ed. Colin Gordon. Translated by Colin Gordon, Neo Marshall, Joseph Mepham, Kate Soper (New York: Pantheon Books, 1980), 146–165.
16. In *Power/Knowledge*, 63–77.
17. Shyam Selvadurai, *The Hungry Ghosts* (New Delhi: Penguin, 2013).
18. See Note 6.

13

Failed Hijrat?
Cultural Mourning, Refugees and *Muhajirs*

Yeh hijrat to nahin thi, buzdilli shayad hamari thi,
ki hum bistar pe ek hadi ka dancha chod aaye hain.
                    d   h
(This was not hijrat but perhaps our cowardice,
we left behind a skeleton on the bed, Mujahirnama 35)

The diaspora which comes into existence through force of circumstances is without a homeland. It does not know whether its origins still count or does it have to begin from this new land and permanently live with new histories between forgetting and remembering. The exodus or migration of the Muslims from other parts of India lying outside the demarcated area for Pakistan is an indication of this uprooting. This condition applies most to those affected by political partitions along geographical lines be it Korea, Vietnam, Germany, India or any other country. They face a peculiar situation not existent in the case of jahazi bhai or an exile such as Joseph Brodsky. Moving from known to the completely unknown is a traumatic experience but very different from the move from known to known with the division in the psyche and with the knowledge that one has to define a new national identity and think of another territory defined by international boundaries as homeland. What about the old homeland? A place where one has grown up and where one has roamed about in the neighbourhood and absorbed cultural traditions? Is culture vested in a religious framework? Then again, the physical space of the home its walls, its gardens, where do they surface in our memory? Qurratutain Hyder briefly migrated to Pakistan but returned to India as her roots were here.[1] Many families were divided as Attia Hosain has recalled in some of her works. People we know and who are our friends have their daughters married to people in Pakistan[2] and vice versa, forcing us to realise that communities exist beyond borders. The human relationships refuse to accept physical boundaries. This can happen elsewhere as well but the relationship between the two halves of a former whole is subtly very different from all other migrations and where the concept of homeland has at least a double application, at least for a couple of generations, if not more.

When permanent migration due to the formation of a new country takes place, it involves loyalty to a new flag and derecognition of a common past. The history of the past is placed within a new locational politics. And while Pakistan may recognise the Arabic origin and the history of the Mughal India, it does not necessarily work with Indian history before 1947. Its interests extend to the formation of the Muslim League and the Muslim heritage. The past is divided and truncated. But the individual psyche hoards its memories and refuses to derecognise the past in its entirety. Can the Indian migrations to Pakistan be termed as diaspora or not? This question has been raised earlier but not really answered. Perhaps we need to make a slight distinction between resident Muslims and those who migrated to the area. Pakistan itself does this by referring to these migrants as *muhajirs*, a word derived from Hijrat, the Prophet's exodus from Mecca to Medina and those who migrated to Medina were referred to as *muhajarins*. People with ties back home do have a homeland or at least a birthplace and a shared history, a common past, neighbourhoods, and memories. The diaspora can and does think of the homeland in varied ways – with love, regret or even disgust. And it also forgets and gradually lends itself to cultural transformations. Where then is home?

All over India, there are several refugee colonies, especially Tibetan, forming almost self-contained communities and preserving their cultural and religious traditions as they engage in rehabilitation work. There are other such as the refugees from Bangladesh but they find a familiar culture to anchor their identities in. Even the language is shared. Refugees from East Bengal and West Punjab similarly sought shelter in the existing identity known as India despite memory and economic dislocations. To live in a refugee colony, to work out new requirements for personal space and belong to a community is a slow process. But the fact of a 'cluster' enables a community formation, which homogeneity may be absent if migration patterns are linked to class, location or time. Manas Ray in the article 'Growing up a Refugee' in the Roy-Bhatia volume elaborates upon this.[3] The fact of having been a refugee leaves a scar on one's psyche which comes alive the moment discrimination or violence takes place as Gulzar in his film *Maachis* (later scripted in his book, *Two Tales of My Times*) also speaks about this.[4] The past always leaves its shadow on the present as memories are reawakened. In the Roy-Bhatia anthology in which Ray has an article, there is another article and this is on the *muhajirs* in Pakistan titled 'Eternal Exiles in the "Land of the Pure": Mohajirs in Mass Transit'[5] by Amber Fatima Riaz, this article explores the other side of migration. The difference between the two articles over and above location and nature of conflict, is that while Riaz focuses on fictional narratives, Ray focuses on personal history and political shifts.

The word *muhajir* is in common parlance and indicates an outsider status, one who is an immigrant and does not belong. The Muslim migrants to Pakistan from the territory that constituted India got to be known as *muhajirs*, especially the ones from UP and Bihar. But many others like Sadaat Hasan Manto also did not feel at home if their birthplace lay in India. Manto was born in East Punjab and identified himself with Bombay, Intizar Husain in a small town in UP and some of his fictional characters live in Bihar. At a deeper level if non-belonging defines the *muhajir*; estrangement comes wrapped in this non-belonging. When a community is snapped, when brother faces brother in the battlefield, or because part of the family has migrated and the ancestral house is declared evacuee property, estrangement possesses the individual psyche. Attia Hosain was in London when the Partition took place, she decided to stay in England and retain her British citizenship from the pre-independence period. She did not return to India because the family was divided by individual choices of new nationhoods.

Instead, her writing went underground as a silence descended on her.[6] Hosain writes in a piece published in *The Independent* in 1988, 'I felt I was not capable of writing, in full measure, about the sufferings of divided Muslim families' (Second Thoughts: Light in a Divided World', 219).[7]

But the consciousness of being an outsider is most forcefully brought out by Intizar Husain in his short stories, especially the 'Unwritten Epic', where Pichwa, divorced from his community, voluntarily follows his friends to Pakistan only to be humbled and rejected. There is no job for him, he is a mere outsider, a *muhajir* who cannot be accommodated amongst the citizens.[8] Pichwa's dilemma is shared by many another immigrant. Similarly Husain's 'A Letter from India' traces the family's routing and re-routing scattered in different countries, once the connection between homeland and nation has been snapped. They are wanderers abroad, unwanted claimants. In their homeland they are forced to visit the graves of their ancestors in the dead of night.[9]

It is in *Basti* that the desolation of the soul is intensely reflected in silence and darkness of the city. No one is at peace. People are either lost in prayer (as their only solace) or in nostalgia with hopes of a return. Or else they look towards political strife for a change in their situation. It is in *Basti* that Husain first moots the idea of hijrat and of eternal exile though he presents it through the narrative structure, fragmentary in time and space. He had earlier talked about it in some of his interviews (see Memon, Introduction to *Basti* xvii-xviii).[10] There is no return possible. Zakir the protagonist has a typical Shiite name (Memon xii) and is a teacher of history. There are many echoes in the novel from 'A Letter to India', (or the other way around depending on which was written earlier). The past is constantly present and constantly being talked about, place names like Rupnagas and Vyaspur are used. But the city is nameless, it is just a *Basti*, a settlement, and does not necessarily form a community. Instead they are like mice scurrying into dark corners. Umar Memon in his Introduction to Pritchett's translation of the novel, writes:

> Zakir, the historian, whose name means 'one who remembers', walks through his time and space with the graphic memory of Shiite suffering. The more the world around him

crumbles into chaos, the more he withdraws into himself in what appears to be almost a scramble for a very private kind of salvation through the Shiite principle of the interiorisation of suffering. (xiii)

As one reads the works of Intizar Husain, the realisation dawns on one that a large number of narratives are interwoven as themes work through connections. Many of his short stories such as 'City of Sorrow'[11] and 'A Letter from India' are lingering below the surface in his novel *Basti*. Shadows, fog, nameless people and faceless bodies in unidentifiable cities make a surrealistic mosaic – liftable from its location and applicable to almost all situations of violence, homelessness and dislocation. The human being is trapped.

The intellectual discontent surfaces in the writing of many a contemporary writer whether *muhajir* or not. Manto whose birth place was in East Punjab and whose real emotional ties were with Bombay felt restless and unhappy, and took to heavy drinking. He ran into debt and was subjected to humiliation. Recalling his life and reminiscing about him, Rahi recounts how he was underpaid for his work, 'In my opinion, Manto began to die the day he set foot in Pakistan' (708).[12]

Faiz Ahmed Faiz, though not a *muhajir* (his birthplace was Sialkot), was also a disappointed man at the time of Partition and his subsequent political involvements sent him to prison and later into exile. Kamila Shamsie's novel *Broken Verses* is a fictional account of Faiz's exile. His ghazal ' *yé dâgh dâgh ujala, yé shabgazidar sahar/intizar tha jis ka yé voh sahar tó nahin* ' (August 1947),[13] speaks volumes for his pain. This dawn is not the dawn we had longed for. Amongst the ones who did not migrate is Rahi Masoom Raza who, in his novel *Aadha Gaon* (*A Village Divided*)[14], expressed his anguish at the politics of the Partition. The Muslim psyche was deeply pained at the division in the community as a consequence of the Partition and the resultant feeling of estrangement. Munawar Rana, an Urdu poet and a post-Partition child, lives in India but his long poem *Muhajirnama* is a catalogue of the losses which the immigrant, the outsider, one who is not a son of the soil has to suffer. Estrangement can creep in, if not on the home soil, then when one visits Pakistan.

Rana gives an account of one such occasion when he went to Pakistan to participate in a *mushiara* (a poet's meet). Nervous and anxious as to how he would be received, he went on to voice the other side of the picture giving an account of all that was abandoned and had to be abandoned in this migration. One of his articles which is included in a prose collection and is also the introduction to the poem *Muhajirnama* titled, 'Hum khud udharne lagte hain turpei ki tarah', (we ourselves get undone like a seam come open) gives an account of his Pakistan visit.[15] He writes about how the post-Partition generation was even afraid of shedding tears (14). He imagines himself into the past is one with the migrants. Quoting another poet, Dr Naseemumujaffar, he refers to a couplet: *Tum ne ghar choda, chalo tum to muhajir ho gaye, hum yahan hazir rahe aur gair-hazir ho gaye.* (You left your home and became a *muhajir*, we stayed here but were rendered invisible). Rana comments on the concept of hijrat, the meaning of which has never been sufficiently explained or scrutinised. In Rana's view, it has never been treated as a partition or separation, and asks if going to Pakistan was hijrat then why are Punjabis and Sindhi who had to flee Pakistan, not called *muhajirs*? (15).[16]

Partition was also a loss of history. Where was Pakistan's history to begin from? Was it going to disown all territorial affiliation with India? How was it going to erase legends and stories shared by the two countries such as *Heer Ranjha* grounded in the soil of the country? There is a short story by Ahmed Salim 'Ishtaria', a proclaimed offender, a man who is wanted by the police and they have pasted posters to that effect all over the place. The wanted man is none other than Waris Shah, the author of one of the best known versions of the romance of Heer Ranja.[17] And when terms like 'banvaas' (exile) are used in poems, the reference is clearly to the *Ramayana* and the *Mahabharata*, and these mythological references form as much part of the Muslim psyche, as almost everyone in India. How can the fact of migration erase it?

Debro A. Castello, in an article 'Borders, Identities, Objects', refers to the act of migration as a transference which leaves much behind. Though Castello's reference is to Latino writing, some of the examples have meaning for the *muhajir*. Castello refers to a story by Gonzalez Viana 'El Libro de Porfirio' where the family brings with them their donkey loaded with their stuff, Viana comments in his story, 'The truth is we would all have liked to bring our donkey, house, public clock, bar and friends, but coming to this country is like dying and one can only bring what one has on, along with hopes and grief.'[18] Castello proceeds to comment on this fable and points out that the burden of the allegory is the heavy cost of immigration. Not only the material components of culture are laid amiss, even the psyche is fractured and the cracks are visible in day to day life, fears and anxieties. This is a special kind of mourning, 'what Ricardo Ainslie calls "cultural mourning", which involves working through the loss of loved individuals, but also familiar cultural forms' (Castello 117). Objects, myths and memories constantly encroach upon the new cultural spaces and mental images. Munawar Rana's understanding of estrangement encompasses both – the feeling of estrangement on his native soil as an Indian Muslim, a feeling pushed on to him by political ideologies around him. as also, the outsider's sense of loneliness. There are numerous references to Babri Masjid in his work. His prose writings also talk about the vulnerability and the loneliness he experiences, In his long poem, he points toward what the muhajir has left behind and sacrificed. In one couplet he writes, *yeh khudgarzi ka jazba aaj tak hum ko satata hai/ki hum bête to le aaye, bhatija chod aaye hai* (Our selfishness still haunts us, we brought our sons, but left behind our nephews). The reference goes beyond kin to friendship, and is a painful reminder of disrupted communities, divided families and memories. He recounts the innumerable undone tasks and the incomplete transference from one land to another. If it was to be a migration, they should have gone back to Arabia, the land of their ancestral past. There is a strong strain of cultural mourning in Rana's poetry and a feeling that while the *muhajirs* took with them what ever they considered valuable, they left behind Iqbal's poetry, the implied reference is to the lyric *'Sare jehan se accha Hindustan hamara'* (Our country, Hindustan, is the best in the world). The poet Mohammed Iqbal wrote this in the early years of the twentieth century. He also wrote another lyric *'yeh mera watan hai, yeh mera watan hai'*. But the Partition has attacked the idea of nationhood and the indivisibility of a shared cultural heritage. These have left behind deep scars, anguish and conflict.

A number of Muslim narratives turn back to history and to 1857, which is more an evidence of their participation in the 1857 war or Mutiny as the British referred to it, and their claims on nationhood and less of their defeat. Intizar Husain's work is suffused with an atmosphere of commonalty, of shared cultural space and festivals. The fact that at some point the paths began to diverge, is a long history of political shifts.[19] Referring to the presentation of Rupnagar as an idyll in *Basti*, Memon comments: 'The hypnotic idyll, which breaks upon the senses with its evocative beauty, underscores the beginnings of a faintly tragic note; the perception that the paradisiacal time and space of Rupnagar, seemingly impervious to change, have finally succumbed to the corrosive powers of time.' (Introduction, *Basti* ix). It was the Partition that turned Husain into a fiction writer (quoted by Memon xvi). In this interview with Memon, Husain expresses his personal feelings about Hindu-Muslim relationship, which he felt were heading towards more and more amalgamation. Seeped in the Sufi tradition, he could trace commonalities of vision despite different theories of creation. Religion, he felt, was not a sufficient bond for a nation (Memon xix).

Husain's early reading of *Arabian Nights* and a later more mature reading of the *Mahabharata* and the *Jataka Tales* is deeply interwoven into his writing, carrying on the process of bringing cultures together and also of exploring the mystery of human life. *Basti* is crowded with myths; the very beginning is an interconnective myth. Bhagatji tells his followers, 'So children, the earth rests on Sheshji's hood. Sheshji rests on the tortoise's back. When the tortoise moves, Sheshji quivers, the earth shakes, and an earthquake happens' (4). Partition is one such earthquake. The other cultural myth provides another version. The ocean expands and Mount Qaf is surrounded by a serpent and 'there is a cow with four thousand horns, and the distance between one horn and another is five hundred years' journey' And any movement part of the cow and the change of horns on which the earth rests can cause an earthquake (5–6). These conversations between Bhagatji and Abha Jan are from Husain's childhood.

The narrative of *Basti* is an interweaving of myth, memory and autobiography. The two lengthy interviews he gave – one to Umar Memon and the other to Alok Bhalla[20], reflect this beginning the novel with reference to Bhagatji, stories of creation and the causes of earthquakes, Husain moves on to monkeys and men, 'Leaping from roof to roof, the monkeys came. It seemed that they would all come down into the street but they only milled about the parapets, shrieking and screaming. Then suddenly they fell silent, as though some terror had gripped them. Then the walls began emptying'. The rest of the story continues with a description of an uninhabited forest on the edge of which stood the Black Temple, an empty temple as if for centuries no prayers had been said. In this unreal atmosphere of fear and terror, even the sight of another man strikes terror in one's heart (20–21).

Interlacing references from Hindu myths, Buddhist tales, lullabies, folk songs with Muslim history, Husain moves on to festivals – Janamashtami – and romances such as the love story of Laila–Majnu. The cultural past is so much with Zakir that Bi Amma tells him, 'Why were you born in our house? You should've been born in some Hindu's house' (31). As the young men, Zakir and his friends, discuss ideologies endlessly, they are also obsessed by the uncertain future. The question foremost in their mind is 'What's going to happen?' (36). Religions intermix in his mind:

> From the Black Temple to Karbala, from Karbala to the Fort, from the Fort to the Ravan Wood … . Everything was as before but perhaps he had changed his relationship with the Black Temple, with the big pipal tree, with the pipal's monkey, with the silent enclosures of Karbala, with the Ravan Wood, with the banyan tree standing in the midst of it, perhaps with Sabirah too. (45)

The coherence underlying the text requires more than one reading and travelling back and forth with the narrative, not merely to perceive the continuity but to make connections between the interiorisation of the past and the silence of the exterior. Sabirah, his childhood friend, though an absent character, constantly surfaces in his thoughts and at times in his conversations. She has remained in India, even when her family has moved away to Dhaka. And even when her mother decides to migrate, Sabirah stays on as an evidence of her belonging to India and signifies a past that Zakir has lost.

Time travels but the world doesn't change, there is always this cohabitation of fear, uncertainty, terror and cruelty. Dreams remain dreams, they never really come into their own. The political atmosphere prevailing in this unnamed city is held captive in the shifting laws in this process. It is the human being who is subjected to suffering. One of these horror stories is told to them by a man, that when he travelled to Pakistan, he was only in his early twenties and his hair was all black, but when he reached it, 'my hair was white and I was alone' (82). The violence, the abandonment of kin, the total dislocation – all connive to lead them to ask why does this happen – were Cain and Abel stepbrothers, were all the brothers amongst the Mughals, step, or was it some unrecognised emotion in them which led them to violence?

Despite the fact that Intizar Husain has often claimed that he is not interested in politics, *Basti* is a political book over and above the personal anguish. The dictatorial regime is a constant shadow and with the resistance by East Pakistan, the civil war transformed into a liberation struggle, violence, uncertainty, and loss stare them in the face. The presence of the past is always a part of them, there is no way they can move beyond it. The moment one leaves one's land, it no longer honours any claim by you and a feeling of being abandoned takes possession. The journey to the self is thus a troubled, lonely one of orphans. The cultural pasts surface in Husain's narrative strategies as a tribute to his cultural mourning. The connectivity from one story to another, the interwoven references surface in both the traditions. One is of the *Thousand and One Tales* and the other of the *Jataka Tales* and *Katha Saritsagar*. In his collection, *Shehrzaad Ke Naam*[21], Husain has two stories referring to Shehrzaad: 'Shehrzaad Ke Naam' and 'Shehrzaad Ki Maut' ('In the Name of Shehrzaad' and 'the Death of Shehrzaad') which are about storytelling and comment on the eternal storyteller, who retreats into silence when memories are lost. One needs reminders to reconnect with reality. Shehrzaad's storytelling mesmerised both the listener and the storyteller, muting the cruelty of one and the fear of the other. She narrated these stories as a survival strategy under threat of death. 'Shehryaad Ki Maut' also bring forth the need for the storyteller to become a listener (*Shehryaad Ke Naam* 32–33). Once the fear of death is removed, she has lost the power to tell stories. Does that mean that loneliness, fear and anguish form the creative ground for narration?

In, 'Shehrzaad Ke Naam', the opening sentence is 'These days my story is going through a crisis, The moment I sit down to write, something happens to disturb me' (136). The particular indication is towards events in India especially the demolition of Babri Masjid (though names are not mentioned). Other crises also mount up – atomic experiments, war exercises, hate campaigns. The storyteller can participate in none of them, has no power to stop them; all he can do is tell a story, a story which is history as well as response, a story which moves across time to man, and across time from a stream of past, present and future. A story underlined with allegorical meanings – Hatim Tai's adventures, the princess held captive in the castle, and the mystery of her laughter. A mystery dwells in every story, history is revised and the mask of the enemy is seemingly impenetrable, broken through (141–142). As he revives his need to write, he ends the story with an assertion, 'After all, I am not engaged in any *jihad*, I have to write stories as long as I can and the way I can, the night has not yet ended, the story too has to go on' (144, my translation from the Hindi version).

In 'A Chronicle of the Peacocks', Husain travels backwards from the Pokaran atomic test to the war in *Mahabharata* wrapping in the violent events of history with his own ecological concerns. Somewhere in the newspaper, two items had appeared together: India's atomic bomb underground test at Pokaran and the fear of 'the peacocks of Rajasthan as they had flown up screaming into the sky' (199).[22] His memory goes back to the time he had seen the peacocks in all their glory in Jaipur and his imagination tries to cope with the post-Pokaran scenario. And as he attempts to visualise, he has a vision 'of a lonely peacock on a distant hill. He seems battered and bruised ... before I can reach the hill, he rises into the sky screaming with terror and disappears' (200).

The Pakistan-Iraq war comes into his mind as well as the pollution caused by bomb explosions and the threat they hold for birds. Everyone is engaged in conflict, 'Saddam Hussain against his countrymen, the Iraqis against Kuwaits ...' (201). Story after story, myths, conversations held in the past, stories from the Old Testament and from the Sufi tradition, all come together, coherent in the manner they feed into each other. 'War transforms man utterly', and then follows the story of Ashwathama. Arjuna and

Ashwatthawa, both used the dreaded weapon Brahmastra but while Arjuma recalled it, Ashwatthama did not. Men out to destroy all life. And then his mind turns to Meerabai's samadhi and the dargah of Khwaja Moin-ud-din Chisti (205), two messengers of peace and goodwill. Good and evil constitute the eternal truth of human life and live side by side. Every culture, every religion has it but what is missing is the human recognition of this truth – a non-realisation which leads to separation, division and hijrat.

Several of his stories, expressive of a cultural past, adopt the Jataka stories form, deal with birds: mynahs, parrots and tortoise wrapping the narrative in myth and using Hindu characters. It is this ownership of the *muhajir* in this look back toward the cultural inheritance which marks Husain's work. Briefly, I turn to his story 'Tortoise'.[23] It features the Bodhisattva, and voices both the fears of mankind and the need to speak out. If total silence is thrust on one, it amounts to death. Husain also uses the Hindu philosophy of rebirth – a goat, a Brahmin in some past life is born a goat in this, while Bodhisattva, born a tree, is capable of assuming at once the form of the Buddha ('Tortoise' 64). The lesson of peace is advocated in different ways, violence begets violence, and evil encompasses everyone the moment we go looking for it or working up hatred against others. Several episodic stories follow one another. In 'The Story of the Parrot and the Mynah', a story which has travelled all the way to India from Iran and has taken root in the subconscious minds of the people, 'Tuti-Mynah ki Kahani', is normally narrated in households, has invariably a didactic purpose, and the birds are guardians of moral values. In Husain's narrative, the target is human inventiveness. The parrot and the mynah are perpetually arguing because, as one of the birds explains, they have always lived in cages built by men and not in the freedom of the forest, 'men have invented many things but the strangest of all inventions in the cage' (102).[24] The conversation between the birds is very revealing and loaded with meaning and the implication that intelligence does not necessarily lead to wisdom. Human beings do not have enough wisdom to realise that they are their own worst enemies, that the self destructive urge is inherent in them. In this story also the Kurukshetra war crops up where the battlefield was soaked with blood (108) as does a reference to Cain and Abel, where the dead body of a brother becomes Cain's burden (110). The theme of fratricide runs through Husain's work as a powerful symbol of Partition riots. Like violence, guilt is always with us as the nameless men in the 'City of Sorrow' realise only when they finally become faceless and nameless.

In going over the shared cultural pasts, and adopting narrative forms which act as constant reminders both of the past and the loss, Intizar Husain is holding to a culture that coheres his inner being. Loss is experienced through separation as in *Basti* when Zakir and Sabirah are separated, never to marry or meet again, separation comes as death of a beloved one and the consequent sense of bereavement, as also by the loss of familiar sites, cultural objects, landscapes, friends and communities. As Ricardo Larios has observed in an analysis of Mexican immigration to Oregon, psychological theorists have worked with this sense of loss – Freud, Engel, Abraham, Klein, Leowald and several others.[25] Larios explains this further by relating it to identity formation, which in early childhood teaches one to differentiate between 'me' and 'not-me'. It is the mourning for this loss which prevents utter disarrangement or disintegration, it holds one together, 'On leaving the homeland immigrants experience loss, not only of loved ones, but also of cultural objects practices, etc.' (Larios 83).

By working with the cultures that were woven into each other in the land of his birth, and which permanently inhabit his psyche, Husain externalises this loss through his narratives. While Rana works with the sense of guilt that possesses one, '*Muhajir keh ke duniya is liya humko ko stati lai//ki hum aate huye kabron mein shajra chod aaye hain*'/The world hurts us by referring to us as muhajirs, because while migrating we have left behind our genealogical roots (*Muhajirnama* 43). This has a resonance in *Basti* where the importance of graves is emphasised as well as in 'A Letter from India'. Rana further questions whether hijrat implies a break in centuries old relationships (44). And again:

Mujahir is liye kehlayenge
Hum rahti duniya tak
Kisi ka saath chuta hai,
Kisi ko chod aayen hai

(we shall be referred to as *mujahirs*/for the rest of our lives/for we have snapped ties/and left many behind).

There is not only this mourning and a sense of estrangement but a whole questioning of the Partition as a political act, an act which has neither led to peace nor freedom. Such is the human condition. The past lives in our minds, and memories cannot be erased. They can only be lived with.

NOTES & REFERENCES

1. Qurratulain Hyder, in her novel *Aag Ka Dariya* (1970), translated as *The River of Fire*, traces the history right from Buddha's time through to independence. He central characters retain the same names with some changed religious affiliations, a fact which goes on to show the inter-religious crossovers. The combination of water and fire in the title reflects upon their individual agencies of vitality, fluidity and fecundity of life. Archetypal symbols of merger and destruction they are also cleansing agents the last phase of the novel is located abroad where the students got together to discuss the future. The novel has heavy personal reflections.
2. There is sufficient evidence of this all around us. For instance Ajmer has a sizable Muslim population and many of them have their kin in Pakistan and vice versa. Visas and immigration patterns also reflect the same.
3. See Manas Ray, 'Growing up a refugee' in *Partitioned Lives: Narratives of Home, Displacement and Resettlement*. Eds. Anjali Gera Roy and Nandi Bhatia (Delhi: Pearson Longman, 2008), 116–145. Ray focuses on West Bengal and discusses the economic and political issues as well as community clusters and violence. Similarly, the TV serial *Buniyaad* based on Manohar Shyam Joshi's script (available in print) describes the rehabilitation process of West Punjab refugees over three generations.
4. Gulzar, *Maachis* in *Two Tales of My Time*. Translated by Devina Dutt (New Delhi: Rupa & Co., 2008), 87–191 110–111, 131–132.
5. Amber Fatima Riaz, 'Eternal Exiles in the "Land of the Pure": *Mohajirs* in Mass Transit', *Partitioned Lives*. Eds Anjali Gera Roy and Nandi Bhatia, 2008. 214–226. *Mass Transit* is the title of a novel by the Pakistani writer Maniza Naqvi (Karachi: OUP, 1998). The word *muhajir* phonetically should be spelt with a 'u', the Anglicised

spellings are mohajir. I am using *'muhajir'* in the rest of this essay but retain Riaz's spellings for reference to her article.

6. For further details see R.K. Kaul and Jasbir Jain, *Attia Hosain* (Jaipur: Rawat Publications, 2001), also Hosain's autobiographical novel *Sunlight on a Broken Column* (1961, New Delhi: Heinemann, 1979). Some of her short stories published just a year or so before her death are also very revealing.
7. Attia Hosain, 'Second Thoughts; Light in a Divided Worlds', Appendix in *Attia Hosain* by R.K. Kaul and Jasbir Jain. 218–219, 219.
8. Intizar Husain, 'An Unwritten Epic', Translated by Leslie Flemming and Muhammed Umar Memon in *Stories About the Partition of India*. Ed. Alok Bhalla (New Delhi. Harper Collins, 3 vols in single edition, 1994, 1999), 633–657. In this connection also refer Sudhir Chandra's essay 'Partition as Hijarat and as Slave Trade: Reading Husain's "An Unwritten Epic"', in *Reading Partition/Living Partition*. Ed. Jasbir Jain (Jaipur: Rawat Publications, 2009).72–86.
9. 'A Letter from India', Translated by Vishwamitter Adil and Alok Bhalla in *Stories About the Partition of India*. Ed. Alok Bhalla, 1999, 96–110.
10. Muhammed Umar Memon, Introduction, *Basti*. Translated by Frances W. Pritchett (New Delhi: Harper Collins, 1995, 2000). vii-xx. Memon's Introduction quotes from his interview with Husain, 'A Conversation between Intizar Husain and Muhammed Umar Memon'. Translated by Bruce R. Pray. *Journal of South Asian Literature*. 8, 2, 1983, 153–186.
11. 'The City of Sorrow', translated by Vishwamitter Adil and Alok Bhalla in *Stories About the Partition of India*. Ed. Alok Bhalla, 1999, 377–394.
12. 'Friends of Manto Reminisce About Him', Appendix 3 in *Bitter Fruit: The Very Best of Saadat Hasan Manto*. Edited and Translated by Khalid Hasan (New Delhi: Penguin, 2008), 704–708. This volume also contains several other memoirs. See Appendices, especially the one by his nephew, Hamid Jalal 'Uncle Manto', 679–700 and Manto's own, 'Manto on Manto' (671–674), a self-critical piece. In the essay 'To my Readers' (655–661), he speaks about the anger in his heart which has 'turned into sorrow. I am sad, very sad' (659).
13. Faiz Ahmed Faiz, The poem titled 'The Morning of Freedom, August 1947' in the English translation is titled in the Urdu original as 'Subeh Azadi: August 1947' Shiv Kumar's *The Best of Faiz* has the Urdu original (in Arabic script), the Roman version and the translation (New Delhi: UBSPD, 2001), 55–56.
14. Rahi Masoon Raza, *Aadha Gaon* (1966) English translation by Gillian Wright, *A Village Divided* (New Delhi: Penguin, 2006).

15. Munawar Rana, Introduction *'Hum Khud Udharne Lagte Hain Turpei Ki Tarah'* in *Mujahirnama* (Hindi, New Delhi: Vaani Prakashan, 2011, 2013), 9–29.
16. *Ibid.,* extract from the poem *'Muhajirnama'.*
17. Titled originality 'Ishtaria' (Urdu) translated as 'Proclaimed Offender' by Nirupama Dutt in *Stories From the Soil'* (New Delhi: Penguin, 2010), 249–251.
18. Qtd by Debro A., Castello in the article 'Borders, Identities, Object's in *Border Poetics De-Limited*. Eds Johan Schimanski and Stephen Wolfe (Hanover: Wehrhahn Verlag, 2007), internet pdf. accessed 25 August 2014.
19. Mushirul Hasan's collection of addresses, speeches and essays on the subject of divisive nationalism is very eye opening see Hasan edited volume *India's Partition: Process, Strategy and Mobilization* (New Delhi; OUP), 200.
20. See Interview with Alok Bhalla, 'Partition, Exile and Memories of a Lost Home'. Translated from Urdu by Alok Bhalla and Vishwamitter Adil in *A Chronicle of the Peacocks*. Ed. by Alok Bhalla (Delhi: OUP, 2004) 209–250.
21. Intizar Husain, *Shehzaad Ke Naam*. Translated by Khurshid Alam (New Delhi: Vaani Prakashan, 2008).
22. 'A Chronicle of the Peacocks', English translation of 'Morenama' in Intizar Husain's collection *A Chronicle of the Peacocks: Stories of Partition, Exile and Lost Memories* (New Delhi: OUP, 2004), 199–208. The Hindi version is available in the above mentioned collection *Shehrzaad Ke Naam*.
23. 'Tortoise' in *A Chronicle of the Peacocks, 2004. 59–78.*
24. 'The Story of the Parrot and the Mynah' *ibid.,* 101–111.
25. See Ricardo Larios's essay on cultural mourning, *Ay dolarya Me volvito a dar:* Loss and Cultural Mourning among Mexican Origin Immigrants to Oregon. 77–94 internet reference accessed 26 September 2014.

Note: In this paper I have, in the interest of consistency and accuracy, made several adjustments. Intezar is also spelt Intizar – I follow Intizar; *mujahir* is spelt as mohajir in anglicised versions, I have used *muhajir*, which is closer to the Urdu pronunciation; and also for the quotation of Faiz's ghazal, I have used Shiv K Kumar's version with diacritics whereas I have not used it elsewhere.

14

The Diaspora Zeroes in on the Borders

Increasingly, writers from Pakistan are writing about the porous borders between Pakistan and Afghanistan. Kamila Shamsie's latest novel *A God in Every Stone* works on the history of the town as it was in the 1930s moving constantly between the British Cantonment and the local people and embedding itself in past histories. But earlier in *Burnt Shadows*, Raza Konrad Ashraf is first attracted then trapped by the Afghan struggle. Fatima Bhutto locates her novel *The Shadow of the Crescent Moon* in Mir Ali, a border town and Nadeem Aslam in *The Blind Man's Garden* also concentrates on the same area. What does this border signify? Adventure, mystery, loss, danger, conflict or escape? Khaled Hosseni, a diasporic writer from Afghanistan in his first novel *The Kite Runner* not only uses Peshawar as an escape route but also details the arduous journey. In *A Thousand Splendid Suns* both the Afghan-Pakistan and the Afghan-Iran border zones are sketched out in detail. Miriam and Laila make a failed trip to the Afghan-Pakistan border.

The zeroing in on the border region is indicative of a larger political concern. As Nadeem Aslam has observed 'History is the third parent.'[1] History is also made up of the past and its stories are capable of sending tremors to the body. The North West Frontier Province, as the area was known in undivided India, had a reputation both for its brutality and its generosity. It neighbours Khyber Pass which has for generations been a trade route and an entry point for invaders. Tribal people and tribal culture are part of this region. It has a past history of Afghan control, the Sikh Empire and the British rule, even if one were not to move any farther back than the eighteenth century. As part of Pakistan, the Pashtun area has a history of separatist struggles. Mir Ali, the city where Fatima Bhutto sets her novel, is even closer to the border. One can well imagine the diverse population of this border territory. The Afghan war with its turbulent record of different enemies and ideologies – the Soviets, Muhujudeens, Americans and the Taliban – each placing the people under a state of near permanent curfew, and leading to want, deprivation and orphanhood also brought into the border zone, a large number of Afghan refugees. As such it is both a haven of refuge and a place of violence and has come to play a significant role in politics and the writing about the war zone.

Pakistani diaspora writes about India as part of memory as in the early sections of the *Burnt Shadows*[2], Dilli is remembered as it was in 1945. Lahore is the centre for Mohsin Hamid's *The Reluctant Fundamentalist*[3] and is the cultural response to 9/11. There are also some narratives of the dictatorships in Pakistan as in Shamsie's *Broken Verses*[4]. But the choice of the border as location is an evidence of both human and political concern, closely tied to the land. Or the diaspora moves further afield to the cities of Afghanistan as in Nadeem Aslam's *The Wasted Vigil*[5].

The war in Afghanistan has been an international war with major powers testing their strength and diplomacy on foreign territory and in the process, encroaching in innumerable ways on rights and independence. The border areas also house several intelligence services and the entanglement of young Raza is not merely with exploration and adventure but ends up as a serious involvement with the Taliban and the CIA. *Burnt Shadows* is a complex novel and covers several decades, many countries and violence in different manifestations. Beginning with the atomic explosions and its affects on the lives of people, it goes on to the Partition, and its many dislocations, and the political reasons for the individual's choice of nationality, the loss of agency and finally with all escape routes leading to death. Casualties govern the course of human life.

Burnt Shadows begins towards the end of the Second World War, when Hiroko and her fiancé are caught in the atomic blast in Japan and while Konrad dies, Hiroko escapes with severe burns but their two lives are intricately linked together for all times to come through memories of the time spent together and later through Hiroko's friendship with Konrad's half-sister. The explosion at Nagasaki left behind loss, scars and radiation. Lost and bereaved, Hiroko travels to Delhi, to Konrad's sister and her husband, a relationship which develops as a continuing strand right through to the end and across generations. The Burtons' hospitality, the meeting with Sajjad Ashraf, the learning of Urdu, Mussourie and Partition all happen in quick succession In between is a honeymoon trip to Istanbul and the return home brings exile from India. Being a Muslim, Ashraf who was not in India at the time of the division, cannot come back. Much against their will they move to Karachi.

Hiroko has kept nostalgia at bay, but now with her young son growing up, the past floods her mind. Ashraf and Hiroko had negotiated the rough edges in their marriage and learnt to understand each other but now Raza turns back on her accusing her of being too western, 'I can't ask any of my friends home ... with you walking around showing your legs. Why can't you be more Pakistani?' (130). The creeping fundamentalism is catching up with them and cultural roots are hardening. This is the early eighties. Hiroko's foreignness begins to invade her mind as she relates to her group through a consciousness brought to her by her own son. How does one survive in closed societies? Terms like Islamic and unIslamic are tossed about. And Raza, pulled emotionally in different directions, panics and fails his exam. His mind goes completely blank. It is at such a delicate point in their lives that Harry, the son of the Burtons, visits them.

Language is a strong bond. Harry had learnt Urdu from Ashraf and Raza is multilingual but language, even as it reaches across, does not necessarily lead to tolerance or an emotional binding. The border comes into their lives at a time when Raza is confused and pulled towards different directions, 'uncertain' of his place in his own country, unsure of his relationships and looked upon as a deformed product of the radiation in Nagasaki (189). The past has caught up with him in many ways. Any new identity seems attractive. He speaks Pashto and is mistaken to be an Afghan. When asked, he wonders why has the question arises when the Soviets have invaded Afghanistan, 'but in the last four years, as increasing number of refugees made their way into Pakistan, it had become something less than unusual for Raza to be identified as an Afghan from a Mongol tribe' (164). It is from this moment that he acquires a second identity, and calls himself Raza Hazara. At home, he is Raza Ashraf. And he strikes a passing friendship with a fourteen year Hazara boy Abdullah; another link, like the relationship with Harry, which is going to follow him all his life one representing Taliban and the dangers in Afghanistan, the other the CIA and access to intelligence. Not that Raza is conscious of either. His main interest in striking up an acquaintance with Abdullah is to buy a present for his father at a bargain price from the Afghans.

Raza is attracted to America on account of his own failures and the rejection by his girlfriend. Feeling lost and twice branded, 'you could be a bomb-marked mongrel or a failure but not both. Not for a second, both. And them he thought a single word America' (191) and that became his destination. From this point onwards, Raza sinks increasingly into the trouble zone, heading 'all the way north through Pakistan in a truck ... . And to Peshawar to the training camp' (211). Raza goes missing allowing himself to be sucked into the movement, into the rugged terrain, up the mountain. And the first causality is Sajjad, shot by a man he was approaching to inquire about Raza. This is Hiroko's second loss – first Konrad Weiss, who had stayed with her, then Ashraf who was her emotional strength.

Raza's return home is full of desolation, followed by another departure in search of other escapes, engagements and nationalities. Hiroko leaves Pakistan with neither Sajjad nor Raza to hold her back. In the end, Raza's attempt to help Abdullah, the boy who had betrayed him to the militants, lands him in the captivity of the Americans, this time betrayed by Kim, Harry's daughter. History repeats itself in mysterious ways. A gesture of loyalty ends up in betrayal. Hiroko begins 'to understand for the first time how nations can applaud when their governments drop a second nuclear bomb' (362).

This is border poetics being lived out on multiple borders – Pakistan and Afghanistan, the US and Canada, between loyalty and betrayal, the self and the other and between the past and the present. The surface crossings are never enough, they too are traps coiling around one, Raza's journey away from home kills his father but gives him no new life, his idealist faith in friendship with Abdullah comes to naught. Harry who comes to catch up with the past is himself trapped in the CIA connection and finally the white man's power becomes a source of reverse racial hatred. All kinds of communication fail as the simple gesture that Raza makes brand him an agent who was identifying Harry and thus a murderer. *Burnt Shadows* is a narrative of pain and anguish, of border crossings that lead to exile (Hiroko and Ashraf's marriage and honeymoon bring them to Pakistan), of the atomic blasts casting their dark, long shadows on the future. Raza, a child of a radiation-affected mother finds no relief, and his compulsive move towards atonement for other people's sins ends in captivity, loneliness, torture and likely death. The individual is minimised in this power game as the impersonal forces are for too strong.

Contrasted to Raza's journey towards his end, is Amir Agha's which is a journey of penance requiring him to muster up courage which he never had. He is pushed into it by Rahim Chacha and allows the opportunity to work towards a slow self-redemption. *The Kite Runner*[6] allows space for the individual to relate. Amir's journey would have ended differently if Hassan's son had not helped him, or later, if Soraya, had not worked patiently by his side. The underlying web is a collaborative one, once again placing the individual within relationships. While the earlier part of the novel is almost linear in its narration as the two boys are enveloped in a relationship of power and submission, of love and hatred, it is Rahim Khan's letter that forces a crisis of conscience, goes back in time to unravel the complexity of relationships, makes Amir see his father differently and relate to Hassan in a bond of blood. This coming together of the past and future comes together in Peshawar. It is here that the real tragedy of feudal lives and of violence is placed in full glare, with all its strengths. Rahim Khan's loyalty and compassion are two strong forces which enable Amir to look within and move beyond mere surface happenings. The hospital, Sohrab's attempted suicide, his fear of being abandoned, the American immigration laws – all come together in an intense emotional play, revealing Peshawar as a city of both hospitality and danger, as a place of refuge and of hope.

The insecurity and impermanence which marks the lives of border dwellers is worked out in all its political moral and personal implications in Fatima Bhutto's *The Shadow of the Crescent Moon*.[7] Moving further towards the edge, the narrative is located in a town called Mir Ali. It is Eid and Eid prayers have an added significance in a Muslim's life but in:

> Mir Ali, where religion crept into the town's rocky terrain like the wild flowers that grew quietly where no grass ought to have grown, you chose your mosque carefully. Fridays were no longer about the supplicants; they were about the message delivered for them by faithful translators of the world's clearest religion. In Mir Ali you were spoilt for choice. (2)

The peaceful forms of prayer for peace and harmony are being fast replaced by politicised messages of hatred and division, of violence and orthodoxy. No one is safe and no one is an individual, they are other Talibanis or not Talibanis. As every day begins with narratives of loss and condolence gatherings, a common mourning and fear has descended on households. Histories of past wars are unfolded as many a generation is sacrificed to violence. Inayat, the father of the three boys, had fought in the war in 1950 in the first battle for Mir Ali, against the armies of Pakistan. The next two decades were spent by the resisting forces in 'hiding, torture camps and unknown and unmarked cells across the country' (17). There was nothing left to bequeath his sons except memories of a lost struggle for soon the state stepped in with all its might for acquisition and possession. People attempt to escape to Afghanistan, some succeed and some get caught and killed. Mir Ali remained an isolated place held by a hostile governance in its own land and cornered off from the rest of the world. Most Pakistanis thought of Mir Ali with the same hostility they reserved for India or Bangladesh, 'insiders, traitors who fought their way out of the body and somehow made it on their own without the glory of the crescent moon and star shining overhead' (19).

Against this history of being broken and held, the people have an urge to escape to a wider world, especially Inayat's eldest son

Aman Erum, who wants to travel to England, America or Canada, to free markets and the world of capitalism, to cross the frontiers of this border location, a country by itself within a country. Decade after decade the strife had continued for more than half a century with the people and the state in direct confrontation. Is this the fate of all unresolved identity situations in border areas? The state was fighting its own: 'Town by town, civil wars were lit by the wide-scale violence of the army a violence that finally reached its zenith on the war on Terror' (22). Thus in this war-torn area, the three brothers move in different directions – Aman seeking his future on other shores no matter what the cost in terms of love and betrayal; Sikander, a medical man, a bereaved father, handling a grieving wife who is now hysterical and uncontrollable while the youngest, Hayat is the only one left to remember his father's narratives of the past and care for the cast-off love of Aman, the tribal girl Samarra.

The narrative flows along three or more time frames: the clock time on this Eid day when the past and the present meet and when histories of men, politics and families are unfolded, the temporal time of happenings which travel to this point and the personal time of this point and the personal time of memories. Time travels through space – Mir Ali, the tribal hills, the border, the escape routes and other lands. Beginning at 9.00 on Eid day, the narrative has eight sections – 9:00, 9:25, 9:53, 10:12, 10:27, 10:45 and then 11:39 and noon – a tale of three hours but the histories covered range over lifetimes, from one generation to another. Student uprisings, the abductions and torture mark the incidents which lead to processions, demonstrations and further resistance; 'Mir Ali never did transcend its enemies' (132).

Rebels and refugees reinforce each other's forces, men who have abandoned homes and do not fear either death or men. All their belief is vested in religion – the *sunna*. They crowd in on inhabitants with their violence and fundamentalism. Mina and Sikander are stopped by the Taliban on the way to a woman who is undergoing a difficult birth. In almost a surrealistic manner, the hysterical Mina shoos off the Talibs and goes on encircling them as if to keep them within that circle, to block all their escape routes. The Talibs, desperate in their frenzy, had bombed the hospital not caring for men or life. Hayat is trapped by his own father's obsession with the past. Tired he 'wants to be done ... . He is tired of sacrificing and living among the ghosts of history' (218–219), while Aman is the only one to go ahead sweeping aside all barriers including those of love and life. He sacrifices Samarra to his own ambitions, handing her to the enemy (228). Fatima Bhutto has written her homeland in dark ink, violence and death around every corner, with the future blocked and all escape routes closed. A frightening scene when year after year violence continues, religions discover new orthodoxies and all distinctions between law and lawlessness collapse. In this narrative of darkness, border poetics is expanded to work not only with individual lives but also the spatial shifts, the land lives the turmoil.

The Blind Man's Garden is another narrative lived on the border and border crossings. Nadeem Aslam builds the novel around the theme of violence. The four sections have section headings which work like puzzles each asking questions, the first is 'Footnotes to Defeat' foregrounding defeat and the need to explain its origins. It creates a future without hope and sets the tone for further losses. The end is forecast. The second is a repeat of the book's title, 'The Blind Man's Garden' and right in the beginning prioritises the sense of hearing over that of sight, shutting out colour but rendering the blind man sensitive to touch and sound. The third of these is 'Equal Sons' leaving it for the reader to work out the nature of equality and the fourth harks back to Isaiah from the Old Testament, who became a prophet under very critical circumstances, when his country's future was bleak. One thing that strikes one is Isaiah's criticism of foreign alliances. Is Nadeem Aslam hinting at this when selecting it as a section heading?

The main narrative begins with stories and the first of these is the bird catcher's who sets snares to capture birds and sets them free only when others pay for them to be set free. He is also the bird pardoner. A strange tale where suffering is the price for freedom, where ensnarer and freer are the same person and the one who buys the freedom for the birds gets pardoned for his sins. One could think the story ends here but it does not. It travels through the novel to resurface at a later point reminding one of the limits of human intention and will. The bird pardoner is suddenly caught up in his own problems and unable to keep his date with the promise of freedom. Does he add to the weight of his own sins? The bird pardoners's tale sets the tone of the novel weighing between sin and redemption, the attributions of justice, the punishments to be borne, all in a world gone awry. The bird catcher's snare is akin to the violence which surrounds one. The snares are a network of thin steel wires hidden deep inside the canopies, knots that will come alive to hold the birds in captivity. Rohan is unable to accept his explanation for the act and wondered wouldn't it call down retribution on the one who trapped and imprisoned it? (7). Are sinners not going to be punished?

Father and son, Rohan and Jeo, teller and listener of stories let fear and terror hang between them. Jeo is now twenty and they are to take an overnight train to Peshawar, the centre of armed action. Jeo's friend Mikal also plans to travel in the same train unbeknown to Rohan. Jeo's wife Naheed is left behind as her husband (Jeo) and her lover (Mikal) proceed to Peshawar, opening out the emotional aspects of the conflict. Naheed in order to be true to her husband requests Mikal not to visit their house as she must learn to love Jeo (21). Mikal, similarly is torn between his loyalty to Jeo, who is like a brother to him, and the love in his heart. But now past loves have to be buried. The journey to Peshawar is being undertaken because of Jeo's plan to spend a month working with the patients. The US has invaded Afghanistan, disguising its intentions under the assumed logic that 'there are no innocent people in a guilty nation' (6). And as refugees and the injured are brought to Peshawar, all help is welcome. But Jeo and Mikal have something else in mind, this is only their cover plan to allow them to find their way to Afghanistan. They are fully prepared and have been studying maps to mark the route.

It is strange that idealism and patriotism even as they generate courage and creativity also generate hatred and violence. And the latter holds its own fears and fascination. Not content with being in Peshawar, which itself is full of danger and violence, where even the hospital buildings are not safe, parts of the city are an inferno, they find their way to Afghanistan where the Taliban is in power, ruling with a strong religious orthodoxy:

> Every ounce of rage – every rape, every disappearance, every public execution, every hand amputated during the past seven

years of Taliban regime, every twelve year old boy pressed into battle by them … . It was as everything had been eaten. (47)

Religious taboos have an inclination to prosper amidst fear and violence and restrictions are imposed on movement, especially where women are concerned. Unaccompanied by men or unveiled, they are condemned. Even visits to the graveyard are forbidden, ancient practices are suddenly terminated (92). While histories of hatred survive, memories are erased.

Meanwhile the two boys cross over to Afghanistan and suddenly find themselves to be the victims of an altogether different kind of hostility. They are under suspicion, believed to be CIA spies. The maps in Jeo's bag further add to this suspicion. Once trapped, like Raza (*Burnt Shadows*), they find there is no getting away. And in their struggle to get away, distrust creeps into their relationship, childhood friendships are put to test. Betrayals abound, they are abandoned in the wilderness by a van driver who has given them a lift. They are further horrified by the body of a dead man, killed in the name of Allah and Taliban. The two boys even as they seek shelter in a cave feel a moral compulsion to go back and bury the dead man, and this pious act makes them prisoners once again. They are now right in the midst of battle, something they had not bargained for. Vulnerable in all respects, there is no future for them, except imprisonment or death. Jeo is the first victim and his body brought back to the house to bring this violence to the father's house.

Where does Naheed belong, now that she is a widow? Which house, which family? She discovers she is pregnant and her mother wants her to abort the child so that a second marriage is possible; if she does not she will always remain a widow. In both cases the dice is fully loaded against women. Naheed's mother had once been assaulted but when she went to the police, they demanded proof and witnesses. Failing to produce both, she was jailed for adultery. A woman's body is not meant for her children or for freedom or even for the future. She is held prisoner by male priorities and the compulsion to ignore her own wishes and desires in order to survive. Having learnt a bitter lesson, Tara determined not to let her daughter suffer the same way has made up her mind that there is no place for Jeo's child in Naheed's future.

As life and death meet both in the battlefield and in Naheed's womb, the bird snarer/pardoner makes an appearance. His personal mission of offering people redemption had gone awry because his fourteen-year-old son had run away to fight in Afghanistan. He had to leave for Peshawar (116). And since then he has been travelling and making inquires in order to find him who, he discovers, is held a prisoner in Afghanistan. This has been the turn of event from October to end-December. The infighting, the innumerable groups involved in fighting with the Taliban and the Americans against each other, it is no longer possible to distinguish between friend and enemy or to assess who is a collaborator and who a traitor. Rohan, the bereaved father, decides to accompany the bird pardoner and later offers his ruby as payment for the ransom for the bird catcher's son. Imprisonment forms a strong strand in the narrative as people are imprisoned: the Taliban, warlords, their own circumstances, societal customs, unequal gender relations, fundamentalism and blindness. Rohan's eyes are bandaged due to injury and he gropes to find a substitute means of experiencing colour. His vision can be restored but the treatment is too long-drawn-out, besides being costly. The ruby, the only possession he could have encashed, has been given away as payment for the ransom. But the doctor suggests that he sell some building. In the process Rohan discovers that he has known the doctor who was once one of his students but had expelled him because his mother was a prostitute (167–168); the long arm of Islamic justice comes full circle.

Wars kill, religion bounds and suspicions becomes one's second nature. Who can one trust, when one's own power to resist torture has its limits? Mikal is in prison. He does not even know whether Jeo is dead. The Americans who hold him now want to break him (191–193), and the American terror is as bad as Taliban's. It is feared that they will invade Iraq and Iran and if Pakistan disobeys, take over Pakistan as well. Rohan's house, of which he was not willing to sell even a part to get the treatment for his eyes, is requisitioned. War has no mercy, no compassion, and no concessions. As journeys of adventure, of escape and of destruction are described, the geography of the area is laid open in great detail Peshawar, Afghanistan border, Waziristan, and histories of defeat, of failed mutinies, of lost battles haunt the people's memories. War is omnipresent. The world, no matter where, has perhaps always been like that. Ruthlessness, being cruel and teaching others to be merciless is the new code of war, religion and education as well. Amidst this the tender sapling of human feeling survives in men such as Rohan (though he has his own rigid moral values) and in Father Mede. Rohan's garden is constantly a character by itself. It is a meeting place, a place for walks, for being close to nature and also serves as a burial ground (for the dead birds who perished in the snare). One day Mikal walks into the garden and along with him enters another past of conspiracies, camouflage, revenge and of lies and Mikal, once again, finds himself a co-prisoner of an American. There is no logical way to get out of it. Moments of escape, of freedom and of reunion are brief.

The sections successively go on getting smaller. The fourth is the briefest. It begins with an epigraph from the Book of Isaiah. And in this, as in the earlier ones, the garden is a recurring presence, Rohan nursing the flowers, Naheed taking over his duties, tending to the plants, the plants multiplying on their own, refusing to perish or be denied life. Finally, the house becomes one with children and a domestic scene in the kitchen. Have happier times finally found their way to them in the blind man's garden?

Naheed has made a rope-guide for Rohan to enable him to walk in the garden, by tying cords from place to place, connecting them to make a rope-walk substituting Rohan's eyes as well Naheed's hands. The garden is with them as it always was. Rohan used to tell Jeo and Mikal that before the knowledge of botany, *'Flowers in their infinite variety and lack of human order were said to be proof of God's existence'* (372, italics in original). Now when much has been lost and there is a gentle lull to the act of violent living, Rohan,

> touches the germinating seeds with his fingertips and recites a verse from Koran. *It is God who splits the seed and the fruit stone. He brings forth the living from the dead and the dead from living ... .*
> (415)

The diaspora writes home with love and suffering and pain, recalling the political and the religious bonds that trap their future, recording human struggles for survival and carefully tending love and compassion. The border is important to them for it closes escape routes or camouflages terror as adventure; the borders exist for them even without physical visibility – felt but not seen the closing in of imperial powers on them; the frontier is of significance not only because of its territory and tribal histories but also as a place of refuge and hope. Amir Agha *(The Kite Runner)*, an Afghan finds hope and healing here. But the young men of Pakistan get caught in traps not of their own making as they seek adventure and explore spaces. These in-between spaces question conventional notions of identity and nation. But more than all else, borders test one's ability to survive, to remain human. Nevertheless it is an active destabliser where identities and nationalities are concerned; a permanent influence on family ties.

NOTES & REFERENCES

1. Nadeem Aslam, *The Blind Man's Garden* (New Delhi: Random House, 2013) 5.
2. Kamila Shamsie, *Burnt Shadows* (London: Bloomsbury, 2009)
3. Mohsin Hamid, *The Reluctant Fundamentalist* (New Delhi: Penguin, 2007). This has been made into a film by Mira Nair.
4. Shamsie, *Broken Verses* (London: Bloomsbury Publishing Pic, 2005. New Delhi: Penguin, 2005)
5. Nadeem Aslam, *The Wasted Vigil* (London: Faber and Faber, 2008).
6. Khaled Husseini, *The Kite Runner* (London: Bloomsbury, 2004).
7. Fatima Bhutto, *The Shadow of the Crescent Moon*. New Delhi: Penguin/Viking, 2013.

15

The Children of Jahazi Bhai
Histories, Cultures and (Dis)Continuities

The inheritors of an indentured ancestorship have now a double or a triple homeland - India, the new environs and the even newer hyphenated identities. Where do they belong and how do they relate to the past? Where does India come into their writing? They too write 'home' or 'homes', as it is never easy to break away from inheritance, or family environs and upbringing The reflection is there in names, rituals, festivals, the epics and the eternal dream of return. Dispersed over various different destinations - the Caribbean islands, Mauritius, Fiji, Africa, Malaysia, this 'coolie' population has infiltrated mainland cultures. Their sense of identity and presence is ordinarily related to the degree of political power and their educational levels. Despite a sizable presence in the Caribbean, Cheddi Jagan[1] was the only one who came into power, in Fiji and in Mauritius the histories have been different.[2] In post apartheid South Africa, Indians have fared better than the blacks. But in the process what they remember is a culture fragmented and sheltered in individual memories, and what they retain is a certain genetic inheritance. As Gurbhagat Singh observed in his essay, 'Expatriate Writing and the Problematic of Centre: Edward Said and Homi Bhabha', that 'expatriate writing is the work of the exile who has experienced unsettlement at the existential, political and metaphysical levels. With this experience, he/she has unsettled the philosophical and aesthetic systems'[3]. It is the loss of a centre and what remains is a mixed, selected and at times contradictory remnants of a cultural past. Thus it becomes important to explore the nature of their memory of the past, inherited through custom, language and hearsay narratives. Equally important is the manner of recollection and the contribution of this inheritance to their sense of identity. Where do they belong? Do they write home or homes, having by now grown roots elsewhere and, perhaps moved on to a third homeland? Does the uppermost layer of belonging erase or replace the past?

V.S. Naipaul is a major example. Between his *A House for Mr Biswas* and the volume *Letters Between a Father and Son*[4] lies the exile's narrative – a search for security which the house symbolises, along with status and independence, a breakaway from the more prosperous in-laws' family; the letters share the struggle, the hatred for the Trinidadian world (also reflecting a self-alienation), and the dreams of Sreeprasad so carefully nurtured during his economic and literary struggles, all the while dreaming of a place in the sun. Naipaul's journey to the third homeland and his acceptance of it (reflected in the *Enigma of Arrival*)[5] overlays all earlier homelands.

But the fourth generation writers reflect a different world. They are more grounded in trying to understand their double layered identity and family histories traced through birth and death records, building up an archival resource material. Frank Birbalsingh's contribution to consolidating the Caribbean identity needs to be recognised in its fullness. His two anthologies *Jahajibhai* (1988) and *Jahaji* (2000)[6] have focussed mostly on the younger writers who are discovering their own place and, in the process, questioning their ethnic identity as well as their Indian inheritance. Birbalsingh examines their uneven relationship to the society in which they have lived ever since birth. He works through their demographic distribution and the reasons for their marginalisation as well as the ideological pull towards radicalism, their compulsion to live with the word 'coolie'.[7] When the past is so powerful, there is every need to negotiate it. And for that there was also the need to move away from the imperial influence and the British writing that had formed part of their school syllabus and general reading. It is an interesting curve as the Queen's English is replaced by the reality of semi-literate populations, a pidgin form full of Indian language words which have gone through several transformations of meaning, pronunciation and spelling.

Sasenarine Persaud's 'Mai, Mai, Mai'[8] works through four generations – Nani, Ma, Ma's children and grandchildren Concerned mainly with women, it works both with woman-woman and man-woman relationships. Persaud also focuses on the male psyche - Papa, Shiv, the sons and the son-in-laws and then the grandson as they relate to the strong female lineage, women who reflect independence, strength and anger, the latter often self-destructive. Persaud's portrayal of Nani reflects a stereotype, the clichéd trope of mother/mother-in-law interfering with the marriage of her children either through presence or through gossip. But in this it captures a very Indian situation emanating from the joint family syndrome. It is a large family, Shiva is the youngest and also the most alienated from his father because of Nani's interference. It is only when his separated father is near death that Shiva discovers that a remark had been falsely attributed to him by Nani that Shiva was not his son, an accusation that affected the father-son relationship. Shiva, incidentally, is a spitting image of his father, and his resemblance itself refutes the supposition. Nani had never 'a good word for Pa, always bad mouthing him' (99), and thus causing Shiva to be perpetually angry with the world. A mere fourteen year boy he is the first to reach his sister Satya's home when there is a quarrel between Satya and her husband Baiju. Despite Satya's rebellion and Baiju's compliance that mother-in-law and mother should be kept out of their lives, the rupture does not heal. But Satya doesn't come home. She stays alone, 'she didn't want another man', but lived with her children. The narrator of the story, a younger sister recounting the past comments, 'It was like seeing Ma and Nani all over again. She went to the Brahma Kumaris and fell in love with their yoga and meditation. Nothing else was good enough for her, none of the old pujas, not even some of the foods' (100).

India is present in the family patterns, in the generational conflict, the poojas and meditation and also the Hindi movies. It is present in their language, in the sibling relationship. But Canada is also on the horizon, an attraction, an escape route, a different world. Home and the ancestral past are in-between situations. 'Mai, Mai, Mai', a narrative of barely ten pages brings to the reader the problems, irony and tears of a four-generation family caught between their 'karma' and their determination unsure of which is going to overtake the other.

'Swami Pankaj',[9] Rabindranath Maharaj's account of the attraction of the Indian version of spiritual peace, is a circuitous route to the self as Pankaj, the protagonist, sways between different worlds – India, West Indies, Canada. The initial labour that was exported from India, hailed from an agricultural background and was dominantly a rural population. In the new home too they were employed on the plantations and farm work presented a shared past. Pankaj too is a farmer and had always lived with the dream of following the sages to the hills of the Himalayas and while living with a dream, he had grown into independence, struggled to expand a small land holding first to five acres and then a hundred, winning for several years the farmer of the year award. Then he moved to Canada and became a taxi driver. But he was not happy. What does a man want: success, money, importance or peace? Finally he is on his way to India returning to the theme of internal goodness and good will. He has come to believe in 'smells', of what we as human beings impart to our environments through our thoughts, actions and desires. These are the source of illness or wellness. A human being is very much like a plant and may or may not grow when transplanted. Before leaving for India, he tells his friend that his dream has always stayed with him.

Madeline Coopsammy and Christine Singh turn to the issues of racism, discrimination and identity. The Caribbean identity is baffling with so many different cultural strands flowing into it. Who are they and where do they belong? Like Cyril Dabydeen in his story, 'Going to Guyana,' the dominating thought is 'Did I still look Asian'? (Dabydeen 120).[10] Amelia Joseph, the protagonist in 'The Insiders', is well-educated, has a good academic score and is now looking for a job. When she goes to meet a bank manager, doubts assail her mind:

> My handkerchief was twisted into a tight rope in my palm and my skirt tightened and I hurt when I sat down. Perhaps he'll insult me. With a population of more than ninety per cent of black people on the island, somehow banks like these had managed to keep the racial composition of their employees as pure as the crystal mountain streams.[11]

Only occasionally there were some Chinese, Indian or mulattoes employed, and the last also those with 'flattened and combed' hair. Being a non-white in the job market, was an obstacle impossible to surmount, no matter how hard you struggled to counteract it. The skin of your colour would remain the same. Getting a job was difficult, and one with a degree of status attached to it, even more difficult. At the end of the interview Amelia realises:

> Now it was brought home to me what I really was. *You're only a little coolie girl*, as Santa Marians would say. *You have a brown complexion and long straight black hair, and though you are proud of your ancestry, in this town you'd be better off if you had some white blood* in *your veins.* (68)

Christine Singh's 'The Job Interview'[12] narrates a similar experience except it doesn't lodge the guilt in Kris but in the system that engulfs him. Kris's mother speaks her West Indian mixed English, while Kris has picked up western social practices and speech. His full name Krishna is now westernised to become Kris. When he chooses football over cricket, his father scolds him for rejecting his heritage, leaving it unsaid whether cricket is Indian, West Indian or British heritage. And by his choice of playing football, is he trying to move outside his multilayered past as well as the colonial domination? All along he has resented being labelled West Indian and felt cornered when sent to a school that welcomed his countrymen. Somewhere in the past, food habits have got mixed, the Indian spicy food somewhat abandoned in the West Indies, is now being replaced by bean dishes, American hamburgers and French fries (165). Born in England, Kris is engaged in a perpetual struggle to shake off his parents' West Indian and their parents' Indian pasts, but it seems almost an insurmountable hurdle. The load is heavy and comes with a history and England does not live up to providing an equal opportunity to all – British, coloured or immigrants. Though the story begins on the day of the interview, moving backwards it captures the past of the cluttered inheritance. Their economic contribution is underplayed as is the exploitation inherent in the indenture system. Kris finds himself on the defensive where food preferences and colonial pasts are concerned. he starts keeping a diary, an account of the rebuffs he has encountered amongst his schoolmates, a pile which grows every day adding to his anger. Is he as Englishman, a West Indian or Indian? When his prospective employer asks him:

'Where are you from, son? It's not a difficult question.'

Kris slowly turned his eyes upon Mr Cowan's and spoke softly, furtively.

–'I really don't know'. (172)

One is bound to ask whether the problem of roots is peculiar only to the twice hyphenated or to all immigrants. Ronnie Govender thinks of himself as an African, while fully retaining the Indian cultural inheritance. Those who anchor themselves in another country have only two ends to negotiate, but those who move further abroad add additional baggage. Even black writers such as Caryl Phillips[13] are conscious of the discriminatory racial practices and in Christine Singh's 'The Job Interview', the problem emerges an all its complexity and multiplicity. Do they belong somewhere or are they permanent nomads?

Another question one needs to address is the dream-like nostalgic present heralding back to a past, which is remote and unreachable. Like Rabindranath Maharaj's 'Swami Pankaj' Shani Matoo's 'Sushila's Bhakti'[14] carries resonances of the cultural past. As Sushila unplugs the telephone and starts meditating, concentrating on her yoga practice, trying to relax, hold her breath and release it, the material concerns, the price of things, the approval and disapproval of others constantly encroaches on her meditation. Into this is introduced the Indian cosmetic 'mendhi' (mehndi)[15] foreign to the Trinidadian tradition. The material is pliant, has an unfamiliar fragrance and it colours your hands and this takes her back to Pandit Maharaj's pooja ceremony at her parents' home. She is insistent on her Brahmin identity and Indianness, the 'brown skin, the purest legacy left to Indians generations away from India'. Sushila is aware that roots are diluted, languages overlaid with others and 'religion held into only by this thin straps of festivals' (178). The ultimate question of belonging clearly points out that all civilisations have developed from emigration - the origins are veiled in the past, 'where the heck did the Indians in India come from? ... .

How far back need I go to feel properly rooted?' (178). And over and above India, back home is Trinidad, as images of Muslim and Hindu festivals come together in her memory. Between remembering and forgetting, it is the image of her grandmother that beckons her mind. As she mixed *mehndi* paste together and coloured her painting, she felt her self being excavated from a vaguely remembered past, memories which filled her with ecstasy and confidence.

Despite remembered pasts and lived presents, the transformations that creep upon one or one's children take one by surprise. Ramdath when he goes to receive his son Pooran at the railway station, when he comes home from his city college, has doubts whether the boy who has got off, is his son Pooran. Overwhelmed by the transformation in his appearance, Ramdath is further shocked when the boy tells him, 'Babooji... de teacher say we have to forget everything we learn at home, an learn only what he say.'[16] (3). But home learning has its uses. Ramdath had taught his son how to plant cane, the mother had taught her son to look after himself while the teacher's teaching will be about the world. The question of erasure or forgetting is not relevant. A person is made up of mixed pasts, learning and teaching as the teacher himself tells them in his science class 'your shoes, your clothing ... the food you eat ... . and even you, my dear fellows are made up of cells ... . There is no substance whose composition is not, contained in these elements' (4). So where is the question of erasure? His classmates laugh at his *roti* and spinach, and call them cardboard and grass. Mr Hopkins, their science teacher watches this encounter between two cultures and from then on pays special attention to Pooran but when the same Mr Hopkins puts a little puppy to sleep the ruthlessness of the act repels Pooran who now decides to go back to the fields with their nurturing life.

Hindu mythology and the stories from the past enter their lives through names and images. The name Ramkissoon immediately calls forth both the *Ramayana* and the *Mahabharata*. But Elahi Baksh points towards the peasant origins, by tracing the word kissoon to *kisan* – farmer-rather than the playful Hindu God Krishna.[17] Loud-mouthed, self-opinionated man called a propagandist, Ramkissoon is the typical *mohalla* man, seeking to thrust his presence on one and all. His home, outside the residential coolie quarters, immediately announces his separateness. Ramkissoon's cottage recalls Mr Biswas's house and points toward the protected security and independence which Naipaul's Biswas and Shiva's rooting in the family (Persaud), and land in 'Pooran, Pooran', represent. These are ways of belonging and carry with them a fierce pride in possessions that are symbolical.

Though Ramkissoon reads borrowed newspapers – a day old or several days old – his memory stores the news which he uses both for political arguments and distance patriotism. Once the argument runs into the performance of the Indian cricket team versus the West Indian team, he is sure that Hazare had once scored a century in the Indo-Australian match before the West Indian Headley achieved the same feat. Back to the newspapers for confirmation. The narrator acknowledges a silent loyalty to India, even as they were wracked by 'quality ambivalence' in not prioritising the West Indian loyalty (19). But even that culture of Guyana, friendly, comfortable, boastful and full of small quarrels, is done away with as many of the younger generation move to the 'cold northern refuge' Canada. The stories in *Jahaji*, one after the other, foreground issues of belonging, rootedness, identity and colour as the literate and illiterate live together and when the new together and when the new world is 'cold' and at times ruthless and indifferent, when equality remains outside their orbit and each narrator, listener and protagonist asks: Where do I belong? Where is my origin? It is something lost in the three-month ship journey, when many of their kind perished?

In another country, Malaysia, the Indian inheritors of the jahazi experience, a different society despite similarity with the West Indian experience, exists. In an article 'Aliens on the Land – Indian immigrant workers in Malaysia' in *The Malaysia Chronicle* (author not mentioned), the journey of Indian immigrants from 1880s is commented upon. 'Indians' were the most marginalised of workers. They resided in closed plantation societies in frontier zones and the plantation symbolises the boundary of their existence. Further, the writer observes, the vagrancy laws, their illiteracy and inability to speak any of the two languages - Malay and English – current in Malaysia, 'intensified their isolation and vulnerability. They were trapped in an unending cycle of dependability and poverty on the plantation.'[18]

How does one rise out of this quagmire? Education is one route, political power a powerful supplement (as it happened in Mauritius) and migration a third. K.S. Manian the inheritor of a colonial past rose out of the past through education and has gone on to become a writer with a deep understanding of the Indian immigrant's psyche as affected by memories and environs. In a Preface to his volume of short stories, *Haunting the Tiger*,[19] he writes about his own creative experience. Though there is the intolerable struggle with words, 'it is the country of imagination, which can be devastating and exhilarating, that holds the writer in its thrall' (ix). Manian holds two of the stories in the volume 'The Eagles' and 'Haunting the Tiger' as significant representatives of his experience, understanding and insight. Manian's narrative strategy is constantly moving beyond the visible to the landscape to capture the interface between the mind and the environs and works wildernesses. 'The Eagles' works with a plantation background. Significantly, both the stories begin with the presence of an old man. In 'The Eagles' it is the death of the 'old Man of the Town' (47)[20] and in 'Haunting the Tiger', the opening line is 'The old man had trouble dying' (37).[21] But the stories move in entirely different directions bearing testimony, in the first to social change, the casting off of servitude, the move towards a less feudalistic life, while in 'Haunting the Tiger' the young man is Muthu himself, when he was energetic and powerful enough to aspire to conquer the world and to take up challenges. 'Haunting the Tiger' is an inward looking-narrative which works through dreams and restlessness, the same restlessness with which he had grown up. As the story moves between the present and the past, two presents come face to face as the old man's thoughts are opened out to the reader. It takes time to realise that Muthu and the old man are the same person.

How many selves does a person have and how is the transition from one to the other take place? His eight-year self died when his mother died, when the fact of loss compelled him to look within. Then his marriage, which he went through all the time disapproving the rituals. His new wife was 'the strangeness he had to give himself up for, to know. He had to, he had told himself, actually jump out of his skin and be refashioned to fit into the life with her' (37).

Memories of an experienced past replace ancestral pasts, but cultural myths of creation and loss still dominate. The moment of death, no matter how difficult, is also a time of internal reckoning, Malaysia was a land of forests, landscapes which were dense and dark, mysterious and lightening: it is the outside world, so difficult to enter and understand. The symbolisation of both the tiger and forest comes through as an exterior space which needs to be known confronted and conquered, a battle of interiority with exteriority. Muthu doesn't want to remain an outsider, he wants to belong. His parents never have belonged. Disgruntled 'they want to return to the country from which they had come. "They can give up this land for a life they've known" he thinks. But what do I have to give up?' Overtaken by the need to possess, to have something to give up, if an exchange has to be made, he feels 'what better way to know the country than to hunt down a beast that knows it well?' (38). Knowledge is a way of belonging, of adapting, of understanding. It means learning the language of the other. Slow explorations on the fringes, forays into the forest with a gun in hand, learning to move noiselessly, practicing to 'haunt' the tiger. The need to know the other takes hold of him, the forest becomes his favourite haunt, his need to possess is an obsessive idea. The dense landscape merges with Muthu's mindscape as he lay dying. But the existential problem of belonging still remains.

But in order to *see*, through all veils and covers, you have to have eyes that can see the intuitive vision. Zulkifli who lives on the edge of the forest tells him that boars can't be killed; they are not enemies and the forest is not an enemy country. One kills them only when they destroy crops. Muthu's way of knowing, of seeking power over the other, is a misguided one. Belonging can never take place through confrontation, conquest or killing the other. 'Haunting the Tiger' is as much about the estrangement of an immigrant as about relationships. The vision that needs to be developed can develop only through dialogue; it has to come through mediation. Were his parents wiser than him? But then their home country perpetually beckoned them. They did not belong, despite the fact that they nurtured plants. But it is doubtful whether he belongs despite the difference in his perspective, grounded as he is in another inheritance, another language, different rituals and social practices located within a caste system and an inherited past with all its baggage can he reach out to other and discover himself? '"I can't get lost", he tells himself ... .' (40). Is this a positive assertion or a voiced fear: 'I know this place and hence will not get lost' or 'I cannot afford to get lost?' Muthu wonders how as to how does one grow up; is it by becoming fearless, or by taking a decision or by learning to be independent? Manian's language is loaded with adjectives 'threat thick silence', and again 'fearful silence' (41). The phenomenological sharpening that he has developed has helped Muthu grow a personal antenna. The forest speaks to him, engulfs him and makes him feel both angry and helpless. The moment of a final reckoning is at this time, when he is dying and something in him refuses to die: 'The old man struggled with the anger his younger self had felt long ago'. Zulkifli had told him time and again, that the tiger can't be shot and can't be possessed (41). Only centuries of living here can lead to an understanding of the ground. You have to belong and not remain on the fringe. Muthu's parents go back to India, they had always remained transients or temporary residents. Having stayed on, he needs to belong more than ever before. The battle is not between two opposite forces but located in the mind. The fact that he stayed behind is also motivated by a desire to break his father's hold on him, the imposition of another will. One needs to think like the 'other', get into the mind of the 'other' as in a game of chess. Zulkifli wants Muthu to think like the tiger, to make the leap. But Muthu fails to make the leap, the leap which should have been of the mind is now of the body, as the spirit flies.

The Indian past, the Tamil culture are all over in 'The Eagles' where Ganesan, a dhobi's son, is possessed by a similar urge for power, the need to defy authority, to bypass tradition, to be independent. The long waits in the big house, his stepmother's remarks, his friend Govindan's snides are all irksome. This is a transplanted society and cultures travel not only through traditions and practices but also through films and their heroes like MGR. A reality of another world is carried over to a foreign land and the immigrant's mind moves in different directions, trying to take them both in and cohere them. The eagles must learn to fly, to break away from the social scorn and marginalisation.

Manian's rooting in Malaysian culture is equally visible through Ganesan and Muthu as in his other stories such as the 'Terminal'.[22] He also looks at the Indian from outside ('In Flight' 27).[23] One of his stories 'Project: Graft Man' is a veiled analysis of the kind of social engineering the modern society indulges in as well as the forms of hybridities that are necessary for cultural transplantation. 'Project: Graft Man' can be read in several ways – as a kind of Wellsian (H.G. Wells) experiment, recurrent in several dystopian novels as well as a cultural narrative of human engineering. The very opening sentence uses the word 'experiment', one carried out over a period of fifty years, building up a foundation for a future researcher with the purpose of testing the 'impact of power ... on the production of a new breed of men ...' (132).[24] The laboratory is controlled by a director, located in a central urban township but on its fringes (perhaps to remind human beings of their native origins) are planted carefully selected men to be used as guinea pigs. The conditions of the selection are many – background, susceptible personalities, docile and malleable, and of a representative nature so as to create a uniform society. It kept the selectees in ignorance and was at heart vested in the sense of superiority of the selectors. Social progress and change act as agents of transformation as all inputs and the environs are totally controlled.

Two men (subjects!) are noticeable in the 'anonymous crowd' – Datuk the grandfather and Hari the grandson – men of different generations. They are being used for entirely different tasks, Datuk, the grandfather, is often called in for consultation and Hari is constantly subjected to sessions, a kind of brainwashing exercise. Hari begins to sense the changes creeping into him, as his thoughts are crowded with images of featherless chickens, of cockerels being sacrificed and his mind totally exposed to his engineers. Hari's thoughts constitute a running commentary on his grandfather and his rising importance. They are also a reflection of a sense of shock as he is called upon to change his values (138). Is this transformation the price of survival? People are the final product and hence thought control has to be developed as a perfect mechanism. But Hari is a 'complete waste' (142), as he is the native who carries his past with him. Reflection, privacy and introspection work contrary to the project which requires the human material to be a non-thinking product Manian gathers in this at least two narratives: the refusal to change and the compulsion to change. The last is being forced through technology, thought control and globalisation – all symbols of power. In itself the graft man is a powerful symbol of diasporic dislocation and the fact of being caught between two opposing forces.

The third and fourth generations of jahazi bhai, live in this mixed world, where identity, colour and status jostle with each other. What should they remember and what forget? How do they take root in their present locations – through history, further migrations, modernisation, ambition or a final transformation? There is a great deal they cannot forget, the culture internalised within them, their homes and linguistic roots. They cannot give up their imagined homelands, even if they give up nostalgia. In the double-layered concept of home, the shadow of the original is ever present.

NOTES & REFERENCES

1. Cheddi Jagan came to power in 1953 but because of his Marxist ideology, the British intervened. He came to power once again in 1961 when he became Prime Minister of British Guyana.
2. The immigration to Mauritius began in 1834 while to Fiji it began in 1879. In Mauritius the people of Indian origin are in a majority of 68 per cent and the country is viewed as a successful multicultural society. In Fiji the Indian power suffered a blow on account of two coups – one in 1987, the second in 2000, leading to further migrations. See Christine Stuart's article, 'Indians in Mauritius and Fiji', (pdf. www/jsu-edu//2000. Henderson State University, accessed 9 October 2014).
3. Refer Gurbhagat Singh 'Expatriate Writing and the Problematic of Centre: Edward Said and Homi Bhabha', *Writers of the Indian Diaspora*. Ed. Jasbir Jain (Jaipur: Rawat Publications, 1998, 2011), 21–29.
4. *A House for Mr Biswas* (New York: Alfred A. Knopf, 1961), *Between Father and Son: Family Letters* (London: Little Brown, 1999).
5. *The Enigma of Arrival* (London: Vintage Books, 1987).
6. *Jahaji Bhai* (1988) and *Jahaji: An Anthology of Indo-Caribbean Fiction* (2000), both edited by Frank Birbalsingh and published by Tsar Publications. The word 'jahaz' would be spelt with a 'z' and not a 'j'.

This is the effect of dislocated languages. I have used *Jahaji* wherever referring to the title and 'jahazi' when referring to those who have travelled this long ship journey foreign lands (The Urdu sound z is captured by the phonetic symbol z not dz).

7. See Introduction, *Jahaji* (Toronto: Tsar Publication, 2000), vii-xxxiv, xvli.
8. *Ibid.*, Sasenarine Persaud, 'Mai, Mai, Mai', 97–107.
9. *Ibid.*, Rabindranath Maharaj, 'Swami Pankaj', *Jahaji*, 40–49.
10. 'Going to Guyana', *Jahaji*, 108–121. Also see Cyril Dabydeen, 'Shaping the Environment: Sugar Plantation or Life After' in *Writers of the Caribbean Diaspora*. Eds. Jasbir Jain and Supriya Agarwal (New Delhi: Sterling, 2008), 11–25.
11. Madeline Coopsammy, 'The Insiders', *Jahaji*, 63–69, 63. In fact 'coolitude' like negritude, in a word commonly used to mark this heritage. The word was coined by a Mauritius poet.
12. Christine Singh, 'The Job Interview', *Jahaji*, 157–172.
13. Refer Caryl Phillips, *The European Tribe* (New York: Vintage Books, 1987, 2000).
14. Shani Mattoo, 'Sushila's Bhakti', *Jahaji* 173–181.
15. Words are spelt the way they are pronounced, hence mehndi becomes 'mendhi' and proper nouns similarly acquire different spellings. Time, distance and society have brought in many linguistic shifts of speech.
16. Ismith Khan, 'Pooran, Pooran', *Jahaji*, 1–14.
17. Elahi Baksh, 'The Propagandist', *Jahaji*, 15–30.
18. 'Aliens in the Land – Indian immigrant workers in Malaysia' *The Malaysian Chronicle*, 28 February 2013. www.malaysiachronicle.com/Accessed 8 October 2014. author not mentioned.
19. K.S. Manian, *Haunting the Tiger: Contemporary Stories from Malaysia* (London: Skoob Books Publishing Ltd., 1996).
20. 'The Eagles' in Manian, *Haunting the Tiger*, 47–67.
21. 'Haunting the Tiger' in *Haunting The Tiger*, 37–46.
22. 'Terminal' *Haunting the Tiger*, 1–21.
23. 'In Flight' *Haunting the Tiger*, 22–36.
24. 'Project: Graft Man'. *Haunting the Tiger*, 132–142.

16

To India with Love
Rushdie, Ghosh and Mistry

The eighties began with a new wave of writing with the postindependence generation coming of age. Salman Rushdie's second novel *Midnight's Children*[1], though received controversially, not only won him recognition and the Booker Prize but began a new tradition in non-sequential writing using language without fear, no longer treading carefully so as not to break the rules of the Queen's English, no longer conscious of being exposed only to the western eye but consciously and deliberately writing home. Five years later came Amitav Ghosh's *The Circle of Reason*[2], which opened up other doors and windows in cultural frameworks and questioned the epistemological monopolies of the west. He located his novel in a semi-rural environment and built on the motif of weaving which has innumerable metaphorical and historical connotations. And, again after another gap of five years Rohinton Mistry made his presence felt on the literary scene with *Such a Long Journey*[3] and filled up another gap, the missing ethnic space, in the representation of Indian culture. Unlike Rushdie and Ghosh, whose characters travel through different territories, Mistry spreads his image of reclamation broadly in a societal complexity through the happenings in a Parsi colony Khodadad in Mumbai.

They are all first generation immigrants – Rushdie mainly in Britain, at times in New York, a British citizen and knighted like Naipaul. (But we hardly ever speak of Sir Salman!) Ghosh lives in the States but of recent years has begun to divide his time between

India and the US. He, to the best of my belief, retains his Indian citizenship. Mistry is settled in Canada. His work, except for a few exceptions, is located in Mumbai and captures the political scenario from an ordinary man's perspective. All the three writers either question or redefine the postcolonial. In their involvement with personal, political and cultural histories, they work through memory and defy the frameworks of master narratives, each inventing his own as they engage with narration and denarration in the same space, Rushdie most of all. He literally confessed in his essay 'Unreliable Narrator in *Midnight's Children*' that this unreliability is deliberate and conscious.[4] Of them Mistry is closest to a centred story, the wandering marked only through memory. As Myrian Sepúlveda Santos has observed, 'The grand narratives about the past, the linear history of sequential events, and the evolutionary appraisal of human beings' achievements have been strongly denounced as invented traditions, instruments of power and constraining practices.'[5] The concern with Indian realities now works in opposition to past practices. Between them a new India as well as a new diasporic vision is presented and though some of these concerns surface over and over again in their writing, I propose to focus on these early novels which are in some measure autobiographical beginnings and locate them.

Midnight's Children has a central character Saleem Sinai, and the narrative, partly autobiographical and partly located in magic realism, opens up the history not only of a divided nation but of a psyche subjected to similar pressures. He relates to India with love, 'looking at it as at an old family photograph', which evokes multiple memories. Rushdie weaves together not only the two dominant cultural strands but also the narrative traditions as inherited from the *kissa* and the *katha*. Bold and unafraid, he plays with factual histories and linear time. Saleem Sinai's unreliability as a narrator captures for the reader the bewilderment and uncertainty of the time, the elusiveness of the 'real', its constant revolution, multiple angles and myriad perspectives. Details, which the hero provides about his birth, lie in-between the autobiographical and the imagined. It is difficult to ascertain the depth of either or distinguish the thin line that separates them even as it welds them together.

Rushdie requires us to share his past and participate in his engagement with reclaiming and reliving it. Through this he also claims his land of birth and expresses the share that it has in his reflections. No matter how difficult it may be to recreate it or enter that phase of one's life, it is difficult to forget it, to separate it from one's consciousness. But distanced in many ways, as with the fatwa and the banning of *The Satanic Verses*, his visits home get involved in controversies, and are as difficult as staying away. The absurdity which he feared through Saleem Sinai (*Midnight's Children* 9) has come to encompass his existential self – born in India, citizen of England, a Muslim by birth but hounded by them he is constantly pushed into multiple exiles and yet, surprisingly, he belongs through his memories. Rushdie dismantles existing frameworks so thoroughly that one has to wade through fantasies, imagined realities, myths, a multitude of characters that change midstream and encompass a whole world from illiteracy, orality to east-west knowledge systems flowing into each other. The novel travels through different locations and places. Kashmir, Agra, Bombay, back up north to Lahore then eastwards to Dhaka and Saleem's memories too tend to fluctuate, a perpetual game of lost and found. By the end of the novel his intended bride Padma is replaced by Parvati. In a comment on the writing of the novel, Rushdie said that it was 'an attempt to reclaim my Indian origin.'[6] In an interview given to Jack Living, he also observed that *Midnight's Children* despite the first person narration is intended to convey that 'everyone's story is part of someone else's.'[7]

Read as history, *Midnight's Children* works at least at three different levels: personal life story, a nation's history of division and loss both of a common past as well as a sense of direction, and an imagined history of situations where difference melts away to knit people together through names, relationships, and marriage. Underneath the fantasy and the magic realism is a factual account which works with every political happening of significance in more than half a century – Cabinet Mission, Five Year Plans, States Reorganisation Committee, Sanjay Youth Brigade, party poll symbols, all of them. In fact, Rushdie right at the beginning juxtaposes two narrative traditions: 'once upon a time' followed by a date, 15 August 1947 (3). Thus history and imagination are brought together – imagining, recording, creating – and work with factual happenings in the life of this child-nation and an imagined past, as seen through baby – eyes. The birth of the free country on the same day, literally makes it his twin.

The use of his grandfather's past, his amazing love story – through the perforated sheet, a symbolical representation of a culture which is just opening out to external influences – he brings out the centrality of Kashmir as his place of origin and uses it to trace the history of the pre-Independence years. The Wavell Commission, the Simla meeting, the division, all fall into place to go ahead and work with freedom and after, through to the Emergency, just behind him, when he wrote the novel. Moving fast forward, he arrives at 15 August 1947, the day of Saleem's and the country's truncated birth, the dawn of freedom and then the story of his growing years, nursed and nurtured by people from very different backgrounds, representing the different castes and religions. This is an internalisation of the possibilities that a lost history held. Saleem's narration of the past is part hearsay, part imagined and filled out and framed within comic incidents. An attempt at analysing the different aspects would automatically be a lesson in the ways knowledge comes to us. The choice of names such as Lifafa Das bring alive abstract characters out of a comic strip. The ingredients of an adventure story are all present – trapdoors, assassination plans, eerie silences, conspiracies, underground threats to life and Ravana gangs – reflecting the internecine quarrels for power that all history is laced with.

As space is partitioned, beginning with the perforated sheet and in 1947 drawing up of the Radcliffe line, time is also partitioned with the clocks in Pakistan half an hour ahead of India. The Sinai family works through the streets of Delhi. Connaught Place, Red Fort, Chandni Chowk, Purana Qila and the General Post office, each marking a historical phase and together they lay out the geography of Delhi. *Midnight's Children* hums with life and brings in the smell of different cities, their mulling crowds and their culture. Rushdie through Saleem writes,

> Reality is a question of perspective; the further you get from the past, the more concrete and plausible it seems – but as you approach the present, it inevitably seems more and more incredible. Suppose yourself in a large cinema, sitting at first in the back row, and gradually moving up row by row, until your nose is almost pressed against the screen. (197)

This is how Rushdie reads the past and the same cinematic frame he is advising his readers to adopt, in speed, compression and evocation.

Amitav Ghosh writes about Bengal but the location is not identified by any one city. He moves across space both inside the country and outside it. His very first novel looked at the post-Pakistan reality as many Hindus continued to stay there and the migrations that occurred because of the atrocities of the Pakistani army during 1971, leading to the formation of Bangladesh. Where does the shadow line exist?[8] Memories and relationships constantly cross it. But migrations, voluntary or motivated by escape, do form a part of his writing as much as the return home. *The Calcutta Chromosome*[9] works like a detective story as mysterious boys come to sell fish, as railway lines stretch into unknown areas and the mosquito carrying the malarial infection remains elusive. One of the dominant strands is the process of research and the researcher. The reader is taken through a whole line of earlier researches located in different geographical spaces, all of which have contributed to the final discovery. And most important of all is the role of the cleaning woman, Manglabi who intuitively selects a slide to be placed under the microscope. Through these journeys and the selection of the slide, two things are stressed. One, that no single person, country of culture is solely the agent of discovery and two, knowledge through scientific means in itself is never really enough, it needs to be supplemented by intuition. Two systems are contrasted dismantling the idea of a one-way flow of knowledge and of a single power centre.[10] This very idea exists in his earlier novel *The Circle of Reason*.[11] The proclamation implied in the Enlightenment of the superiority of reason and the presumption that it will progress linearly is dismantled; but it doesn't work that way. Reason moves in a circle and works through different emotions. Epistemologies are created by a whole lot of extra-rational factors. Science is a fascination for Ghosh in almost all his novels and his training in anthropology works in this novel as well as in *The Hungry Tide*.[12] Similarly he chooses as his shadow-heroes persons of science – Ronald Ross, Marie Curie, Louis Pasteur – and they represent a counterpoint to Indian knowledge systems.

When eight-year-old Alu, recently turned orphan, comes to Lalpukar to his uncle's home whom he has never met, the uncle

Balaram runs inside to get hold of his measuring tools. His interest in phrenology is an obsession and Alu, so called because of his potato-shaped head, is his target. Balaram, a school teacher is a man who goes contrary to all superstitions, irrational thinking and most of the social practices. The dominant figure in the village is Bhudeb, a wealthy man, the owner of the school with social authority and a desire to gain prominence. But Bhudeb is a man with little knowledge and even less imagination and is a constant source of provocation for Balaram. In his persistent pursuit of phrenology, Balaram discovers that his assessments are fairly off the mark. Alu, at age ten, is a voracious reader, a keen observer and a good learner. His interests were wide, 'He would read almost anything he happened to find in Balaram's study, history, geography, natural history, biology.... And not just in Bengali. It had taken him very little time to learn English' (29). He would try to read French with the help of a dictionary and could speak several languages. Later he learns weaving and becomes an expert, making good money out of it. Balaram confesses to his friend Gopal that he had perhaps made a mistake. His obsession with Reason had guided all his activities and pursuits. The biography of Louis Pasteur had been his constant companion, a legacy he passed on to Alu. He was also fascinated by C.V. Raman. But in the end the Louis Pasteur book is only fuel for a funeral fire. The reader gradually realises that through the whole interaction of Balaram and Alu through the experiments in phrenology, somewhere at the back of it all, Ghosh is critiquing the use to which practical sciences were put by imperial races. Towards the end of the nineteenth century, psychological and racial theories were built not merely on scientific observations but were geared towards the dark races. Lombroso's researches are present in Joseph Conrad's *The Secret Agent* (1907) and the body and brain centred racial theories that validated slavery. Ghosh by pushing forward this example of phrenology gone wrong is exposing these discriminatory approaches. Balaram, half-guided by his own knowledge of phrenology, and half because Alu had stopped going to school, takes him to the weaver Debnath, requesting him to take Alu as an apprentice. Alu is overjoyed. The world of meaning is in direct contrast to the machine:

Man at the loom is the finest example of mechanical man, a creature who makes his own world as no other can, with his mind ... . It [the loom] has created not separate worlds but one, for it has never permitted the division of the world. The loom recognises no continents and no countries. It has tie the world together with its bloody ironies from the beginning of human time.

It has never permitted the division of reason. (59)

The Circle of Reason through its central arguments related to science and the continued resistance that human behaviour offers to it through a practical working rationality which is far more encompassing of social attitudes, traditional individual intuitions and inclinations expressing the will of a person, has presented an understanding of Indian history. I see in Balaram's fascination for science a reflection of the beginnings of what is referred to as the Bengal Renaissance and the attraction of reason and science. The period of 1830–1860 was the beginning of this exposure to different kinds of thought – reason, science and revolution. The various reforms introduced by the religious movements were also an outfall of this. The Gandhian movement with its emphasis on self-reliance, self-respect and self-occupation forms another discourse in the novel. Alu is an entrepreneur, he organises his sales; he is an artist with imagination and his work is in much demand. The loom, the *charkha*, the wheel is Janus-faced. It looks towards both directions: the industrial revolution which went into industrialisation and productive self-employment leading to a holistic life, which brings mind and body together. The juxtaposition of two attitudes is a continued concern with Ghosh who recognises the strength of emotions and intuition, which are part of meditative processes as well as India's knowledge systems.

Gopal, a close friend of Balaram, takes a somewhat different position. A man of literature, he was elected president of the Rationalists days student during his. The task before the Rationalists was 'applying rationalism to everything around them' and in his study of Sanskrit and its classics, he was 'no longer in doubt that here were very curious parallelisms between the ideas of the ancient Hindu sages and modern science' (49–50). Thus, there was no opposition and the west did not have a monopoly. Instead there was always some overlapping and the directions had been different.

The political debates of the period, the attraction towards anarchic and revolutionary movements find a place to complete this portrait of a Bengal township. The revolutionary movement acts as a catalyst in Alu's life, changing it from his contented and peaceful life in Lalpukar to that of a fugitive from law. Suspected of terrorist activities, there is no other option but to disappear with the police inspector Jyoti chasing him all over the world. From here the travels begin, space is opened out, a constant cat-and-mouse game is played; there are encounters with other cultures and Jyoti begins to understand the working of Alu's mind and sympathises with him. As the novel moves towards its close everything becomes weird, unreal, a world in a flux. Is this the diasporic experience? Rituals have to change, old customs improvised, the funeral rites are made of substitutions and altered. One is true to the spirit of the thing but not to actual procedures The movement in *The Circle of Reason* is from homeland to other shores, other experiences and cultures and the adjustments this new world requires, Ghosh in his resistance to the word postcolonial and the Commonwealth Prize is engaged in unravelling the threads of west-centricism both in scientific domination and cultural stereotypes of the east. In the process, the intention is to discover the eastern pasts and unveil them, bring them to light. These histories are not marked by dates or recorded knowledge but are marked by personal pursuits, the everyday human life, live and failure. In a later novel, *The Glass Palace*,[13] which seems different at the surface, he extends this process of decolonisation to East Asia, moves outside India to Burma and later Malaysia. The young boy Rajkumar who begins his journey as a helper in a tea shop and then through his own entrepreneur ship and determination rises in both wealth and authority, serves as a counterpoint to the feudalistic stereotype of the coolie, The history of the freedom struggle, the logic behind the desertions in the British army during the Second World War, all point towards an alternative. *The Glass Palace* is perhaps one of the few novels to highlight the idea that went into the formation of the Indian National Army (INA) else why did Subhash Bose join hands with Fascist forces? The historical account goes far beyond dates, events and happenings to present psychological insights into the working of the mind of suppressed people as well as the dilemma of choice that confronted the Indian soldiers in the British army. There is a significant comment on the affiliation of the diasporic Indians working in these regions, affiliation to the home country:

> And India – what was India to them? The land whose freedom they were fighting for, this land they had never seen, but for which they were willing to die? ... . India was the shining mountain beyond the horizon, a sacrament of redemption – a metaphor for freedom in the same way that slavery was a metaphor for the plantation? (522)

Ghosh like Rushdie, deals with the uncertain and unreliable. In *The Calcutta Chromosome*, dates are not factually correct, the real discoverer is lost in mist, ghost trains lead nowhere, railway tracks are terminated in the midst of wilderness, the boy who comes to sell fish appears and disappears mysteriously, like a genie. A great deal of emphasis is laid on written records but, at the same time, hearsay, stories, gossip carry their narrative right into their midst. In *The Circle of Reason*, even knowledge is transmitted through different mediums and methods: formal, earthy experiences and the teaching of traditional skills through a 'guru'. Alu learns his trade but outgrows it to become an artist, weaves the 'maya' motif which becomes a craze. But his uncle pursues knowledge through the written word. The final tossing away of *The Life of Louis Pasteur* which has been with the narrative right from the days in Presidency College, is a remarkable gesture of declaring freedom from borrowed, second-hand knowledges. The intermix of different knowledge systems is a useful ignition but the original needs to be recovered. Rationality does not move through linearities, reason doesn't grow by degree; it moves back and forth, digs and excavates. If Rushdie is 'reclaiming', Ghosh is 'excavating'. Hence the semi-rural environment, and his refusal to be defined only by urban space, Ghosh also blurs boundaries. Hence, his rejection of 'postcolonial' in the statement he made in answer to a question was because 'I grew up in India which was a place not a pre-something or post something'. And later he refused to be as a Eurasian Regional winner for the 2001 Commonwealth Writer's Prize. He objected to the valourising of a 'particular view of the past or present, in creating as it were, a literary 'bloc'. I believe the idea of the 'commonwealth' does represent a certain reading, of the past and present...' (63).[14] Engaged in exploring past histories and validating indigenous knowledge systems, Ghosh's purpose is to dwell on human nature which constantly, consciously or unconsciously, is engaged in self-knowledge, and simultaneously learns and discards, innovates, invents and compromises where necessary. It is thus that civilisations grow.

Such a Long Journey is Rohinton Mistry's debut novel and is located in a Parsi residential complex in Bombay. Other spaces are introduced through happenings but the central characters do not move out except towards the close. Though their minds do travel. Parsi life is opened out in all its details, dress, prayer rituals, the constant pressures both monetary and political and the crowded space. At one point the question is asked: Is there no place for minorities? The community ties are strong and supportive. Right in the beginning we are introduced to Miss Kitpitia, loud and shrill and the telephone-keeper and the lame Tehmul whose speech knows no pauses or halts. The centre, however, is in Gustad Noble's family and his friends and it is through this family that the narrative spreads outside. The Chinese aggression, and the Indo-Pak war of 1965 have left a mark on the house indicated by the blackened windows so that light does not filter in, a protection against bombardments. But inside the house there are other worries, illness being one of them. Their daughter Roshan's illness is constantly with them. Their son Sohrab, unwilling to yield to the parental pressure to attempt an IIT entry, moves out of the house. Amidst this is the story of Jimmy Billimoria, said to be working for RAW and the incident when sixty lakhs payment was made to an unidentified person, merely on a phone call allegedly from the PM's office. Billimoria sends this money through a connection in Chor Bazaar to Gustad Noble, who gets another friend to help him deposit the money in a bank through several instalments. But all the time illness is also Dinshaw's constant companion, running parallel to the bank deposits. Billimoria is taken prisoner, Roshan is constantly struggling with a persistent stomach infection, which so far has not been diagnosed. Crises mount up. With Billimoria held prisoner, both Gustad and Noble are in a hurry to get rid of the remaining money. As soon as the last deposit is made, Dinshaw dies in the hospital, finally yielding to the illness, with no one at his bedside.

Illness, disability and stink are all around. It is a disorganised world. The novel opens with Gustad facing eastward to offer his orisons to Ahura Mazda. An early morning time and peaceful, the sparrows chirping and the milkman come to deliver milk. Prayer also forms a strand in the novel. Gustad at times goes to church, with a Christian friend where he follows his actions faithfully to pay homage to the Christian god. Later, he accompanies another friend to a temple with full faith in the miracle cure the deity was reputed for. And he finds a way of solving the problem of the colony's wall being a public urinal by getting a pavement artist to paint holy figures on it. A representative gallery of holy figures comes up and is a positive discouragement to the users. Gustad's open-minded faith and the picture gallery on the wall of the colony are testimonies to a possible everyday world, but they also comment on the Indian society – the living habits, the excessive religious faith almost amounting to superstitious belief and rigid positions. Gustad's actions are an indication of how communities can live together and relate positively to go ahead to form a nation.

Some of the themes such as overcoming financial stringency, the children's contribution by the help they give are further pursued in *Family Matters*[15] where the school-going children take to walking to school in order to save the bus fare. The old man, their grandfather, lies in the kitchen in the small flat and often interrupts the family meals through the claims on his body, at first despised by the son-in-law, he comes to be loved. A similar emotional bond, where the pull of the conscience gets better of Gustad's reasoning, when he makes a trip to Delhi in response to his friend's call to meet him in the hospital where he has been shifted from the prison. Jimmy is on his deathbed. Both the novels: *Such a Long Journey* and *The Circle of Reason* end with deaths and funerals, completing a full circle of lives which have all along been adjusting to their circumstances with makeshift arrangements. One wonders why death, cremation and funeral rites? Is it that they complete the cycle of human life on earth or that they signify cultural absorption, or perhaps because they signify a community come together to mark the departure?

Mistry adds a 'supplement', a Derridean supplement, supplying the absent, filling up the gap in the cultural narrative, in direct contrast to the other two writers discussed here. And though politics enters all his novels, the concern is mainly with representation and a wholeness of Indian reality as far as it can be signified. All his novels stay close to the ground and to Mumbai as it is affected by national politics. His multicultural world has to be multireligious even if man has monopolised God. He looks back home to work from home-ground. Diasporic writing is memory writing – not personal, not merely national but cultural and native. Memory connects as history does not. As Santos points out it builds links between past and present.[16] In the case of the diaspora, it also crosses physical distance thus building up a space-time continuum. Santos reminds us that 'collective memory' encompasses a number of different meanings, 'from more subjective and particular accounts of the past to readings of remote traces inscribed in social codes' (164). When removed from these familiar practices, a fictional memory recall of the way prayers are said or the claims of crowded neighbourhoods and limited spaces evoke images of the way particular communities live but also, for the writer, who is now dislocated bring a past alive. One cannot help but remember for the past continues to persist in our lives. It has made us what we are and shaped our subjectivities.[17] Does the writer create a private world for personal sustenance or is it a historical retrieval? Perhaps, memory narratives when they build up cultural pasts both of the individual and the community, are two-directional. First, they remind us what we are, of our difference and separateness which is of great significance in personal value, and second, locate us in cultural space. Rather than read them as postcolonial, they should be read as cultural assertions, willing to take their own position in the larger world.

Rushdie's work is marked by open defiance, throwing a challenge to all to work with his fantasies and magic realism and create meaning out of the ever-shifting realities where language and meaning are not in unison but constantly tearing apart. Ghosh offers a cultural challenge as he questions established knowledge systems. And Mistry opens a new world of relationships where there is place for everyone, even all the gods. There is fantasy, magic and in some degree miracle performance in all of them even if these live merely on the peripheries. At the centre of these memories is the human being – the ever mysterious man. And India. These diasporic writers turn back to their home country and represent a past that lives in them today.

NOTES & REFERENCES

1. Salman Rushdie, *Midnight's Children* (New York: Avon Books, 1982).
2. Amitav Ghosh, *The Circle of Reason* (New Delhi: Penguin, 1986, 2008).
3. Rohinton Mistry, *Such a Long Journey* (Calcutta: Rupa & Co., 1991).
4. 'Unreliable Narrator in *Midnights Children*', *Imaginary Homelands. Essays and Criticism 1981–1991*. (London: Granta Books, 1991). 22–24.
5. Myrian Sepúlveda Santos, 'Memory and Narrative in Social Theory: The Contributions of Jacques Derrida and Walter Benjamin.' *Time and Society* (London: Sage, 2001). Vol. 10 (2/3) 163–189.
6. Rushdie on the 'Writing of the Novel' in *the Guardian* 26 July 2008. Internet ref. accessed 20 October 2014.
7. *The Paris Review, the Art of Fiction, 2014*. Rushdie interviewed by Jack Livings. Internet reference. The paris review. org/interview/the art of fiction. accessed 20 October 2014.
8. *The Shadow Line* (Delhi: Ravi Dayal, 1988).
9. Amitav Ghosh, *The Calcutta Chromosome* (Delhi: Ravi Dayal, 1996)
10. Refer my essay, 'Agenda, Activism and Agency: Mapping the Postcolony' in *The Politics of Literary Theory and Representation: Writings on Activism and Aesthetics*, Ed. Pankaj K. Singh (New Delhi: Manohar, 2003), 159–175.
11. Ghosh, *The Circle of Reason* (New Delhi: Penguin, 1986, 2008).
12. *The Hungry Tide* (New Delhi: Harper Collins, 2011).
13. *The Glass Palace* (New Delhi: Harper Collins, 2000)
14. Refer Jain, 'Agenda, Activism and Agency' in Ed. Pankaj K. Singh, 159.
15. Mistry, *Family Matters* (Toronto: McClelland and Stewart, 2002).
16. See Myrian Setulveda Santos. (footnote 5 above) *The Politics of literary They and Representation.*
17. See Santos, 164–65.

17

Cultural Interpretations/ Representations in Film of the Indian Diaspora

Nostalgia, Memory or Spoofing?

For more than two decades the cultural scene has been bristling with talk of crossover films, directed, at times also produced, and almost always written by Indians living abroad. These films form a broad category in themselves as they are engaged in an ongoing dialogue with their culture of origin. A host of factors shape and govern the nature of this discourse: whether they are first or second generation immigrants, the nature of the host culture – whether England with its history of a long relationship with India or Canada and the USA – and the location both of the director/writer's emotional self and of the filmic narrative. Another factor is of the viewership. Even if the targeted/imagined viewership is neutral, the cultural content locates it at a juncture of at least two different viewerships. Thus, it would be natural to ask how does this determine the content and the frames of this cinema. How does this affect the making of meaning?

There is a distance to be travelled from culture to art. Described as a semiotic system, in itself culture is an abstraction – it is felt, lived, variously internalised and rebelled against – but it is elusive in its very nature, held together by certain practices, myths, beliefs and symbols. Clifford Greetz commenting on its nature writes: 'Though ideational, it does not exist in someone's head; though unphysical it is not an occult identity' (*The Interpretation of Cultures*. London: Harper Collins, 1993: 10–11). Between the two extremes of a reificatory and a reductionist approach, there is a third possibility of looking at culture as a living, evolving entity, an organic body capable of growth and of being able to relate to it at that level. Is the diaspora able to do that or is it caught between nostalgia, a return to the past and its own distancing from it? Diaspora films may, for the purposes of discussion, be classified into three main categories. True, there is plenty of overlapping in themes and concerns but the targeted exposure and the directorial thrust in the selection of the reality they seek to represent, form the basis of this threefold classification. First, there are the in-between films where a constant negotiation takes place between home and the outside, between inherited values and social practices, often between two generations and always between two cultures. This forms a wide range of growing-up narratives such as *Anita and Me* based on Meera Syal's novel and *Bhaji on the Beach, American Blend* and even *The Namesake*. This theme infiltrates into most films located in host cultures. The second category borders on this but the conflictual situation is a bizarre mix, full of stereotypes and caricatures and in general a fun atmosphere is created. At one level these films are a sign of maturity, at another they evoke an entirely different set of responses from the audiences in India and the audiences in the west. The third category is one of diasporic films located wholly in India as for instance Deepa Mehta's elements trilogy and several of Nagesh Kukunoor's films and even Mira Nair's *Monsoon Wedding*.

The first two categories explore the closed world of the Indian household, their attitudes to marriage and sexuality, to the degree of freedom vis-à-vis the degree of protection and contrast this with the pulls of the outer world, which offers a different set of values. The focus is on the 'difference' with its accompanied conflicts and incongruities. These films are compelled by their very nature to work with at least two generations and often three. And occasionally political issues in the homeland also find an expression. Srinivas Krishna's 1991 film *Masala* works with gods and goddesses, real-life situations, cultural stereotypes, visibility or invisibility of minorities, and also the militancy back home. Following closely on the heels of the Air India crash of 1985, it voices both the anger and the tragedy of the explosion. The protagonist Krishna has lost both his parents in the crash; he lives with an uncle who rents his place to the Sikh militants. The camera travels to include many incidents of racist violence. All these serious issues are intermixed with a constant stream of spoofing, making it difficult for the viewer to locate a still point. Krishna, the author-director, came in for a lot of criticism from the Hindu community in Canada primarily for ridiculing the Hindu gods. Titles like *Masala, Mississipi Masala* and *Bollywood/Hollywood* send a clear signal of their in-between status. They mix cultures, and are caught up in a mixed reception. Uma Parameswaran, an Indo-Canadian writer, in an essay 'Problematizing Diasporic Motivation', observes that these comedies are careful not to tread on any other toes 'outside their own ethnocentric community's.' She goes on to comment that this growing tendency to laugh at one self 'perhaps comes from the immigrant sensibility of resorting to self-disparaging humour in order to defuse one's anger at oneself or at others' (*Films, Literature and Culture.* Ed. Jasbir Jain, Jaipur: Rawat, 2007: 14–15). I believe part of it is also a distancing, looking at Indian culture from the outside and freezing its contradictions and stereotypes for iconic representation.

The spoof or partial spoof focuses on the middle class, and plays with the clichéd images of Indian. One such is the famous Indian wedding, with its mixing of generations, a display of silk sarees and jewellery, a get-together for gossip, friendships and animosities and of course a lot of song and dance. These scenes are representative of the Indian wedding now increasingly being celebrated abroad, and in themselves they also nostalgically resurrect a cultural memory. The theme of marriage lends itself to a juxtaposition of arranged versus marriages of choice. Very often, the young want to step out of the frame while their parents try to put them back into it. The insistence on learning to be a good cook is part of this effort. It is amazing to note that a lot of cinematic footage is used on the cooking of meals and scenes in the kitchen, signifying not merely a self-run household but also the Indian obsession with food as essential to well-being. In *Bend It Like Beckham* the maternal insistence is on learning how to cook and to give up playing football. One of the most memorable scenes is when the young girl escapes from her sister's wedding, decked up in a glamourous sari and changes into a sports dress at the back of the car in order to play in a match. It immediately captures the conflict between desire and personal ambition on the one hand and family and cultural expectations on the other.

Another typical scene is the traditional pooja, no matter where the story is located – *American Desi, The Namesake, Fire, Masala* – all of them portray it. It is a dominant cultural motif holding tradition in place and the individual conscience anchored to faith. In *Bend It Like Beckham* (2002) for the sake of cultural authenticity, the Hindu gods give place to the portrait of Guru Nanak Dev, the first Guru of the Sikhs. Acts of worship are embedded in a series of cultural rituals – lighting the incense, the *aarti*, the tika on the forehead, the prasad, the touching of the feet of the elders in order to get their blessings – and these rituals bond the community together even as the young stray away and discard them once they are out. Spoofed or realistically portrayed, they are a slice of life as lived by the diaspora communities when they get together on festive occasions.

American Blend (2006) strikes a different note with the portrayal of the kathak dance instead of a pooja as a cultural artefact. This difference is heightened when it is the American wife, Jamie, married to the Indian Raj, who runs these classes. Again, several of her students are white women and the dance practice sessions become a conjunction of cultures as the black young man who is dating Jamie's daughter steps in with the beat of his dance and three (not only two) cultures meet, reaching across to one another. The in-between films act like a bridge in temporal terms and in the constant contrast between stereotyped icons and the moving away of the young from what they signify, narrate the evolution and change of a living culture. They typify the process of negotiation and adaptation.

Mira Nair's *The Namesake* (2006) based on Jhumpa Lahiri's novel of the same title, is a different kind of an in-between film suffused with loneliness, nostalgia and the anguish of the first generation immigrant. Isolated in a far-off country, their hearts belong back home but their economic resources cannot be stretched to accommodate frequent visits home. The struggle becomes lonelier and lonelier, as communication is also disrupted. The death of Gogol's father in a lonely hospital bed, far away even from his home in America, acquires an added significance as symbolic of the lonely journey of immigration. But the cultural conflicts persist in Gogol's and his sister's life. When their mother decides to go back to India after the death of her husband, the viewer has a mixed feeling – is she happy, is she sad, or is she now torn between two homelands – one of her parents, the other of her children but none truly her own?

The epigraph to Gurinder Chadha's script of *The Mistress of Spices* based on Chitra Divakaruni's novel, (which however doesn't have the epigraph), goes as follows:

> India is an ancient land famed for its myth, magic and tradition. But when the people leave to start new lives in the faraway lands of America and Europe, what happens to the magic left behind? This is an immigrants' tale about keeping the magic alive.

The epigraph frames the film, which works with a selected train of events. A young girl, orphaned, abducted, lands up on an island ruled by the first Mother, who inducts these young girls into the mysterious world of spices and sends them out into different parts of the world to open stores, heal people and serve society. Their gift of 'seeing' what others cannot see rests on the effacement of their own desires. The film deviates from the novel and uses a much focused cinematic frame. Choosing not to dwell lingeringly on the beginning, it sweeps through it, creating a magical aura and then lands us in the *Spice Bazaar* in San Francisco. For the rest, the insides of the shop, its spice-filled jars and the bunch of red chillies strung together, a recurring symbol signifying both danger and desire or the danger of desire, are in constant focus. The outside world enters it through its varied customers – men and women of different ages, nationalities and cultures. The outside world also inhabits her visions. Tilottama can 'see' what other cannot see. The future penetrates her mind.

Departing from the novel where the young Tilottama is placed in 'the body of a bent woman with skin the colour of old sand ... .

They do not know, of course. That I am not old, that this seeming-body I took on in Shampati's fire... is not my own' (Divakaruni, London: Black Swan, 1997, 4–5), the woman in the film is young. Divakaruni's Tilottama carries within her the legend of the Tamil bhakti poetess Auvaiyar, who in order to avoid marriage, through her prayers to Ganesha, attained instant old age. Later, as the narrative rests on the aroused desire in Tilottama, a desire which destroys her gift of healing, this self-imposed disguise of an old body becomes extremely relevant and indicative of a love which does not begin with physical attraction or touch but goes beyond the body, but this is entirely missing in the film. Thus, we have multiple interpretations of culture – one of Chadha, the other of Divakaruni, others still of non-culture readers/viewers, of cultural readers located abroad, and of cultural readers/viewers back home, especially if they are familiar with both the novel and the film. The departure from the body of an old woman subtracts from her image of a witch woman, dispensing magical herbs in an alien world and caught in a conflict between her mission, her old body and the aroused desire in her young heart.

This woman is living out a life prescribed by the Mother, subject to edicts – to serve others and heal them, to place the spices above all else, not to look into the mirror and not to experience desire. The activities she manages are multifold, listening to the personal confidences of her customers, diagnosing their ills, grinding, packaging and dispensing the spices and growing her plants. One of her customers is a grandfather obsessed with the wayward habits of his granddaughter, another is a Kashmiri taxi-driver, subjected to racist attacks, one who feels concerned about her as a brother, and who she can foresee will get hurt in a racist attack, and a third is an American architect, towards whom she feels attracted. It is this desire which destroys her magic, the spices no longer have the desired effect, her basil plant withers away and the red chillies stare her in the face.

How does one read/interpret this film? Exotic, magic, stereotype or a conflict of cultural realities? Is it an allegory of colonial invasion, the loss of environment, of the recovery of homemade products right from the mother's kitchen or nostalgia for vanishing cultures? Or is it about the need to recover, to look not in the mirror but one's own mind? Or plainly and simply give up being superhuman in favour of plain and simple ordinariness? *The Mistress of Spices* (2005) presents a simple world which at heart is complex, distant and inaccessible. Responses are bound to be mixed.

The fear of desire and sexuality is an underlying narrative strand in most diasporic films. In *Bend It Like Beckham*, the young girl is accused of lesbianism, with the community considering it right to act as a moral watchdog. Lesbianism is also a sub-theme in Deepa Mehta's *Fire* where it simultaneously critiques patriarchy and the ideology of sexual denial, propagated alike by religion and nationalist concerns. *Fire* (1996) also has its other margins, the neglected women, the over-worked domestic help who indulges in masturbation, the old mother-in-law, bedridden but still in command in the hierarchical joint family. The themes of arranged marriage, obsession with producing an heir and of sexual deprivation run parallel to the recitals, performances and video projections of the Ramayana, which punctuate the film as the 'eternal' truth that continues to hold the whole society to ransom.

But *Fire*, like the other two films of Mehta's elements trilogy, is located in India as are Mira Nair's early film *Salaam Bombay* (1988) and the majority of Nagesh Kukunoor's films such as *Hyderabad Blues* (1998) *Iqbal* (2005) and *Dor* (2006). Nair's *Salaam Bombay*, happened to be one of the early diaspora films. About street children, it used real street children as actors. Beautifully made in aesthetic terms, it however, came in for a great deal of negative criticism. Was this the India we wanted to project? Poor, homeless, orphaned, neglected. How was it different from the stereotype projected abroad from the starving Indians, the bride-burnings and female infanticide; or from the projection of the drought-stricken African child with an enlarged liver? In such cases, very often, the audiences in the homeland cease to see film as an aesthetic medium but begin to evaluate it as a representative icon. A master artist like Satyajit Ray was also criticised for his film *Pathar Panchali* for its depiction of poverty, with the well-known filmstar Nargis Dutt, then a Member of Parliament, herself joining the chorus.

The debate between aesthetics and the projection of national identity is an ongoing one with responses refusing to be neutral. The consciousness of how the 'other' perceives us, the knowledge that though this is a truth, even if it is only one aspect of the truth, interferes with any entirely aesthetic evaluation. We view the film, get absorbed in it, cannot resist appreciating its cinematography, aware of the atmosphere it has created and the response it has evoked, but then another consciousness intercedes – of our cultural identity. Is it ever possible to see a film as a closed text? Films are layered with multiple subtexts. The visible is only one of the layers and this too conveys different meanings to different audiences. But then there is the historical truth, the ontological real, and the reality of the moment captured in the film lying in wait for future viewers, and quite likely, very different interpretations. Art then reflects contemporaneity as much as it does the past. And its relationship to the future is always uncertain and unpredictable. The Freudian theory of the 'pleasure principle', in his 1920 essay of the same name, takes us beyond the theory of response to the tension that is at the heart of this experience. He proceeds to say that the course taken by mental events is invariably set in motion by an 'unpleasurable tension'. This unpleasurable tension invests the relationship between culture and art i.e. between reality and representation, as well as art and its reception. We would hardly care to remember or think about that which has only given us pleasure during the duration of the viewing.

Of Kukunoor's films, his very first, *Hyderabad Blues*, moves along conventional lines except that it is set in Hyderabad and Southern India gets a representation. But *Iqbal* and *Dor* are unusual films, taking up unusual discourses. Working with margins, personal ambitions, self-growth and national imaginaries all come into play. *Iqbal* takes up the story of a deaf and dumb boy eager to play cricket. He has the potential but no coach, no opportunity and no money. His father, an average villager, is opposed to the whole project and wants him to pick up some skill. All the major concerns of the diaspora like racism, marriage, frozen cultural icons are missing. In fact, it is difficult to remember that it is a film made by a director of diasporic locations. The film centrestages the ambition of the boy, the many obstacles in the course of its realisation including the commercial aspect of sports and the corruption in the selection of players. It is unusual in its double engagement with disability – alcoholism is the other disability from which a has-been good cricketer now perpetually caught in drunkenness, suffers – and to add to this the deaf and dumb boy is from a Muslim family, a religious minority in India, a constant 'other' in communal riots.

In *Dor* (2006), Kukunoor breaks new ground as he takes up the tasks of creating a secular imaginary of the nation something which is faintly perceptible in *Iqbal*, a humanistic discourse crossing all borders of religion, class, cultural traditions and of redefining modernity in terms of values. Working with two parallel stories of two young girls, one a Muslim from the hills of Himachal Pradesh, the other a Hindu from the desert plains of Rajasthan, he proceeds to contrast landscapes, attitudes, differences before bringing them on a level plain. Their lives and narratives converge because of a third space – Saudi Arabia – where their husbands have gone in search of employment. The two men are marginal, in the sense that they are absent, but the narrative weaves around them. One of them, Shankar, the Hindu, dies accidentally and Aamir, his roommate, is charged with murder and sentenced to death. Zeenat then leaves her home, unescorted in search of Meera in order to procure the letter of forgiveness. This is another new theme through which the humanist discourse is set into motion; to be able to forgive requires primarily a sense of self-recognition, then a courage to deviate from the beaten path and finally, in this instance, the ability to rebel against the patriarchal stranglehold. To achieve all this a necessary move has to be made for a personal transformation from a passive role to the acquisition of an agency.

Meera gradually begins to recognise her self. In her journey towards this self-realisation, she needs a prodding from outside. Zeenat acts as the catalyst with her sense of independence and self-confidence, facilitating Meera's choices between life-denying conventions and the upsurge of life in her own body. During the course of this journey the hollowness of the family's sense of honour, the value the parents attach to their son, measured only in terms of money, and the Rajput father-in-law's commercial transaction for the sexual use of his widowed daughter-in-law, all are exposed. Meera realises that widowhood does not kill all desire. Zeenat and Meera use the religious space of a temple for the purposes of meeting and strangely enough, support is extended to Meera by her grandmother-in-law who tells Meera to listen to her inner voice, just as Zeenat had told her to take a step forward as a 'leap of faith'. She steps out to forgive, to relate and to pick up the threads of life. *Dor* literally means thread or string, something that connects. It is a title loaded with multiple meanings. *Dor* is a beautiful film, which despite its concern with a multitude of unpleasant realities, satisfies emotionally, aesthetically and intellectually.

Diaspora filmmakers have travelled and are travelling a difficult path. Their different audiences cannot be neutral; their own commitment to art also cannot be neutral. The act of representation, loaded as it is likely to be with cultural density, can depend on no glossaries or introductions, as the written text can. The written text does have its own vulnerability, but the filmic discourse because of its immediacy has many more. Again political histories of a nation have a tendency to weave themselves into a narrative. *1947 Earth* and *Water* (both by Deepa Mehta) are overlaid with the reform and resistance discourses so integral a part of India's colonial phase. *1947 Earth* has a clear-cut division into two halves, the first with its moments of sharing, mild flirtations, kite-flying and community get-togethers increasingly absorbed in discussing politics; the second unrelieved in its grimness, disruption, oppression, broken friendships and growing hatreds. The rising crescendo is accompanied by intermittent noises in the background – Nehru's 'Tryst with Destiny' speech, the beat of the maid Shanta washing clothes in helpless frustration, the cries and screams of the rioters and then the blasts. Together these combine to reconstruct the anarchy and helplessness of the Partition, which marked the British exit, reversing at one stroke the imperial glory framed in the British films of the Raj nostalgia.

Water goes even further back in time and locates itself in a widows' home insulated against the outside world, with women of different generations living together in a world where desire of all kinds is forbidden. Four characters hold the narrative together: Madhumati – the powerwielder, Shakuntala – the protector, Kalyani – the exploited and Chuyia – the catalyst. Into this house of repression, desire steps in the garb of poetry (that too of Kalidas, a classical Sanskrit poet), and love; and into this narrative of exclusion Mehta introduces multiple subtexts – a critiquing of social practices, of religious corruption, stagnation and power, of the exploitation of the widows by the so-called rich benefactors, and the call of modernity which alienates the young from social concerns. Gandhi and his non co-operation movement run parallel to the main narrative. Gandhi is present in the news, everyone talks of him, the youth are now being attracted towards him, he is the only hope for the margins and, at the end of the movie, Chuyia is handed over to his protection.

Gandhi's presence in all the three movies of the trilogy is a tangible one. *Fire* mimics Gandhi's views on celibacy, *1947 Earth* blames him for the Partition and in *Water* there is a polyphony of voices about him. The eunuch and Madhumati criticise him for challenging the brahminical caste division, Narayan's friend considers him to be of nuisance value, Narayan's mother blames Gandhi for her son's growing patriotism but for Shakuntala, Narayan and Chuyia he is a messiah. Mehta's relationship with Gandhi from 1996 (when *Fire* was made) through 1998 (*1947 Earth*), to 2006 (*Water*) has evolved, her relationship with India has also evolved, significantly her other subtext, which finds a place in all the three films, is the contest between humanistic discourse and violence.

At the end we are left with a whole lot of questions, many of which have no answers or have many possible ones. Why India? Why does the diaspora choose to write about India? In the in-between films, it is their reality; in the shifted location films it is the state of their own in-betweenness. They simultaneously or alternately belong to both sites. Do they choose to narrativise India because of the pull of the homeland, or is it a kind of negotiation with their own love-hate relationship with the mother country, or because India – with all its crazy systems, poverty levels and social problems – sells? Chadha's *Bride and Prejudice* (2004) transfers the Austenian world to India and fills it up with loud nuances but in *The Mistress of Spices*, Chadha professes to the belief of keeping the 'myth, magic and tradition' alive. Mira Nair asks, 'If we don't tell our own stories, who will?' and Deepa Mehta refutes the idea that her target audience is in the west. She is much more fascinated with issues. In several films, in some form or the other the characters point out to the gap: 'This is America – but we are Indians'. A counter-discourse has simultaneously been generated in India with films like *Aa Ab Laut Chale* (Lets' Go Back Home, 1999), *Dilwale Dulhaniya Lejayenge* (The Brave Shall Take The Bride, 1995), *Pardes* (Abroad, 1997) *Swades* (Homeland, 2004) constructing both nation and culture and debating issues of development and dreams which drive one abroad.

Today, with funding and narratives going global, with casts and directorial ventures reflecting varied inputs and locations constantly shifting within a film, a constant process of evaluation has been initiated. Films in their own right are dialogues bridging differences, reaching out and looking not only each other in the face but also oneself in the mirror.

FILMOGRAPHY

Aa Ab Laut Chale. Dir. Rishi Kapoor, Perf: Aishwariya Rai, Akshay Khanna, Rajesh Khanna. Moushimi Chatterjee, 1999.

American Blend. Dir. Varun Khanna, Perf: Anupam Kher, Dee Wallace, Ranjit Choudhary, Kristin Erickson, 2006.

American Desi. Dir. Piyush Dinkar Pandya, Perf: Kal Penn, Purva Bedi, Deep Katdare, Rozwan Manji, Ronobir Lahiri, 2001.

Anita and Me. Dir. Metin Huseyin, Story: Meera Syal, Perf: Kabir Bedi, Chandeep Uppal, Max Beesley, Sanjeev Bhaskar, Anna Brewster, 2002).

Bend it Like Beckham. Dir. Gurinder Chadha. Story: Meera Syal, Perf: Parminder Nagar, Keith Knightley, Anupam Kher, Frank Harper, 2002.

Bhaji on the Beach. Dir. Gurinder Chadha, Perf: Kim Vithana, Sarita Khajuria, Shaheen Khan, Zohra Segal, Akbar Kurtha, Peter Collier, 1993.

Bollywood/Hollywood. Dir. Deepa Mehta, Perf: Dina Pathak, Moushimi Chatterjee, Leela Ray, Rahul Khanna, Kulbhushan Kharbanda, 2002.

Bride and Prejudice. Dir. Gurinder Chadha. Perf: Aishwariya Rai, Nadira Babbar, Anupam Kher, Martin Henderson, 2004.

Dilwale Dulhaniya le Jayenge. Dir. Aditya Chopra, Perf: Shahrukh Khan, Kajol, Amrish Puri, Anupam Kher, Karan Johar, 1995.

Dor. Dir. and Writer Nagesh Kukunoor, Perf: Shreyas Talpade, Gul Panag, Ayesha Takia, Girish Karnad, 2006.

Hyderabad Blues. Dir. Nagesh Kukunoor, Perf: Elahe Hiptoola, Nagesh Kukunoor, Rajshri Nair, Vikram Inamdar, 1998.

Iqbal. Dir. Nagesh Kukunoor, Perf: Shreyas Talpade, Naseerudin Shah, Girish Karnad, 2005.

Masala. Dir. Srinivas Krishna, Perf: Sakina Jaffrey, Zohra Segal, Saeed Jaffrey, Srinivas Krishna, 1991.

Mississippi Masala. Dir. Mira Nair, Perf: Meena, Roshan Seth, Jay, Sharmila Tagore, 1992.

Monsoon Wedding. Dir. Mira Nair, Perf: Leela Dubey, Naseerudin Shah, Shetali Shah, Vijay Raaz, 2001.

1947 Earth. Dir. Deepa Mehta, Perf: Aamir Khan, Nandita Bose, Rahul Khanna, Lilette Dubey, 1998.

Pardes. Dir. Subhash Ghai, Perf: Shahrukh Khan, Mahima Choudhary, Amrish Puri, Apurva Agnihotri, 1997.

Salaam Bombay. Dir. Mira Nair. Perf: Shafiq Syed, Hansa Vithal, Chanda Sharma, 1988.

Swades. Dir. Ashutosh Gowarkar, Perf: Shahrukh Khan, Gayatri Joshi, Kishori Balai, 2004.

The Mistress of Spices. Dir. Paul Mayeda Berges, Story: Gurinder Chadha based on Divakaruni's novel, Perf: Aishwarya Rai, Dylan McDermott, Nitin Ganatra, Kwesi, 2005.

The Namesake. Dir. Mira Nair. Perf: Irfan Khan, Tabu, Kal Penn, Ruma Guha, 2006.

Water. Dir. Deepa Mehta, Perf: Seema Biswas, Sarala John Abraham, Lisa Ray, Manorama, 2007.

18

Overwriting Memory
The Diaspora and Its Present

... the life one has lived is unknowable except in the most superficial of ways, that one is somehow doomed to be a tourist in the landscape of one's past – and the tourist's landscape is one that exists only in imagination, its objectivity suspect, its reality fluid.

– Neil Bissoondath[1]

All it took then in Trinidad was looking for Indians, all it took now in Canada was skin colour. We had not moved one inch.

– Ramabai Espinet[2]

'Son, I am glad you left. We too backward here.'

– Cyril Dabydeen[3]

Who is the diaspora? The reader may notice that all the three epigraphs I have selected are from writings of the children of the indentured labourers, the third, fourth or fifth generation. Additionally, all of them are twice migrants, the second migration taking place voluntarily to a new land, away from the land of their birth and upbringing. The second migration at once provides them with two homelands – one they have known and experienced physically, the other remembered through cultural artefacts, fractured narratives, twice or thrice removed tales and the words that are present in their everyday discourse echoing a faraway past.

The South Asian diaspora, especially with histories of indenture, has been amply theorised and theory, as is expected, is constantly shifting and evolving, negotiating frameworks, approaches and locations change. It is important to ask the question: what is it that enters the theoretical discourse to change the direction? Is it just newness, some unexplored area, a new psychological or philosophical approach or a new piece of writing that challenges existing theories? I am convinced that writing goes ahead of theory and refuses to be framed by it; we theorise in order to locate our own perceptions and responses, and at times adopt a framework which appears to offer space, meaning and newness.

Migrations are in themselves as ancient as known histories – whether we refer to the Biblical journeys or the travels motivated by adventure, lure of wealth, search for land or power. Migrancy and dislocation have always been there but what makes the diaspora significant is that the early journeys were not guided by any of the above motives – not even pure exile. They were out of compulsion and need, and brought with them a denial of a human condition. Today diaspora is an umbrella term which fails to make any distinction between exiles, indenture, slaves, expatriates or employment dislocations. Concepts such as nation, citizenship and human rights have entered the discourse. In fact, the change in the all-inclusive meaning of diaspora, in itself, partly narrates the reason why Vijay Mishra makes a general distinction between the 'old diaspora of exclusiveness ... and the new diaspora of the border ...'[4], but Makarand Paranjape holds a different view. Bringing travel, rural-urban divide and relationships between the two diasporas, he is of the view, 'The diaspora, then, must involve a cross-cultural or cross-civilization passage ... . Also, the crossing must be forced, not voluntary; otherwise the passage will amount to an enactment of desire-fulfilment'.[5] In such a case there would necessarily be some mourning and a mild cultural shock, if any, at the first encounter.

No matter which method we adopt toward defining or un-defining it, no definition will hold all diasporic journeys together whether they are of imperial migrations, settler communities, adoption of a country other than a homeland and tenures of employment in unfamiliar terrains. The last is applicable to the

British in India and meets most of the requirements of Paranjape, including language and religion. William Arnold's novel, *Oakfield, Fellowship in the East*,[6] written while in India is a testimony to the loneliness and trauma. Perhaps an important distinction one could make is between linear and non-linear. In actuality the early South Asian diaspora as contract employees, for whom the dream of return was neither feasible, and later, not even promising, made linear journeys. Today's intellectual and technological migrations are also largely linear with the money power and the dubious mixture of visibility/invisibility. In Canada and elsewhere, racial differences make the immigrants a visible minority but for all else, in terms of agency and power, there is an anonymity attached to the majority. But as Uma Parameswaran once pointed out that the power (and recognition), which the Indian diaspora experiences on a return visit home is like a heady wine. The exchange rate of the dollar and the pound, gives them an additional advantage.[7]

Another subdivision comes into being through the writing in languages, when Punjabi, Gujarati or Marathi writers aboard write in their mother tongues. Associated with this is also a sense of parochialism created both in their homeland as well as hostland. In the latter it builds up a sense of community as magazines, plays and performances knit people together. Even those who write in English often build a sense of belonging on the basis of the language they learnt as their first language.[8] These are some of the ways of belonging, hoarding memory, preserving the past, and in one way putting the traumatic incidents such as Komagatu Maru in the past.

I have in mind three other solitary categories. The first of those who remember and those who forget. During a visit to South Africa, I picked up a collection of short stories by Ronnie Govender, *At the Edge and Other Cato Minor Stories* (1996)[9], which even as they dealt with apartheid in South Africa also carried an Indian past in names and customs. I wrote to him and he responded, not really admitting an Indian past but apparently reflecting it in his writing. I presume he has not visited India. Another work *Black Chin, White Chin* is a novel, which is described as an evocative portrait of five generations of descendants of former indentured Indian labourers and their struggle to build an identity in an emerging South Africa.[10] But the diasporic criticism from India and about India does not engage with these writers who have not migrated a second time or moved to the west, over and have not fallen into the role of a victim, despite their success in intellectual terms. Why? The second of these neglected categories is one of exiles unless they or we have the ability to romanticise them. My reference is to the well-known artist, M.F. Husain, who was also a filmmaker, and had finally to leave India when it became impossible for him to express himself in his chosen mediums due to right-wing opposition, a general hostility and vandalisation of his paintings. Where lay his trauma – here or there? He migrated at the age of ninety-one and later when an honorary citizenship was offered to him by the Government of Qatar, he accepted it. Husain died in 2006 in a foreign land. His death can be mourned by Zafar's ghazal *'Do gaz zameen bhi na mili kuye yaar mein'* (Not even two yards of land was available in the abode of my beloved).[11] For Husain, exile was a one-way journey, a rejection by his country and without the possibility of return, leading to a sense of betrayal and loneliness and hard to live with. Does a Husain need a collectivity to claim diaspora attention?

My third category is the global soul, who has adapted himself to new technologies and globalisation and is a nomad, who makes no claims and belongs nowhere. In fact, Pico Iyer uses an epigraph from Simone Weil's poem, which ends with the line, 'We must be rooted in the absence of a place.' This is a willed otherness, a willed deracination inhabiting spaces which simultaneously expand and shrink. One word Iyer uses frequently is nowarian, embodying within it a sense of constant replacement and perhaps renewal. Iyer is unable to read his native language, has had a travelling childhood, a habit which has persisted in adulthood. He records a meeting with Kazuo Ishigura, who was a child migratory at age five and part neither of Japan, nor of Britain and labelled by his looks as a foreigner in the western world.[12] These experiences of removal and distinction are shared alike by diaspora and global soul. The global soul draws its freedom from a sense of non-affiliation, of being 'loosed from time as much as from space.' Iyer writes 'I had no history, I could feel, and lived under the burden of no home ...' (Iyer 23). He admits that unable to pronounce his given name, he goes by an Italian name. Never been in a position to vote, he has ended up renouncing all democratic participation and locating nation, nationality and rootedness of belonging in a no man's land. Where does one place the global soul in terms of identity and subjectivity, in terms of long-term relationships and the archives of memory?

Having listed the categories that defy collective definitions, I have now to ask myself two questions: why should we, located in India, theorise the diaspora? And if there is enough cause for doing so, how should we set about it? There is reason enough to theorise the diaspora, especially the expressions of relatedness and remembrance, their affiliations with the mother country and the audiences and admirers they find here as also for the recognition at the international level by award-deciding juries on cultural or anti cultural grounds. We need to theorise and evaluate them for more reasons than the one stated above: especially the language writers who have a constant communication with their homeland and are more specific in their treatment of cultural nuances than the writers writing in English, but the latter get a wider academic attention. The fact that a fair amount of academic effort is spent on diasporic studies, obviously by encroaching on the space of the writing in English by the non diasporic ones, is another fact that needs to be examined in terms of academic worth and justification. There is sufficient cause to theorise the diaspora if for naught else, in order to get our bearings straight. Now the other significant question remains: *how?*

Sudesh Mishra in his work *Diaspora Criticism*,[13] has given a detailed account of the major theoretical approaches up to the beginning of the present century. The work appeared in 2006; one can safely assume that the period till 2004 has been covered including that of Paul Gilroy (*Black Atlantic* 1993), Homi Bhabha, Vijay Mishra, Dipesh Chakrabarty and Stuart Hall. There is also another work, Sam Durant's *Postcolonial Narrative and the Work of Mourning* (2004) which like Vijay Mishra's asks the question of remembering: what do we remember and what forget and how are the two processes interlinked. The work draws attention not only to the selective nature of memory but also its counterpart of forgetting and amnesia – willed or not willed. When territorial expanses change and language becomes distant, how does one inhabit a vacuum and make it habitable? I will, however, not go into these aspects, especially not at this point, but would like to respond to Vijay Mishra's 'Diaspora and the Art of Impossible Mourning' and Shiva Kumar Srinivasan's 'Diaspora and its Discontents' both of which work with and reconstruct theoretical issues.

Vijay Mishra takes up the Derridean reference to mourning, signifying a total finality and the impossibility of retrieval. Derrida's *Work of Mourning*[14] is about the loss of his friends and consists of addresses delivered in their memory, mostly as *memoires* and are adieus and recollections: as such the finality of death is what is considered. Mishra by using 'Impossible Mourning' also indicates a definite finality of the past which can never be recovered either physically or emotionally or kept alive through an unchanged memory. It is a loss which has to be remembered as a loss; the journey has been a linear one, in this case the indenture workers' sea journeys. But there is another word in Mishra's title, which calls for attention – 'Art' in the 'Art of Impossible Mourning'. This can have several connotations - art as a practice, as that of professional mourners, a repetitive act, a constant presence which through externalisation and repetition, works as a therapy, and art as a narrative, the telling or imagining of an event otherwise inaccessible, to keep the memory alive for future generations, as a recording. In this connection, it would be relevant to explore the dimensions of memory in Paul Ricoeur's work, *Memory, History and Forgetting* (2004).[15] Ricoeur draws our attention to the finality which a narrative confers on the real (276). He goes on to add that even in historical recounting the past is overlaid, 'the historian's representation is indeed a present image of an absent thing, but the absent thing itself gets split into disappearance, into existence in the past' (280). The past is over but not done with. It is still there in its ghostly existence, caught in the moment, incapable of any flexibility or shift or renewal.

Does this account for the diaspora's constant return to the past, to a history known only through fragmentary accounts and incomplete and rough-edged, half remembered and half forgotten customs, practices and rituals, almost like a distant archives, now in ruins? Caryl Phillips in his *Crossing the Bar*[16] has captured the past through imagined lives, memories of three siblings placed in different spaces and living in the fluidity of time. One part of the jig-saw puzzle is supplied by the diary of the slave ship's captain, an unwilling slave of his compulsions, locked up in the memories of his family. This too is a kind of mourning, an externalisation of an inherited past. It is also a 'resistance to history' in its sidelining of statistics and in travelling back to the point of the beginning after its journey of over nearly two centuries. Recounting, imagining and narrating are acts which simultaneously turn to the past and the future and attempt to construct a bridge. Vijay Mishra, himself, a jahazi bhai, dislocated from Fiji and presently in Australia, commands a certain authority in his glance back. He insists on the work of mourning as a necessary prelude to setting the 'ego free'. Mishra's reference inevitably travels back to the Freudian melancholia, distinguishing between the two – mourning and melancholia. While the first sets the ego free the second possesses it through its failure to objectify the loss.

But as we look at the progeny of the indentured workers, is it not that the 'trauma' is now distantly realised in the form of a displacement and not as an experienced act, that identification with the hostland is more or less complete with the Caribbean past surfacing more often than their ancestors' India, as part of their lives? I have in mind writers like Neil Bissoondath.[17] This gives rise to other related questions such as: why does diaspora writing dwell on the past and what significance does ancestral history have for the recovery of a lost identity? In contrast to the displaced categories, why do writers like Bharati Mukherjee, Salman Rushdie and Rohinton Mistry turn to history, when each writer is so different from the other? And *how* do they remember history? The older diaspora and their generation foreground space – houses, rooms, attics before moving on to landscapes, rituals, customs, practices, the bamboo marriage, while voluntary diaspora circles around cities, Calcutta, Bombay, Bangalore which in themselves are expansive and non definable forces that resist possession. Moreover, if we wish to problematise nation and homeland, how does one surmount the factor of citizenship, divided loyalties and long distance nationalism?

Vijay Mishra, in the essay under discussion, expands on the idea of the proxy newly fabricated homelands (37) constructed on the basis of narrow loyalties, religious histories and new identity formations. Significant factors in this reconstruction are money power and the desire of political power. Sudesh Mishra, likewise refers to this and views it as a resistance to hybridity, and listing a whole lot of works embodying the idea writes,' ... all testify to diaspora as the smithy where menacing forms of ethnonationalisms are ritually hammered out. Such reactionary positions, if not openly then covertly, rely on the *political disavowal of an ethical future* based on recognising the asymmetry of race, ethnicity, nation and culture,' (Sudesh Mishra 76, emphasis mine). I deliberately emphasise the loss of the ethical as well as the underlying anti-modern and pro-feudal position. Do we not have the right to resist and question this? The participants in these moves are mostly the voluntary diaspora, not the ones who left under compulsion. Long distance nationalism is disruptive and has strong links with terrorism and is frightening both in its appropriation of our democratic rights and its hidden hand in fostering a fragmentation of our national psyches. The recent election scenario, the lobbying based on right wing ideologies, new split identities coming into being through divided diasporic selves into a pro-native culture on one hand and, on the other, a pro-western code of living marked with a certain disdain for the homeland. There is an obvious need to question the nature of the impossible mourning, its truth and fiction. Do we locate it somewhere near Lacan's *real* and *imaginary*, both of which are in the long run unreal, or accept a certain degree of homelessness as an unacknowledged reality? Žižek while commenting on the Lacanian concept of the real also comments on the melancholic and writes 'the melancholic is not primarily the subject fixated on the lost object, unable to perform the work of mourning on it; he is, rather, the subject who possesses the object, but has lost his desire for it, because the cause which made him desire the object has withdrawn, lost its efficiency'. Hence melancholy has come to stand 'for the presence of the object'.[18] Again, Kate McGowan in 'The Real' talks about the Wachowski brothers' film trilogy *The Matrix* and referring to it as an interrogation of the real, locates the idea of freedom in the act of thinking and willing, not memory.[19] The real is also a recall, hence a representation and as such is not real.

The second essay, I wish to consider is Srinivasan's 'Diaspora and Its Discontents.'[20] Srinivasan works with the Freudian concept of 'discontent', the 'irremediable antagonism between the demands of the instinct and the restrictions of civilization' (Freud qtd by Srinivasan 52). Moving on to the extension of repression to Marxist critics, he finally arrives, inevitably as it were, at the Lacanian approach to the relationship between the order of the imaginary and the institution of aggressivity, a correlate of narcissism in the human subject.[21] Srinivasan then proceeds to make a valuable distinction between historical and structural as also between a material interpretation of repression and the more intrinsic response in terms of negotiating narcissism and alienation. Repeatedly he uses the combined term 'imaginary aggressivity', by which his emphasis is on identity formation leading to a more stable self and subjectivity. Srinivasan doesn't use the terms which I have, but the moment we disconnect the imaginary aggressivity from the inequity in society the origin of the new emancipatory narrative has to lie somewhere in the individual, especially if, at some point, the Lacanian mirror stage is to be recognised. This supplements Vijay Mishra's view that mourning 'sets the ego free' (36). Except, Srinivasan linking the same imaginary to aggressivity, foregrounds the latter and attributes to it a positive action, rather than an indulgence in historical narratives and traumatic mourning. Trauma in itself is a difficult experience to reconstruct or relive. What we remember of it, except for a sense of loss which lies buried deep down within us, is an imagined recollection of the conscious memory.

Again, when we review the history of visits home vis-à-vis return, the anger and hatred often displayed by the diaspora, the emotional moving away, unable to participate at any existential level, there is an acknowledgement that the return home will fail to reinstate.[22] It is through this psychoanalytical approach the compulsive act of reliving or recreating the past of diasporic writers writing about India, is explained.[23] Srinivasan's query as to why does the subject repeat, voices what many of us have asked: why do they come back to India (emotionally, not necessarily physically), in search of their raw material? Is it a 'pure' renegotiation of memory and space? Or is there some other motive? Because all histories that are imagined do not necessarily rest on known narratives. This is a larger question and the answer will vary from writer to writer, work to work and I'll refrain from taking it up here as it requires expansion beyond the present concern.[24]

Placing the theoretical positions of Vijay Mishra and Srinivasan side by side one is conscious of a difference in their positions and the directions they wish to indicate. Mishra moves through a position of mourning of recall to the emancipation of the ego, while Srinivasan's structural approach is a psycho-analytic analysis (I was initially going to use the word dissection, which is appropriate in its own right). But none of the two critics provides the answer to my question: *Why do we, located in India, then feel the compulsion to theorise their work, a distanced memory of a forgotten and an abandoned home?* I can see two reasons both overlapping with the *how*. True, diaspora writing is uneven: some of it merely exotic, a formula put together, some other more seriously and inwardly involved, close to the heart and echoing Trilling's concept of authenticity, with the relationship to India both a personal and an intellectual engagement, capable of transcending the one to one communication and reaching out to express more existential concerns, but some is only an exercise in India-bashing. The reasons for return are very different in each case. It is not necessarily a search for raw material in the writing which speaks from personal involvement, exploration or historical engagement or a deep-rooted need to know the past, while the exotic, formula writing is a search for newness and difference, an easy at-hand accessibility where myth, violence or stagnancy can be woven into the narrative. There is an urgent need to examine the writing of the diaspora and their impulse to come back in their memory or imagination to Indian themes in a more critical way, than we have done so far.

The celebratory status yielded to all alike, and more especially the virulent ones and exotic manufactured histories, leads us to ask the question how do they relate to us at home? And this is not merely an ideological question; it is more concerned with intention, direction and purpose. Do they appropriate and encroach upon the creativity at home? They are more visible, more easily accessible to the western reader with their own distant eye which dilutes cultural ethos while the writing in India languages, with its unfamiliar cultural nuances is not so easily accessible to them. Arun Mukherjee has accepted this in *Oppositional Aesthetics*[25] and Gayatri Spivak justifies it her introductions to Mahasweta Devi's stories on similar grounds. My own experience of unfolding Indian and Indian diasporic writing abroad confirms me in this view. Ismat Chugtai's 'Chauth Ka Jora' is difficult for the western reader and Ananthamurthy's *Samskara* requires a greater involvement from the reader, while Bharati Mukherjee's melodramatisation of the Kali image in *Jasmine* is so obvious, and any formula narrative about sati, dowry death or the outline of the *Ramayana* narrative or of the *Mahabharata* gets accepted fairly easily. The literary and critical space they initially claim because of their Indianness, appropriates the native space reducing the relationship between us and them to that of *id* and *ego*. I use the Freudian concepts here. The problem is not entirely with the writing but with the uncritical critical reception which has shifted from aesthetics to origins and is often, in the writing in English already governed by the recognition abroad. Is there no qualitative difference between how we read and how the other culture reader reads? Is a literary text totally self-contained and has no connection with the outside or with cultural receptions or locations?

I intend to focus on some Caribbean writers who have migrated, a second migration, to Canada or England, writers who have an ancestral history of indenture, in order to address the question of their relationship to India and the manner in which their writings reflect their inherited memories of the past – Naipaul, Bissoondath, Dabydeen and Espinet. Naipaul's writing is virulent and full of condescension, except for *A House for Mr Biswas*. His travelogues are journeys already performed in his mind or framed by his readings, except for *India: A Million Mutinies Now*, where he identifies with the rising religious aggression and comments upon this vitality. Lacking the space to elaborate further I refer the reader to his *Letters Between a Father and Son* which include several written to his sister.[26] His choices for escape, he feels, are limited: not Trinidad which has no history, not India which has only a historical past, hence another island, Britain where he lovingly relates to the landscape.[27]

Naipaul's *The Mimic Men*[28] is a most revealing text, which recalled even in his Nobel Lecture, described it as a book about colonial men mimicking the conditions of manhood, men who had grown to distrust everything about themselves (2001). It is here that the Freudian relationship between id and ego applies to him. The truth is that we carry the past with us, though we never visit it (*Mimic Men* 185). I draw the reader's attention also to a reference to *Asvamedha*, the horse sacrifice (152–153). Naipaul has always carried his double origin uneasily, hating both, resisting and resenting both but returning to them over and over again. The Naipaulian view is that all revolutions are futile. In his two later novels about India, both of which received unfavourable reviews, *Half-a-Life* and *The Magic Seeds*, Willie is a failure.[29] His involvement in the revolution leads to nothing and a subsequent move to Africa, stresses the same. There is no cause worth fighting for and thus Willie is doomed to sponging on others in England. Nowhere is there any move on Willie's part towards self-reflection, no questioning of the individual's role. The title of the second novel *Magic Seeds* is obvious in its reference to genetically modified, terminator seeds which do not propagate and are sterile.

In contrast to Naipaul, Bissoondath, his own sister's son, opts out the Naipaulian inheritance as does Cyril Dabydeen.[30] The other Dabydeen – David – in England also lovingly explores his past. But what is it they remember from the land of their ancestors? I'll take up only two examples: Bissoondath's first collection of short stories and his nonfiction *Selling Illusions*. The latter is an identification with Canada and a questioning of the official multicultural policy, but the first *Digging Up the Mountains*[31] offers rich narrative experiments with personas, landscapes and imagined constructs, working at several levels of migrations, of belonging and alienation and constructing the self bit by bit by being buffeted about rather than defining it through location in the idea of race, a distant past or an alienated self. The scenes of his childhood memories are from West Indies – not India. Dabydeen, likewise, roots himself in the West Indies, and when he refers to India, it is through picked up symbols. In the story 'Jet Lag' in *My Brahmin Days*, where he negotiates the Naipaulian fear of India, and as the flight lands he reminds himself, 'I was a Canadian entering a foreign land. This was no mere defence mechanism. History dispensed with, Kala Pani vanished. The flux of time and change only … . I was a Canadian in a vast new land' (82–83).[32] (But ironically the officer at the airport includes him in his sweeping statement, 'We are all Indian here'). The problem of belonging is at both levels – race and emotion. India is not a nightmare, people here are as normal and well-meaning and hospitable as elsewhere (refer 'My Brahmin Days'). But all the while he is conscious and accepts the possibility of realising fully well that it is not possible to return to the past and aware that he doesn't belong there. Dabydeen, like Bissoondath, transmutes history through selected events and creates a childhood past in the Caribbean home of plantations. Ramabai Espinet, who is another Caribbean who has migrated to Canada, in her novel *The Swinging Bridge*[33], weaves both her pasts – the immediate and the ancestral – together in the history and its recordings in a family narrative where houses and land symbolise belonging, where the approaching end of her brother Kelly does not make the novel pessimistic or Kelly a passive character.

Coming back to the initial premise – how do we theorise and why do we theorise, it is obvious that there is a need to question existing theories, if our relationships are not to end up in myth-making and generalities, and if we are to capture the changing shifts in diasporic writing, a psycho-analytic approach is most significant, whether it is trauma or discontent or the uncovering of the subconscious. I have used location along with the Freudian *id* and *ego*. We need to recognise and critique, diasporic writing not as an ego evolving itself on our presence but as a different category, calling for judgment on its own ground. Similarly, we need to free ourselves of the easy subordination based on affiliation rather than aesthetics, and recognise our own subjectivity, across our different languages, including English as one of them and bring them together not as a purely academic exercise but as an aesthetic and a historical reality. And this I feel allows us to be objectively perceptive, to evaluate aesthetically and to locate them in history and oeuvre. No work of art is truly independent or self-contained. Exile or forced migration is a 'space-time continuum' that has not been chosen, but once placed in such a situation the constructing of a new society or community is an ethical responsibility, which the writer cannot abandon.

NOTES & REFERENCES

1. Neil Bissoondath, *Doing the Heart Good* (Toronto: Cormorant Books Inc., 2002), 13. The Bissoondath's novel and Rohinton Mistry's *Family Matters* (2003) stand comparison favourably Mistry can a migrant, returns to India for his location, recreates and relives it with love while Bissoondath chooses Canada, but write a narrative equally powerful dealing with relationships between generations.
2. Ramabai Espinet, *The Swinging Bridge* (2003). (New Delhi Penguin, 2004), 78.
3. Cyril Dabydeen, 'Berbice Crossing' in *Berbice Crossing and Other Stories* (Yorkshire, England: Peepal Tree, 1990), 103–115, 111.
4. Vijay Mishra, 'Diasporas and the Art of Impossible Mourning', in *In Diaspora: Theories, Histories, Texts* (New Delhi: Indialog Publication, 2001), 24–51, 26.
5. Makarand Paranjape, Introduction, *In Diaspora*, 1–14.
6. William Arnold (1828–1859) was Matthew Arnold's younger brother who worked in the British administration in India. He wrote several articles and one novel, *Oakfield, Fellowship in the East* (1853), exploring spiritual meeting points between east and west. Critical of the unfriendly and unchristian attitude of his British colleagues, the novel is sad and lonely, William died young at the age of thirty-one.
7. In fact, most of upper class diaspora buy their furnishings and jewellery from India and plan exotic holidays to Goa, Kerala or Ladakh. This for two reasons – the comparatively less expensive material (compared to the west), and also to escape as much of home stay as possible. Some even go to the extent of staying in hotels instead of the family homes. Intellectuals seek more visibility here, writers wish to capture a large reading public. Justifiable reasons but hardly any different from the outsiders.
8. For more details, refer my essay, 'The New Parochialism; Homeland in the Writing of the Indian Diaspora', Included in the present volume.
9. Ronnie Govender is an established short story writer, novelist, playwright. This collection of short stories published by Manx in 1996 is about the lives of the indentured community.
10. Description on the back cover of the novel. (New Delhi: Harper Collins, 2007):
11. Bahudar Shah Zafar, the last Mughal Emperor who was imprisoned in Rangoon after the Indian defeat in 1857. The grave is of utmost significance to the Muslim – his own and those of his ancestors. Intizar Husain in his novel *Basti* and several of his short stories

points out this importance. Refer *Basti* (1979). Translated by Frances Pritchet (New Delhi: Harper Collins, 1995, 2000), 139.
12. Pico Iyer, *The Global Soul* (London: Bloomsbury, 2000) 20–22.
13. Sudesh Mishra, *Diaspora Criticism* (Edinburgh: Edinburgh University Press, 2006).
14. Jacques Derrida, *The Work of Mourning*. Eds Pascale-Anne Brault and Michael Haas (Chicago: Chicago University Press, 2001).
15. Paul Ricoeur, *Memory, History and Forgetting*. Trans. Kathleen Blamey and David Pallauer (Chicago: Chicago University Press, 2004).
16. Caryl Phillips also a child migrant like Pico Iyer, but unlike him is rooted in the historical past. *Crossing the Bar* (London: Pan Macmillan, 1994).
17. Neil Bissoondath, a Caribbean-Canadian lives in the present and is directed towards the future. Refer especially his *Selling Illusions: The Cult of Multiculturalism in Canada* (Toronto: Penguin Books, 1995), where his insistence on recognition as a Canadian. The same year another work came out, *If You Love This Country: Fifteen Voices for a United Canada.*
18. Slavoj Žižek, 'How to Read Lacan-Troubles with the Real.' internet reference www/lacan.com/zizalien.atm.referred. 12 June 2014, 1–7.
19. Kate McGowan, 'The Real', *Key Issues in Critical and Cultural Theory* (Jaipur: Rawat Publications, 2008), 102–119.
20. Shiva Kumar Srinivasan, 'Diaspora and Its Discontents', In *Diaspora* Ed. Makarand Paranjape (2001), 52–67.
21. Srinivasan, see footnotes 6 and 7 on p. 65
22. *Ibid.*, 56–57.
23. *Ibid.*, 57. Though its is equally true that while part of the reason is this somewhere also is the autobiographical impulse, a past which imparts them a distinct identity and which for reasons of its different happens to be highly marketable. Naipaul was one of the first to realise this.
24. Srinivasan anticipates me in his reference to the Partition of India as a traumatic event and the need to explore the psychological traumas of refuges, exiles, *muhajirs* and the dislocated.
25. Arun Mukherjee, *Oppositional Aesthetics: Readings from a Hyphenated Space* (Toronto: Tsar, 1994). All the seven articles in the first part of the book deal with this aspect, 3–66.
26. *Letters Between Father and Son* with an Introduction and notes by Gillon Aitken (Great Britain: Little, Brown and Company, 1999). He

advises his sister in a letter dated 24 November 1949, to look at India as a dead country still running with the momentum of hey day (9).
27. *The Enigma of Arrival* (London: Picador, 2002).
28. *The Mimic Men* (1967) (London: Picador, 2002).
29. *Half-a-Life* (London: Picador, 2001) and *Magic Seeds* (New York: Vintage, 2004). Both are histories of Willie's travels, non-commitment and continued failures.
30. The direct inheritor of Naipaul's version of relationships and recollections through memory, surprisingly is Kiran Desai, a first generation immigrant, who with her very title, *The Inheritance of Loss*, dons a negative mantle and ends up with three static characters and an illegal immigrant, and introduces the Gurkha Land Movement as a strategic intervention in the family saga. But the Indian reception was both feverish and frenzied with a flood of amateur critical papers on the novel.
31. *Digging Up the Mountains: Selected Stories* (Toronto: Macmillian, 1985).
32. *My Brahmin Days and Other Stories* (Toronto: Tsar Publications, 2000) 82–83.
33. *The Swinging Bridge* (New Delhi: Penguin, 2004).

Index

Aadha Gaon, 182
Achebe, Chinua, 3, 6
Adorno, T., 171
Afrindian diaspora, 116, 117
Ahmed, Nazneen, 140
Ali, Agha Shahid, 155
Ali, Monica, 139–140, 144
American Blend, 235, 237
Amu, 157
Anam, Tahmima, 135, 144
Anand, Mulk Raj, 2
Anderson, Benedict, 68
Anil's Ghost, 36–37, 82, 163
Anita and Me, 69
Area of Darkness, An, 92
Arnold, William, 249
Ashraf, Raza Konrad, 194
Aslam, Nadeem, 194–195, 201

Badami, Anita Rau, 154, 155, 156
Bakhtin, M., 55, 73

Bannerjee, Himani, 30, 156
Baran Buhe, 57
Basti, 187, 190
Bend in the River, 4
Bend It Like Beckham, 236–237, 240
Bhabha, Homi, 4, 41, 94, 134–135
Bhaji on the Beach, 69, 235
Bharucha, Nilufer, 47
Bhasha Andolan, 136
Bhutto, Fatima, 199, 201
Birbalsingh, Frank, 96
Bissoondath, Neil, 30, 81, 106, 108, 112, 156, 247, 253
Black Chin, White Chin, 118, 121–122, 249
Blaise, Clark, 147, 159
Blind Man's Garden, The, 194, 201
Bose, Shonali, 157
Bourdieu, Pierre, 55
Boys Will Be Boys, 12, 19

Brah, Avtar, 73
Brennan, Timothy, 148
Brick Lane, 135, 139, 144
Bride and Prejudice, 244
Broken Verses, 13, 16, 19–20
burden, 28, 55, 64, 80, 151, 184, 190, 250
Burnt Shadows, 194–196, 198, 203

Calcutta Chromosome, The, 225, 229
Can You Hear the Nightbird Call?, 154, 156
Castello, Debro A., 183, 184
Cato Manor, 117, 249
Chadha, Gurinder, 238
Chatterjee, Sarat Chandra, 2
Chernilo, Daniel, 16
Chronicle of a Death Foretold, 163
Chugtai, Ismat, 257
Cinnamon Gardens, 174
Circle of Reason, The, 221, 225, 227–229, 231
civil war, 82, 137, 153, 162–164, 171, 187, 200
Conrad, Joseph, 101, 226
coolie, 208
Coopsammy, Madeline, 210
Corneille, Roland de, 159
Crossing the Bar, 252
Cutting for Stone, 129–130, 132

Dabydeen, Cyril, 83, 112, 105, 247, 258
Dark Side of the Nation, The, 30, 156
Dark Swirl, The, 111

Daughters of the Twilight, 126–128
Derrida, Jacques, 7, 252
Desai, Anita, 81
Desai, Kiran, 82
Desirable Daughters, 149
Dharweshwar, Vivek, 29
Diaspora Criticism, 251
Diaspora films, 235
diaspora, 54, 79
diasporic writing in Punjabi, 56
Digging Up the Mountains, 106, 108, 258
Divakaruni, Chitra, 69, 238
Dor, 242
Dreams After Darkness, 154
Durant, Sam, 251
Dying Traditions, 138

English Patient, The, 40, 47, 51
Espinet, Ramabai, 8, 33, 34, 96, 247, 259
expatriate, 66

Family Matters, 12, 15, 23, 231
Field of Cultural Production, The, 55
Finding the Centre, 94, 106–107
Fine Balance, A, 80
Firdausi, 15
Fire, 240
forgiveness, 15–16, 21–23, 26, 132, 158, 174–176, 242
Foucault, Michel, 170
Freud, S., 74
fundamentalism, 25
Funny Boy, 174

Ghosh, Amitav, 37, 82, 157, 221, 225
Glass Palace, The, 228
God in Every Stone, A, 194
Golden Age, A, 135, 140, 144
Govender, Ronnie, 116, 118, 121, 249
Greetz, Clifford, 234
Grewal, Manraj, 154
Group Areas Act, 117
Gunesekera, Romesh, 162, 163, 169–170, 173, 174
Gunny Sack, The, 117, 119, 123, 126
Gupta, Ashis, 40, 46, 82, 138
Gurmet, 71
Guru Nanak Dev, 56

Hamid, Mohsin, 12, 13, 195
Hans, Harbhajan, 60
Hartley, L.P., 105
Haunting the Tiger, 215
Heart of Darkness, 101
Heidegger, Martin, 167
Herk, Aritha van, 113
Heterotopia, 42
History of the Sikhs, 150
Home and Exile, 3–4, 6
Home and the World, 134–135
home, 78
homeland, 78, 85–86, 178
Hosain, Attia, 81, 180, 181
Hosseini, Khaled, 12, 13, 20, 194
House for Mr Biswas, A, 208
Hungry Ghosts, The, 163, 174

Hungry Tide, The, 37, 225
Husain, Intizar, 64, 69, 181–182, 187
Husain, M.F., 250
Hyderabad Blues, 241

identity, 24, 25, 29, 31, 32, 35, 38, 40, 41, 42, 45, 46, 47, 49, 50, 51, 52, 65, 66, 68, 72, 73, 74, 78, 79, 80, 83, 84, 91, 94, 106, 113, 121, 135, 139, 142, 153, 156, 168, 176, 180, 190, 196, 207, 208, 214, 240, 241, 251, 253
Imaginary Homelands, 78–79
In a Free State, 100
India: A Million Mutinies Now, 97
Inhuman: Reflections on Time, The, 58
Iqbal, 241
Iqbal, Mohammed, 184
Island of a Thousand Mirrors, 163, 166
Iyer, Pico, 250

jahaji bhai, 208
Jahaji, 208
JanMohammed, Abdul, 6
Jasmine, 149
Jhabvala, Ruth, 81

Kanaganayakam, Chelva, 156
Kandasamy, Meena, 98
Kanthapura, 111
Karodia, Farida, 116, 122, 127
Khan, Sorayya, 12–13, 25, 138
Kirkpatrick, Jeane, 153

Kishore, Giriraj, 3
Kite Runner, The, 12, 14, 20–23, 194, 198
Krishna, Srinivas, 235
Kukunoor, Nagesh, 235

Lahiri, Jhumpa, 70, 80, 237
Lamming, George, 90, 91–92, 95, 105, 107
Larios, Ricardo, 190
Letters Between a Father and Son, 92, 208
Location of Culture, The, 4, 41, 94
London Ki Ek Raat, 2
Lopez, Barry, 41
Lyotard, Jean Francois, 58

Maachis, 158, 180
Magic Seeds, 258
Maharaj, Rabindranath, 212
Mahasweta Devi, 79
Manian, K.S., 215
Manto, Sadaat Hasan, 180
Markandaya, Kamala, 2, 81
Marquez, G.G., 163
Masala, 235
Matoo, Shani, 212
McGowan, Kate, 254
Meatless Days, 12, 14–15, 17, 19
Meer, Fatima, 3
Mehta, Brinda, 57
Mehta, Deepa, 235, 240
Memon, Umar, 181, 185
Memory, 7, 11, 14, 18, 23, 232
  unreliability, 44, 114, 155, 232

Middle Passage, The, 93, 106–107
Midnight's Children, 44, 221–224
Mimic Men, The, 93–97, 100, 257
Mir Ali, 194, 199
Mishra, Sudesh, 251, 254
Mishra, Vijay, 12, 66, 248, 252–253, 256
Mistress of Spices, The, 69, 238, 244
Mistry, Rohinton, 12, 15, 25, 81–81, 114, 163, 221, 230, 232
Mohanty, Chandra Talpade, 56
Monsoon Wedding, 235
mourning, 12, 253
muhajir, 180–181
Muhajirnama, 182
Mukherjee, Arun Prabha, 31, 67, 256
Mukherjee, Bharati, 81, 147–149, 156, 159
Munaweera, Nayomi, 163, 166, 167
My Brahmin Days, 105, 106, 112, 258
Mystic Masseur, The, 83, 111

Naipaul, V.S., 4, 81, 83, 91–92, 98–101, 106–107, 208, 257
Nair, Mira, 235, 237, 240
Namesake, The, 235, 237
Namjoshi, Suniti, 81
Nanackchand, Ami, 117
Naseemumujaffar, 183
1947 Earth, 244
Noontide Toll, 163, 169, 173
Noor, 12, 25

Ondaatje, Michael, 36, 40, 47, 82, 162–163, 167
Operation Bluestar, 147, 157
Oppositional Aesthetics, 31, 256
Other Secrets, 128

Paani, 70
Pahla Girmilya, 3
Palace of Illusions, The, 69
Parameswaran, Uma, 8, 78, 249
Paranjape, Makarand, 248
Parmeswaran, Uma, 73
Pathar Dabi, 2
Pathar Panchali, 240
Persaud, Sasenarine, 209
Phillips, Caryl, 212, 252
Pleasures of Exile, The, 91, 95
plural, 16, 26, 30, 31, 34–36, 38
plurality, 28, 30, 32, 38
post-colonial, 4, 5
Punjabi diaspora, 65
Punjabi diasporic writing, 57, 72

Rahman, Anisur, 36
Ramaswamy, Sumathi, 130
Randhawa, Ravinder, 82
Rao, Raja, 111
Rastogi, Pallavi, 117
Ray, Manas, 180
Ray, Satyajit, 240
Raza, Rahi Masoom, 182
refugee, 2, 3, 20, 29, 65, 66, 78, 83, 101, 137, 154, 176, 179, 180, 195, 197, 200, 202

Reluctant Fundamentalist, The, 13, 24, 195
Riaz, Amber Fatima, 180
Ricoeur, Paul, 252
Rishtey, 60–61
Running in the Family, 162
Rushdie, Salman, 56, 68, 79, 81, 162, 221

Sacred Hunger, The, 47
Sahgal, Nayantara, 2, 85
Said, Edward, 5, 6, 29, 66, 78
Salaam Bombay, 240
Salim, Ahmed, 183
Sandhu, Sukhdev, 140
Saanghera, Balbir Kaur, 72
Santos, Myrian Sepúlveda, 7
Satanic Verses, The, 223
Secret Agent, The, 226
Secular Criticism, 5
Sekha, Harpreet Singh, 57
Selling Illusions: The Cult of Multiculturalism in Canada, 30, 106, 156, 258
Selvadurai, Shyam, 162, 163, 173, 174
Shadow of the Crescent Moon, The, 194, 199
Shahnama, 15
Shamsie, Kamila, 12, 13, 19, 20, 194
Shehrzaad, 187
Sheikh, Farhana, 82
Shohat, Ella, 4, 5
Sincerity and Authenticity, 8, 68
Singh, Christine, 210–211

Singh, Gurbhagat, 207
Singh, Jarnail, 69–70
Singh, Khushwant, 150
Soja, Edward, 42, 169, 170
Sorrow and the Terror, The, 147–149, 156, 158–159
space, 3, 8, 11–13, 15–16, 18, 20–21, 23–26, 29, 32, 36, 42–43, 51, 54–57, 73, 85, 96, 97, 113, 118, 121, 141, 142, 144, 156, 167, 169, 170, 180, 181, 185, 198, 206, 224, 225, 230, 232, 248, 250, 252, 253, 257
spatial, 12, 15, 42, 170
specular, 6
Spivak, Gayatri, 31, 66, 79, 84, 256
Srinivasn, Shiva Kumar, 254–256
Such a Long Journey, 221, 230–231
Suleri, Sara, 12, 20, 25
Sura so Pehchanian, 57
Swinging Bridge, The, 8, 33, 35, 259
Syal, Meera, 69, 82, 235

Tagore, Rabindranath, 134, 135

third space, 40, 41, 42, 52, 66, 67, 81, 82, 242
Thousand Splendid Suns, A, 194
Toymaker from Wiesbaden, The, 40, 42, 44, 51
Trilling, Lionel, 8, 68
two-nation theory, 3

Unaccustomed Earth, 70
Unsworth, Barry, 47

Vassanji, M.G., 33, 82, 116, 119, 123
Verghese, Abraham, 116, 128

Wasted Vigil, The, 195
Water, 243
Wizard Swami, The, 83, 111
Wonham, Henry B., 41
Write to Reconcile, 174
write, 11, 26
writing, 11, 26; writing home, 23

Zaheer, Sajjad, 2
Žižek, Slavoj, 254

JJ — essay on Grem Novak (62-63)

Husain (64) - (260)